AGING WITH A PLAN

AGING WITH A
PLAN

HOW A LITTLE THOUGHT TODAY CAN VASTLY IMPROVE YOUR TOMORROW

SHARONA HOFFMAN,
JD, LLM, SJD

Second Edition

In memory of my parents,
Rabbi Morton and Aviva Hoffman

CONTENTS

Acknowledgments   xiii

Introduction and my personal story   **1**

Why I Wrote the Book   2

A Few Facts and Figures   8

  The childless   11

What the Book Covers   12

CHAPTER 1 **Money Matters: Retirement Expenses,
          Savings, and Fiscal Decision-Making**   **17**

Are Americans Saving Enough?   18

  What medical expenses can you expect as a senior?   20

Retirement Savings and Professional Financial Advice   23

  Take advantage of employment benefits   24

  Prioritize saving for retirement   25

  Obtain professional financial advice   27

  Obtain an interest-free loan if facing a financial crisis   30

Long-Term Care Insurance   30

  Policy costs and limitations   31

  Your financial circumstances   34

  Your age and health status   37

  Hybrid products   38

Reverse Mortgages 39

Long-Term Care Costs as a Policy Issue 41

Financial Preparedness Checklist 43

CHAPTER 2 The Benefits of Community Living 45

The Importance of Social Interaction and
Feeling Useful 47

The Many Forms of Independent Retirement or
55-Plus Communities 52

Independent living or 55-plus communities 53

Naturally occurring retirement communities 54

Village networks 56

Additional services available for independent living 57

Shared housing services 57
Senior centers 58
Meals on wheels 59
Faith-based and nonprofit organizations 59
Programs of All-Inclusive Care for the
Elderly (PACE) 61

Continuing Care Retirement Communities 61

My own CCRC visits 62

CCRC benefits 66

CCRC costs and financial risk 70

Other concerns 75

CCRC without walls 78

Retirement Community Preparedness Checklist 79

**CHAPTER 3 Help with Money, Care, and Home
Management 83**

Daily Money Managers 83

Geriatric Care Managers 86

Elder Law Attorneys   89

Organizing, Adapting, and Selling Your Home   91

   Adapting your home   91

   Personal emergency response and detection systems   92

   Professional organizers   94

   Relocation specialists   95

   Home staging   96

Employing Elder Care Service Professionals   97

Help with Money, Care, and Home Management
Preparedness Checklist   100

CHAPTER 4 Essential Legal Planning   **101**

Advance Directives for Health Care   102

   Living wills   107

   Durable power of attorney for health care   109

   Anatomical gift form   114

   Advance directive for mental health treatment   116

   Barriers to advance directive implementation   118

      Portability   118

      Quality and specificity of instructions   120

      Precedent autonomy   121

   Default surrogates   123

   Hospital ethics committees   124

Power of Attorney for Property and Finances   125

Wills, Trusts, Transfers on Death, and Other Asset
Distribution Instructions   128

   Wills   129

   Trusts   131

   Transfer on death   133

   Other instructions   134

Storing, Disseminating, and Updating Your Legal
Documents   135
Legal Preparedness Checklist   138

CHAPTER 5 **Driving While Elderly**   **141**

Driving and Collision Statistics   143
State Regulation   144
Knowing When to Stop Driving and Making It Happen 150
The signs of danger   150
Having the conversation   151
Finding Transportation Resources   153
The Aid of Technology   155
Driving Preparedness Checklist   157

CHAPTER 6 **Coordinated Care: Treating the**
Person, not Diseases   **159**

The Practice of Geriatrics   162
The shortage of geriatricians   166
Planning for Medical Care in Old Age   169
Finding a doctor   169
Concierge medicine and direct primary care   172
Being a member of your own medical team   174
Involving trusted advocates and obtaining adequate support 179
Coordinated Care Preparedness Checklist   183

CHAPTER 7 **Long-Term Care**   **185**

Nursing Homes   187
Quality of care   190
Costs   194
Observational status   195

Medicaid eligibility 197
Assisted Living 199
Home Care Agencies 203
Hiring Aides Independently 207
Part-Time Care: Adult Day Services 210
Long-Term Care Preparedness Checklist 213

CHAPTER 8 Exit Strategies: Maintaining Control at the End of Life **215**

Hospice and Palliative Care 219
Being an Active Member of Your Health Care Team 223
The problem of overtreatment 224
The power to choose 228
DNRs, out-of-hospital DNRs, and POLST 229
Religious beliefs 232
Medical Aid in Dying 233
Ending Your Life without Medical Assistance 238
CODA 241
End-of-Life Preparedness Checklist 242

CHAPTER 9 Conclusion **245**

Help from the Government 249
What the Future Holds 251
The Importance of Social Life 253
Retaining a Sense of Purpose and Usefulness 254
Write Your Legislator 255
Remain Adept at Using Technology 257
A Final Preparedness Checklist 259

Index 263

ACKNOWLEDGMENTS

First and foremost I want to thank the many relatives and friends who shared their lives and their stories with me. They have taught me so much about the difficulties and triumphs that people experience at every stage, especially when they care for elderly relatives or face their own end-of-life challenges. To my parents and mother-in-law I am indebted not only for teaching me countless life lessons but also for their unflagging love, support, and encouragement. I miss the three of them terribly.

Case Western Reserve University (CWRU) has been my intellectual home for over twenty years and has given me the opportunity to have an incredibly fulfilling career. I am grateful for being included among its faculty and also for financial support for this book project. A CWRU Academic Careers in Engineering & Science (ACES) Advance Opportunity Grant enabled me to do early research, and a law school summer grant and sabbatical allowed me to complete a draft of the project.

The Robert Wood Johnson Foundation selected me for a 2013 Scholar in Residence Fellowship to work with the Oregon Health Authority on the regulation of in-home care. That experience provided valuable insights into this important source of services for the elderly. During my sabbatical semester in 2014, Emory University School of Law welcomed me as a visiting scholar and supplied beautiful office space in which it was a pleasure to work on the book's first edition.

I am grateful to the ethics committee at the University Hospitals Cleveland Medical Center for exposing me to the complexities of numerous elder care issues and enabling me to be an active participant in discussions of treatment controversies as well as decision-making for incapacitated patients without proxies. I have also learned much from staff members at a number of continuing care retirement communities that I visited and hospices that cared compassionately for my loved ones.

Several readers of early drafts provided comments that helped me improve the manuscript significantly. They are Jaime Bouvier, Naomi Cahn, Cassandra Robertson, and Tony Moulton. Jennifer Armstrong provided detailed edits and suggestions that were invaluable. Leon Gabinet and Joan Burda were generous with their time and contributed a great deal to my understanding of wills, trusts, and estates. Their help provided a strong foundation for my treatment of these matters in the book. Numerous other colleagues offered inspiration and advice and ensured that I would not lose faith in this project.

A special thank you to four research fellows at CWRU School of Law whose work was vital to this book: Stephanie Corley, Tracy (Yeheng) Li, Rebecca Smith, and Mariah Dick. Halden Schwale and Drew Snyder also provided very capable research assistance.

Many thanks to my fabulous team of editors at Anthem Press: Molly Grab, Megan Greiving, and everyone involved in line editing the manuscript. They did wonderful work and had infinite patience for my many questions.

Finally, my deepest thanks go to my husband, Andy. For the past 16 years, he has been a loving husband and an intellectual partner. He has made my work better and my life far richer.

INTRODUCTION AND MY
PERSONAL STORY

As often happened in those days, my lunchtime conversation with a colleague drifted to the subject of eldercare. My husband and I had been immersed in caring for elderly relatives who were in their mid-80s and beyond. During an 18-month period in 2013 and 2014, we lost my mother, who died at the age of 84; Andy's mother, who died at 93; and my father, who died at 87. My friend revealed that she was coordinating care for her mother, who was in her 90s, had advanced dementia, and lived in another state. I said that sometimes I felt that our parents were lucky because at least they had us to help them, and that I have begun to worry about my own aging because Andy and I have no children. Then my friend surprised me by saying that she enjoys a very close relationship with her only son, but what she fears most about aging is that he will come to dread visiting her and will consider contact with her to be an unwelcome obligation. Having a devoted child, therefore, was hardly a comfort when she contemplated her later years.

This book, *Aging with a Plan*, began with my own effort to identify strategies that I could adopt to minimize the potential pitfalls of aging. It also grew out of a desire to help my contemporaries who may find themselves suddenly immersed in caring for elderly relatives, a sometimes overwhelming task for which little in life prepared us. It is meant to be a concise but comprehensive resource for middle-aged people who have much to gain from thinking ahead.

This second edition is fully revised and updated. It was completed in 2021, a year that will long be remembered for the COVID-19 pandemic.

In the process of researching and writing, I have learned a great deal. Too many elderly individuals refuse needed professional caregiving because of its costs and the loss of autonomy it involves; some undergo aggressive medical interventions that exacerbate rather than improve their conditions; and others end up in facilities that are inadequately staffed and whose services at times border on neglect. Yet I have also found much reassurance. I am convinced that many other people in their 40s, 50s, and early 60s can benefit from the knowledge I gained and from investing some effort in planning for their later years as well as for those of their loved ones. As I learned the hard way, in the midst of crisis, it is very difficult to make the best possible decisions if you have never contemplated the matter at hand.

WHY I WROTE THE BOOK

"Shoot me before I get to be like my [mother, aunt, grandfather]" is an only half-joking comment I've often heard from individuals who are involved in caring for the elderly. Yet, as much as Americans plan for their futures earlier in life, few of us dare think about and plan for frailty, which could extend over years or even decades of our lives. *Aging with a Plan* aims to change that.

The book is anchored in both my personal experience and my professional expertise as a professor of law and bioethics at Case Western Reserve University. I am also a member of the Ethics Committee at Cleveland's University Hospitals, which often grapples with difficult treatment decisions for incapacitated elderly persons who do not have other decision makers. My interest in issues of health law, bioethics, and caregiving stems in part from a 15-month period in the mid-1990s in which I suffered my own medical crisis and shortly thereafter became a caregiver for my then 65-year-old mother, who underwent extensive treatment for breast cancer.

The first time I thought seriously about my mortality was in the spring of 1994. I awoke in the early morning hours of May 4 to the most severe abdominal pain I had ever experienced. I struggled to think clearly. Was it a stomach flu? Was it menstrual cramps? I got out of bed and walked doubled-over to the bathroom. I took two aspirin, fought my urge to shriek in agony, and tried to find the least uncomfortable position, alternately sitting, lying down, and pacing in my small one-bedroom apartment. I could not believe how piercing and unrelenting the pain was, and nothing would relieve it.

I was 29, single, and had no family in Houston, where I had been living for four years. It turned out that I had a large (eight by five by five inches), borderline malignant ovarian tumor. I underwent major surgery, but, to my relief, I did not need chemotherapy or radiation. As soon as the tumor was discovered, my parents, who lived in Michigan, rushed to Houston, and friends remained by my side so that I was rarely left alone until well after my hospitalization. Six weeks after the surgery, at the end of June, I resumed my full-time work schedule. I weighed 98 pounds, having lost 10 pounds, and tired easily, but life slowly returned to normal.

And then came a phone call in the third week of November 1994 that would dramatically change everything once again. My mother, or Eema, as we called her in Hebrew, was diagnosed with breast cancer following suspicious findings on a routine mammogram. She wanted to take advantage of my living in Houston and have her surgery at the renowned MD Anderson Cancer Center. Thus, my parents and three younger sisters made a pilgrimage to Texas, and my one-bedroom apartment turned into Hoffman family headquarters.

Eema had a full mastectomy to remove her right breast along with 12 lymph nodes on December 7, 1994. The surgery was successful, but we soon learned that 6 of the lymph nodes were positive for cancer. She would need both chemotherapy and radiation, with treatment lasting well into the summer.

I don't remember any serious family discussion of next steps. Instead, I remember only Eema's announcement:

> I'm going to stay in Houston for all of my treatment. I will live with Sharona, and everyone else can visit when you want to.

I had not contemplated this possibility before, but I did not object. It was reasonable for Eema to want to be treated at a premier oncology center, so I embarked on this journey with her, though not without trepidation.

And thus began what ironically became one of the most wonderful periods of my life. I had not been particularly close with Eema during my first three decades. She was more a strict disciplinarian than a friend. By contrast, the nine months I spent with Eema in Houston were a gift that introduced me to a person I had never known before. Eema suddenly blossomed into a gregarious, adventurous, and fun-loving woman who looked and acted decades younger than her 65 years.

We attended numerous lectures and community events. We also frequently went to the theater and took advantage of half-priced tickets that were available one hour before the show began. Eema even developed a surprising interest in eating out, though she had previously always preferred to eat modest meals at home.

I would tease Eema and tell her that she was exhausting me with all this running around.

"You're supposed to be sick, and I'm supposed to be having a very boring year, stuck in the apartment taking care of you. Instead, you don't let me stay home at all."

In response she would squeal in delight and acknowledge that she didn't recognize herself.

"Who knows what's really in this chemo? It is giving me a complete personality overhaul."

Eema's energy, initiative, and magnetism impressed me to no end. Her health care providers loved her. My friends adored her. Even Freddie, the woman who delivered our mail, was extremely fond of her because Eema made a point of going downstairs to the mailboxes to chat with her as she worked. Freddie asked about Eema whenever she saw me for years thereafter.

Eema completed her eight cycles of chemotherapy and then underwent six weeks of radiation treatment. She left Houston in August 1995 and was cancer-free for almost eighteen years. She died on May 17, 2013, of what turned out to be pancreatic cancer.

I often think back to the dramatic years of 1994–95. I was both a patient with a serious illness and a caregiver for a prolonged period of time. I learned firsthand about the triumphs of modern medicine and the challenges and complexities of the health care and insurance industries. I also learned a lot about caregiving. I know how important family, friends, and community are in difficult times. And I have an acute awareness of how much time, effort, and money may be required to meet all the needs of a loved one who is very ill.

Eema and I were sustained by the devotion of our friends and by our own close bond. We looked forward to visits, phone calls, and mail, and we made a point of going out and interacting with others as often as possible. The many months we spent together were also a highlight for me because I felt at my most useful, and Eema was generous in expressing her gratitude every day. For others whose health is failing, it is very challenging to maintain robust social lives and a sense of purpose. The importance of social interaction and feeling useful are major themes throughout this book.

My experiences led me to become increasingly interested in medical matters and ultimately to devote my career to health law and bioethics. A decade after graduating from Harvard Law School in 1988, I returned to school to pursue an advanced degree (LL.M) in health law at the University of Houston Law Center and then obtained a faculty position at Case Western Reserve University (CWRU) School of Law, where I serve as codirector of the Law-Medicine Center. I have also earned a doctorate (SJD) in health law from CWRU.

I have written *Aging with a Plan* in order to find answers to the many questions and anxieties that I have about growing old without an obvious source of informal caregiving. In 2013, Eema suffered terribly during a 10-day hospitalization before her pancreatic cancer was diagnosed, and we switched her to hospice care for the final two days of her life. But in some ways, she was very fortunate. Once it was clear that Eema's condition was serious, her four daughters dropped everything and rushed to be with her, and we left the hospital only to get a few hours of sleep at night. We also were not shy about pressing doctors and nurses to do everything possible to relieve her pain, and we easily reached consensus about pursuing comfort care when it was clear the end was near. Eema took her last breath while deeply asleep and surrounded by her children.

Thereafter, our father, though he was devastated by the loss of his wife of 54 years, enjoyed the benefits of having four devoted daughters. One of my three sisters resided minutes away and was extremely involved in his care. She visited frequently, filled his pill boxes, and coordinated all of his care. The rest of us, who lived out of state, called multiple times a week and visited as often as we could. When it was clear my father was dying in late 2014, we once again gathered together and held a round-the-clock vigil by his bedside during his final days.

My old age will inevitably be different. My husband, Andy, is seven years older than I, and we have no children and no large, extended family. Moreover, in October 2013, at the age of 55, Andy was diagnosed with Parkinson's disease. Although this illness progresses slowly, he will become increasingly disabled and will likely need assistance from paid caregivers, which could deplete our savings. These circumstances worry me. If

I reach old age and experience the inevitable deterioration of my health, will I have a strong support network, as I did when I was sick at 29? In the absence of children, will there be trustworthy people who can regularly help me with medication, transportation, finances, and the like? If I live independently late in life, will I have the fortitude to give up driving when that is prudent or to know when it is time to seek professional caregiving or move to a nursing home? And what if I become one of the millions of elderly people with cognitive impairment and dementia? How can I even begin to contemplate that possibility?

Over the years, I have learned that many share my anxiety about having to be self-reliant late in life. What can be done? One option is to simply focus on enjoying the present and not "waste time" fretting about potential future misfortunes. But a need to manage and plan is deeply embedded in my nature. Letting the chips fall where they may is not. You can always hope to die in your sleep, but this is very unlikely. According to one study, only 10 percent of people who die of natural causes experience sudden death with no prior diagnosis of a potentially fatal illness.[1] Some torments, like the onset of dementia, are currently outside of human control. But other hardships, like social isolation and a lack of purpose can be overcome or be avoided with sufficient effort.

In the spring of 2007, I spent a sabbatical semester at the Centers for Disease Control and Prevention, working on public health emergency preparedness. All of us have recently experienced a public health emergency in the form of COVID-19. We have seen the tragic consequences of failing to plan for a global pandemic and of not taking it seriously enough. COVID-19 also vividly demonstrated how unpredictable life

---

1. Mary Elizabeth Lewis et al., "Estimated Incidence and Risk Factors of Sudden Unexpected Death," *Open Heart* 3, no. 1 (2016): e000321.

can be. Whatever your age, you may be healthy one week and gravely ill the next, needing trusted people to make critical decisions for you. If we are not educated about the challenges of our later years, we may face unnecessary suffering and avoidable disasters. This book, therefore, serves as a guide to aging preparedness.

A FEW FACTS AND FIGURES

The challenges of aging are of utmost importance to American society and will only grow in significance in the coming years and decades. If you are like me and are past the half-century mark, you are among a large wave of people who are changing the age demographics in this country.

In 2019, 16.5 percent of the population, or 54 million people, were age 65 and over,[2] up from 3.1 million in 1900.[3] Those who are 85 years old and older numbered 6.5 million in 2018, compared to just over 100,000 in 1900. Experts predict that by 2040, the 85 and older population will grow to 14.4 million.[4]

"Baby boomers," defined as those born between 1946 and 1964, began turning 65 in 2011. The 65 and older population is projected to expand to 78 million by 2035 and to constitute

---

2. Erin Duff, "Share of Old Age Population (65 Years and Older) in the Total U.S. Population from 1950 to 2050," September 28, 2020, https://www.statista.com/statistics/457822/share-of-old-age-population-in-the-total-us-population/.

3. Administration for Community Living & Administration on Aging, "2019 Profile of Older Americans," Administration for Community Living & Administration on Aging, https://acl.gov/sites/default/files/Aging%20and%20Disability%20in%20America/2019ProfileOlderAmericans 508.pdf (May 2020): 5.

4. Administration for Community Living & Administration on Aging, "2019 Profile of Older Americans," 3.

21 percent of total US residents.[5] In fact, the US Census Bureau predicts that in 2035 seniors will outnumber children under 18 in the United States, of whom there will be only 76.7 million.

In 2019, life expectancy in the United States was 76 years for males and 81 years for females.[6] Life expectancy is an average that varies with age, and thus the outlook is even better for individuals who have already lived to be 65, because they have survived the hazards of infancy, childhood, and young adulthood.[7] Women who are now 65 can expect to reach age 85 and their male counterparts can expect to live to be 83.[8]

Although many seniors achieve longevity, they do not necessarily do so in good health. According to the National Council on Aging, 80 percent of older adults have at least one chronic condition and nearly 70 percent of Medicare beneficiaries have two or more.[9] Most commonly, seniors have hypertension (67 percent of men and 75 percent of women), heart disease (28 percent), diabetes (28 percent), cancer (19 percent), stroke (9 percent), and arthritis (54 percent).[10]

5. US Census Bureau, "The U.S. Joins Other Countries with Large Aging Populations," US Census Bureau, updated October 8, 2019, https://www.census.gov/library/stories/2018/03/graying-america.html.

6. Erin Duffin, "Average Life Expectancy in North America for Those Born in 2019, by Gender and Region (in Years), *Statista*, September 20, 2019, https://www.statista.com/statistics/274513/life-expectancy-in-north-america/.

7. Maggie Koerth-Baker, "Death of a Caveman: What Swedish Babies and the Stone Age Can Teach Us about Life Expectancy and Income Inequality," *New York Times Magazine*, March 24, 2013, 14.

8. Administration for Community Living & Administration on Aging, "2019 Profile of Older Americans," 5.

9. National Council on Aging, "Healthy Aging: Fact Sheet," National Council on Aging, revised July 2018, https://d2mkcg26uvg1cz.cloudfront.net/wp-content/uploads/2018-Healthy-Aging-Fact-Sheet-7.10.18-1.pdf.

10. Administration for Community Living & Administration on Aging, "2019 Profile of Older Americans," 17.

Furthermore, as of 2021, 6.2 million Americans were afflicted with Alzheimer's disease, almost all of whom are seniors.[11] Many more live with other forms of dementia.[12] Recent research, however, provides some encouraging news concerning dementia. One study found that dementia rates among US residents who are 65 and older dropped from 12 percent in 2000 to 10.5 percent in 2012.[13] Several other studies confirm a decline in the prevalence of dementia in the developing world.[14] This drop is likely attributable to better education and health, including control of blood pressure and cholesterol through medication and good health habits such as regular exercise and proper nutrition.[15]

---

11. Alzheimer's Association, "2021 Alzheimer's Disease Facts and Figures," *Alzheimer's & Dementia* 17, no. 3 (2021): 1–104, at 19. More specifically, according to the Alzheimer's Association, "the percentage of people with Alzheimer's dementia increases dramatically with age: 5.3 percent of people age 65–74, 13.8 percent of people age 75–84 and 34.6 percent of people age 85 or older have Alzheimer's dementia."

12. Alzheimer's Association, "2021 Alzheimer's Disease Facts and Figures," at 19.

13. Péter Hudomiet, Michael D. Hurd, and Susann Rohwedder, "Dementia Prevalence in the United States in 2000 and 2012: Estimates Based on a Nationally Representative Study," *Journals of Gerontology: Series B* 73, suppl. 1 (2018): S10–S19.

14. Olivia Petter, "Dementia Rates Are Falling in Europe and the US and Experts Credit Decline of Smoking," *Independent*, March 21, 2019, https://www.independent.co.uk/life-style/dementia-decline-rates-smoking-tobacco-prevention-study-harvard-school-public-health-a8833136.html; Alzheimer's Research UK, "International Research Shows Dementia Rates Falling by 15% per Decade over Last 30 Years," Alzheimer's Research UK, March 20, 2019, https://www.alzheimersresearchuk.org/international-research-shows-dementia-rates-falling-by-15-per-decade-over-last-30-years/.

15. Gina Kolata, "Dementia on the Retreat in the U.S. and Europe," *New York Times*, August 3, 2020, https://www.nytimes.com/2020/08/03/health/alzheimers-dementia-rates.html.

Nevertheless, experts estimate that dementia cost American society a staggering $305 billion in 2020.[16] Much of the burden of caring for this population falls on family and friends. According to the Alzheimer's Association, over 11 million Americans provide unpaid care for Alzheimer's disease and other dementia patients, supplying approximately 15.3 billion hours of care in 2020.[17]

But many individuals lack adequate support systems. Federal government statistics reveal that in 2019, women who were 65 or older were twice as likely to live alone as men in that age group (9.7 million vs. 5 million). Overall, 28 percent of seniors who are not in facilities live by themselves.[18] The Alzheimer's Association estimates that this figure includes 26 percent of dementia patients who do not live in long-term care facilities.[19]

The childless

A significant segment of the US population remains childless throughout life. As of 2018, according to the Pew Research Center, 14 percent of women in the age group of 40–44 had never given birth.[20] In 1976, the figure was only 10 percent.

---

16. Alzheimer's Association, "Costs of Alzheimer's to Medicare and Medicaid," Alzheimer's Association, March 2020, http://act.alz.org/site/DocServer/2012_Costs_Fact_Sheet_version_2.pdf?docID=7161.

17. Alzheimer's Association, "2021 Alzheimer's Disease Facts and Figures," 36.

18. Administration for Community Living & Administration on Aging, "2019 Profile of Older Americans," 4.

19. Alzheimer's Association, "2020 Alzheimer's Facts and Figures," 425.

20. Gretchen Livingston, "They're Waiting Longer, but U.S. Women Today More Likely to Have Children than a Decade Ago," Pew Research Center, January 18, 2018, https://www.pewsocialtrends.org/2018/01/18/theyre-waiting-longer-but-u-s-women-today-more-likely-to-have-children-than-a-decade-ago/.

In her moving memoir, *Blue Nights*, Joan Didion writes about the death of her only daughter less than two years after she lost her husband. In a poignant passage with particular resonance for me, she recounts her efforts to fill out medical forms in physicians' offices:

> Sitting in frigid waiting rooms trying to think of the name and telephone number of the person I want notified in case of emergency.
> Whole days now spent on this question. This question with no possible answer: *who do I want notified in case of emergency?*

She could think of no one and left the space blank on the paper.[21] Many others who lack close relatives must face similar dispiriting moments. A major purpose of this book is to offer resources and recommendations for those who will be aging without nearby family members to whom they can turn for assistance.

WHAT THE BOOK COVERS

Aging with a Plan offers one-stop shopping to those who wish to prepare for their own aging and that of loved ones. I explore a variety of relevant social, legal, financial, and medical issues. I elaborate on the importance of developing a robust social life, intellectual interests, and ways to maintain a sense of purposefulness that will not fade late in life. In the words of a friend who is a geriatric social worker, the key to good aging is to "stay active physically, mentally, and socially."

In general, my guiding question is this: What should middle-aged individuals contemplate, study, decide, and do to be as well-equipped as possible for their own aging and that of loved

---

21. Joan Didion, *Blue Nights* (New York: Vintage, 2011), 185.

ones? Furthermore, at a broader, societal level, what cultural, attitudinal, and legal changes are required to improve the prospects of the elderly, especially those who cannot count on others to care for them? What should baby boomers, with their strong political voice and economic power, be striving and lobbying for?

In brief, I address the following topics in this book's chapters.

- In Chapter 1, I explore some of the costs that individuals may incur after retirement and discuss the importance of retirement savings and of obtaining professional financial advice. I provide guidance as to how to obtain financial counseling and begin a savings program and analyze in detail two particular financial products: long-term care insurance and reverse mortgages.
- Chapter 2 describes several types of retirement communities with a special focus on continuing care retirement communities. I argue that seniors should not lightly dismiss the idea of living in a community setting because of the importance of maintaining social interaction and intellectual and civic engagement throughout life.
- A major concern for independent seniors without close family members is whether anyone will be available to help coordinate their care, pay bills, and provide the support that others receive from their children and nearby relatives. In Chapter 3, I explore a variety of emerging options for professional help, namely geriatric care managers, daily money managers, elder law attorneys, professional organizers, and experts who can assist with adapting a home to accommodate disabilities or with preparing it for sale.
- In Chapter 4, I discuss and critique a variety of documents that are essential for purposes of legal preparedness: durable powers of attorney for health care, living wills, organ donation forms, advance directives for

mental health treatment, durable powers of attorney for property and finances, wills, and trusts.

- I dedicate Chapter 5 to the fraught issue of driving by the elderly. I examine the following questions: (1) Do elderly drivers have reason to worry that they are a danger to themselves or others on the road? (2) How do state laws handle driver's license renewal for older drivers? (3) How can families tell whether elderly relatives are at risk of unsafe driving? (4) How should you approach conversations with elderly loved ones regarding this sensitive subject? I also discuss transportation alternatives that are available in some communities and emerging automobile technologies that will enhance seniors' ability to drive safely as they grow older.
- Chapter 6 focuses on the changing medical needs of people from middle age onward and the importance of obtaining coordinated care, ideally from physicians with geriatric expertise. I also outline strategies for becoming an active, educated member of your own medical team and building strong support networks in case of illness or disability.
- In Chapter 7, I discuss the long-term care needs of the elderly and existing options for such care. To this end, I analyze the benefits and shortcomings of nursing homes, assisted living, home care, and adult day care services. I also provide guidance to help you do your research and make appropriate choices concerning long-term care.
- Chapter 8 analyzes end-of-life care and the degree to which you can maintain control over it. I discuss medical aid in dying (available in a handful of states), the ability to decline unwanted life-prolonging treatment, "do not resuscitate" and POLST orders, palliative care, and hospice programs. Thinking about the end of life might seem like a depressing thing to do, but engaging in soul-searching about our preferences, knowing what choices

we'll have, and discussing these matters with loved ones should facilitate end-of-life decision-making for ourselves and those in our care.

Since my husband's Parkinson's disease diagnosis, I am more aware than ever of life's uncertainties. I am often reminded of the old adage that "people make plans and God laughs." The diagnosis came at age 55, when we believed that Andy had many, many years of good health and full strength ahead of him. Parkinson's disease is a degenerative neurologic condition caused by loss of dopamine cells in the brain, and patients often live for decades with it. We simply do not know what the future holds for us in terms of Andy's disease progression, ability to work, care needs, and expenses. At the same time that we must accept considerable uncertainty (a particularly difficult proposition for me), we must also try even harder to put safeguards in place so that our future is as secure as possible in terms of finances and opportunities for social, intellectual, and civic engagement.

Planning ahead can be critical to maintaining a good quality of life as you age even when you suffer health problems, loss of loved ones, and other misfortunes. By contrast, facing a crisis without having thought about potential next steps can be overwhelming. Crisis can come in many forms: sudden illness, death of a spouse or partner, or worsening mental or physical impairments that rob people of the ability to take care of themselves. Without planning ahead, these adversities can leave elderly individuals without any good options, unable to socialize, to remain active and independent, and to enjoy the pleasures that make life worth living.

Planning for your later years entails not only taking concrete steps, such as writing a will and an advance directive, but also learning about the problems that the elderly encounter, such as obstacles to effective medical care and driving challenges. Learning about these matters will not only help you think through how you might address them when your time comes but will also empower you to help aging loved ones in the more immediate future.

With adequate planning, the long-term impact of hardships can be diminished. Furthermore, planning ahead can prevent the loss of autonomy that so many seniors fear. For example, having a trusted substitute decision maker can alleviate anxiety about what financial and medical decisions will be made for you if you lose decision-making capacity. Likewise, living in a high-quality retirement community can be a solution to the problems of social isolation and inactivity in old age.

In short, the book strives to develop sound approaches to building sustainable social, medical, and financial support mechanisms that can increase the likelihood of a good quality of life throughout the aging process. In other words, I aim to develop a plan that will be useful to me and, more important, to you.

CHAPTER 1

MONEY MATTERS: RETIREMENT EXPENSES, SAVINGS, AND FISCAL DECISION-MAKING

One of my concerns as the wife of a Parkinson's disease patient is my financial welfare when I am older. How long will Andy be able to work? How much money will we spend on his long-term care needs given that such expenses will not be covered by insurance? Will I have to retire early in order to become his caregiver? Will I have sufficient funds to be comfortable in my retirement and enjoy my later years?

Many decisions about retirement, living environment, health care, and other matters related to aging depend at least in part on finances. Money may not buy happiness, but being financially comfortable can make it easier to live a satisfying and enjoyable life after retirement. Your ability to follow several (though certainly not all) of the recommendations outlined in this book will depend on having adequate resources, and, therefore, I address money matters upfront.

Baby boomers will become eligible for full social security benefits between the age of 66 and 67 if born before 1960 or at age 67 if born in 1960 or later.[1] Thus, millions of Americans could live for two or more decades after retirement. With what

---

1. Social Security Administration, "Benefits Planner: Retirement," Social Security Administration, accessed December 20, 2020, https://www.ssa.gov/planners/retire/agereduction.html.

money will they support themselves? This chapter discusses strategies that you can implement in middle age to maximize the possibility of having a financially comfortable older age.

ARE AMERICANS SAVING ENOUGH?

I have heard friends joke: "My kids are my retirement plan." In reality, however, contemporary parents more often find themselves supporting adult children than being supported by them. According to the Pew Research Center, in 2020, 17.8 percent of 25- to 34-year-old Americans lived with their parents.[2] In addition, approximately three million grandparents are raising grandchildren.[3] Furthermore, a 2019 Merrill Lynch/ Age Wave survey found that parents provided financial support to 70 percent of sons and daughters who are ages 18–34, including over half of those in their early 30s. Almost three in five millennials (those born in the 1980s and 1990s) stated that their lifestyles depended on this type of support, which totals $500 billion a year nationally.[4] But this largesse often is to the financial detriment of parents, who sacrifice their retirement

---

2. John Creamer, Emily Shrider, and Ashley Edwards, "Estimated 17.8% of Adults Ages 25 to 34 Lived in Their Parents' Household Last Year," United States Census Bureau, September 15, 2020, https:// www.census.gov/library/stories/2020/09/more-young-adults-lived-with-their-parents-in-2019.html#:~:text=Estimated%2017.8%25%20 of%20Adults%20Ages,Their%20Parents'%20Household%20 Last%20Year&text=A%20Pew%20Research%20Center%20 report,their%20parents%20in%20March%202020.

3. Kent Allen, "Grandparents Report Success in Raising Grandchildren," AARP, November 6, 2018, https://www.aarp.org/home-family/friends-family/info-2018/grandparents-raising-kids.html.

4. Richard Eisenberg, "Parents' Support to Adult Kids: A Stunning $500 Billion a Year," *Forbes*, October 2, 2018, https://www.forbes.com/sites/nextavenue/2018/10/02/parents-support-to-adult-kids-a-stunning-500-billion-a-year/#29ab14245c87; Janna Herron, "Millennials Still Lean on

savings. In addition, almost all grandparents (94 percent) lavish money on their grandchildren, spending an annual average of $2,562 on them.[5] On the flip side, 20 percent of millennials provide financial support to their parents, and 12 percent of parents with children living at home also care for an older adult.[6]

Many commentators bemoan the fact that most Americans' retirement savings are sorely inadequate. A quarter of American adults have no retirement savings or pensions whatsoever, and the same is true for 13 percent of working people who are 60 and older.[7] One in three baby boomers (33 percent) have between $0 and $25,000 in retirement savings even though many are nearing the end of their careers.[8] This is not to say that workers should be blamed for their savings shortfall. In

Parents for Money but Want Financial Independence, Survey Says," *USA Today*, April 18, 2019, https://www.usatoday.com/story/money/2019/04/18/millennial-money-why-young-adults-still-need-support-parents/3500346002/.

5. Aaron Kassraie, "Nearly All Grandparents Provide Money to Grandchildren," AARP, April 12, 2019, https://www.aarp.org/home-family/friends-family/info-2019/grandparents-money.html.

6. Patty Lamberti, "How to Help Your Parents Financially—without Going Broke Yourself," *Money Under 30*, April 19, 2019, https://www.moneyunder30.com/helping-parents-financially; Gretchen Livingston, "More than One-in-Ten U.S. Parents Are also Caring for an Adult," Pew Research Center, November 29, 2018, https://www.pewresearch.org/fact-tank/2018/11/29/more-than-one-in-ten-u-s-parents-are-also-caring-for-an-adult/.

7. Board of Governors of the Federal Reserve, "Report on the Economic Well-Being of U.S. Households in 2018," Board of Governors of the Federal Reserve, May 2019, https://www.federalreserve.gov/publications/files/2018-report-economic-well-being-us-households-201905.pdf, 4.

8. Northwestern Mutual, "1 in 3 Americans Have Less than $5,000 in Retirement Savings," Northwestern Mutual, May 8, 2018, https://news.northwesternmutual.com/2018-05-08-1-In-3-Americans-Have-Less-Than-5-000-In-Retirement-Savings.

many cases it is the inevitable result of low earnings and the high price of essentials such as housing, higher education, and health care and not a consequence of individuals' choices to spend on luxury items today rather than save for tomorrow.

What medical expenses can you expect as a senior?

Financial resources make it possible to enjoy leisure activities as we age. But even more important, they are essential to obtaining proper medical care after retirement. Even retirees who live modestly can expect to have considerable expenses because of uncovered health care costs.

Some services you might need are rarely covered by insurance—hearing aids, for example. Unfortunately, the cost of a single hearing aid ranges from $1,000 to $4,000, a price that is daunting or completely unaffordable for all too many retirees.[9]

Moreover, even with Medicare coverage, you can sometimes pay exorbitant fees. Some medications, known as specialty drugs, cost upwards of $100,000 per year, and patients who need them pay thousands of dollars out of pocket.[10]

How much money might you need to meet your medical costs after retirement? Fidelity Investments estimates that a 65-year-old couple will need $295,000 (in today's dollars) to cover future medical expenses, such as deductibles, copayments, and the many costs that Medicare does not cover.[11]

---

9. "How Much Do Hearing Aids Cost?" Consumer Affairs, updated September 28, 2020, https://www.consumeraffairs.com/health/hearing-aid-cost.html#.

10. Sharona Hoffman and Isaac D. Buck, "Specialty Drugs and the Health Care Cost Crisis," *Wake Forest Law Review* 55, no. 1 (2020): 55–88.

11. Fidelity Viewpoints, "How to Plan for Rising Health Care Costs," Fidelity, August 3, 2020, https://www.fidelity.com/viewpoints/personal-finance/plan-for-rising-health-care-costs#:~:text=How%20much%20is%20needed%20for,health%20care%20expenses%20in%20retirement.

This figure does not include the very high price of long-term care, such as in-home care, assisted living, and nursing homes. Public insurance programs sometimes cover these expenses,[12] but a large number of seniors must pay for their long-term care services out of pocket.[13]

As discussed in Chapter 7, on average, nursing homes cost approximately $106,000 per year for a private room and $93,000 for a semi-private room. The base rate for a one-bedroom apartment in an assisted living facility is approximately $51,600. The median cost of an aide from a home care agency is $23.50 per hour.[14] According to one source, 52 percent of seniors will need long-term care services during their lifetimes. Women need such services for an average of 2.5 years, and men need them for an average of 1.5 years because they often do not live as long.[15] If an elderly individual needs to reside in a facility or receive round-the-clock care at home, the costs can grow to be astronomical, and it often is not covered by insurance. I discuss insurance coverage in detail below and in Chapter 7.

The Employee Benefit Research Institute's 2019 Retirement Confidence Survey queried 1,000 retirees and 1,000 workers

---

12. According to a Congressional Research Service Report, in 2016, Medicare paid 22 percent of US long-term care costs, and Medicaid paid 42 percent. Kirsten J. Colello, "Who Pays for Long-Term Services and Supports?," *Congressional Research Service*, August 22, 2018, https://fas.org/sgp/crs/misc/IF10343.pdf.

13. National Institute on Aging, "Paying for Care," National Institute on Aging, last reviewed May 1, 2017, https://www.nia.nih.gov/health/paying-care.

14. Genworth, "Cost of Care Survey 2020," Genworth, December 2, 2020, https://www.genworth.com/aging-and-you/finances/cost-of-care.html.

15. Christine Benz, "75 Must-Know Statistics about Long-Term Care: 2019 Edition," *Morningstar*, November 25, 2019, https://www.morningstar.com/articles/957487/must-know-statistics-about-long-term-care-2019-edition; Ellen Stark, "5 Things You Should Know about Long-Term Care Insurance," *AARP Bulletin*, March 1, 2018, https://www.aarp.org/caregiving/financial-legal/info-2018/long-term-care-insurance-fd.html (stating that 48 percent

who were 25 and older. It found that 82 percent of retirees are confident they (and their spouse) will be able to live comfortably for the rest of their lives. Moreover, 67 percent of workers are confident that they (and their spouse) will be able to afford a comfortable lifestyle throughout retirement.[16]

Despite Americans' optimism, reality may be quite different for many. It is safe to assume that an alarming number of retirees will not be able to live comfortably, much less luxuriously. A 2019 study published in *Health Affairs* focused in part on seniors with significant disabilities. It found that only 57 percent of these individuals could pay for at least two years of a "moderate" amount of home care if they liquidated all their assets. Only 40 percent would be able to pay for "extensive" home care after fully liquidating their assets.[17] A second study examined the resources of middle-income[18] seniors. It projected that there would be 14.4 million middle-income seniors in 2029 and that 54 percent of them will not be able to afford both senior housing (such as assisted living and independent living communities) and medical care.[19] Experts estimate that one out

---

of Americans need long-term care for less than a year, 19 percent require it for 1–2 years, 21 percent use it for 2–5 years, and 13 percent for 5 years).

16. Employee Benefit Research Institute and Greenwald & Associates, *2019 Retirement Confidence Survey Summary Report*, Employee Benefit Research Institute, April 23, 2019, 3–4, https://www.ebri.org/docs/default-source/rcs/2019-rcs/2019-rcs-short-report.pdf?sfvrsn=85543f2f_4.

17. Richard W. Johnson and Claire Xiaozhi Wang, "The Financial Burden of Paid Home Care on Older Adults: Oldest and Sickest Are Least Likely to Have Enough Income," *Health Affairs*, 38, no. 6 (2019): 994.

18. Middle income was defined as "annuitized financial resources of $25,001–$74,298 in 2014 dollars" for people who are 75–84 and $24,450–$95,051 for those who are 85 and older.

19. Caroline F. Pearson, Charlene C. Quinn, Sai Loganathan, A. Rupa Datta, Beth Burnham Mace, and David C. Grabowski, "The Forgotten Middle: Many Middle-Income Seniors Will Have Insufficient Resources for Housing and Health Care," *Health Affairs* 38, no. 5 (2019): 851–59.

of seven people who are 65 years old today will be disabled for at least five years before they die.[20]

Those who are parents should be aware that their lack of savings could generate considerable financial obligations for their children. Because many individuals now live into their 90s and beyond, some sons and daughters will be caregivers in their 60s and 70s. Instead of enjoying relaxed retirements, they may find themselves encumbered by caregiving duties and spending their retirement savings on their parents' needs.[21] The law may even obligate children to provide such support. For example, a Pennsylvania court held that a son was required to pay a $92,943 bill for his mother's nursing home care following a car accident.[22] Twenty-seven states (and Puerto Rico) have filial support laws that may require adult children to cover their parents' expenses in some circumstances. States have rarely enforced these statutes, but long-term care institutions may choose to rely upon them as a collection tool.[23]

RETIREMENT SAVINGS AND PROFESSIONAL FINANCIAL ADVICE

It may seem obvious that money is essential to a comfortable aging process, especially if you will age without many close family members nearby who can provide unpaid assistance.

---

20. Susan Jacoby, "We're Getting Old, but We're Not Doing Anything about It," *New York Times*, December 23, 2019, https://www.nytimes.com/2019/12/23/opinion/america-aging.html?smid=nytcore-ios-share.

21. Susan B. Garland, "At 75, Taking Care of Mom, 99: 'We Did Not Think She Would Live This Long,'" *New York Times*, June 30, 2019.

22. *Health Care & Retirement Corp. of America v. Pittas*, 46 A.3d 719 (Pa. Super. 2012).

23. K. Gabriel Heiser, "Filial Responsibility Laws and Medicaid," *AgingCare*, updated June 20, 2019, https://www.agingcare.com/Articles/filial-responsibility-and-medicaid-197746.htm.

However, the statistics above indicate that many may not have internalized this message. In fact, according to the Employee Benefits Research Institute, only 42 percent of workers report that they have attempted to calculate how much money they will require for retirement.[24] Needless to say, this is not an optimal approach to retirement planning.

Take advantage of employment benefits

As a first step, if your employer offers a defined contribution plan such as a 401(k), you should be sure to enroll. Saving through these plans is rewarded with tax benefits because money is taken out of paychecks before taxes. As a simple example, if you are taxed at a 25 percent rate, you receive only $75 for every $100 of your salary. However, if you designate $100 for your 401(k) account, the entire amount is invested because the 25 percent tax is not collected. Moreover, employers often match at least a percentage of contributions, thus adding considerably to workers' retirement savings.

Sadly, 35 percent of private-sector workers over the age of 22 do not have retirement savings plans as an employment benefit.[25] Many more choose not to participate in retirement plans that their employers offer. Only 52 percent of millennials contribute to their workplace retirement programs, while 80 percent of baby boomers do so.[26]

If your employer offers life insurance and disability insurance at little to no cost, you should also be sure to sign up for these benefits. Life insurance will provide your named beneficiary or

---

24. *2019 Retirement Confidence Survey*, 13.

25. The Pew Charitable Trusts, "Retirement Plan Access and Participation across Generations," Pew, February 15, 2017, https://www.pewtrusts.org/en/research-and-analysis/issue-briefs/2017/02/retirement-plan-access-and-participation-across-generations.

26. Pew, "Retirement Plan Access."

beneficiaries with a sum of money upon your death. They can use this money for any purpose, including to pay for your funeral. Disability insurance will pay all or part of your salary if you become unable to work because of a disability.

Life insurance is particularly valuable for individuals of modest means whose families may not have funds to pay burial expenses. If it is possible that this will be true for your family, you should purchase a policy even if it is not available through your employer.

Prioritize saving for retirement

You can also speak to your bank about opening a traditional individual retirement account (IRA) or a Roth IRA. In 2019–21, contributions to Roth IRAs were limited to $6,000 (or $7,000 for those 50 and over), and the money is tax exempt when it is withdrawn.[27]

In addition, deferring retirement for a few years will not only enable you to earn extra income but also raise the amount of your social security payments. The Social Security Administration offers delayed retirement credits to eligible individuals. As the federal regulations explain, "you may earn a credit for each month during the period beginning with the month you attain full retirement age [...] and ending with the month you attain age 70."[28] Full retirement age ranges from 65 for those born before 1938 to 67 for those born in 1960 or thereafter.[29]

Experts advise that you save for retirement even if you have young children and simultaneously need to save for their college

---

27. IRS, "Retirement Topics—IRA Contribution Limits," IRS, reviewed June 18, 2019, https://www.irs.gov/retirement-plans/plan-participant-employee/retirement-topics-ira-contribution-limits.

28. 20 C.F.R. § 404.313 (2020).

29. 20 C.F.R. § 404.409 (2020).

educations. College loans are widely available, but similar borrowing programs do not exist for retirement. And failing to save for retirement may well mean that you will become a burden to your children later on.[30]

Even small savings can accrue to meaningful sums over the years. For example, a sum of $365 (representing saving $1 a day during a single year) would yield $1,577.50 after 30 years assuming a 5 percent interest rate. An individual who continuously saves $250 each month in an account with an interest rate of just 1 percent would have $15,373 after five years of maintaining this fiscal habit.[31]

Those with more financial flexibility should engage in thoughtful retirement planning. There is no magic formula to calculate how much you should save for retirement.[32] Fidelity advises that you strive to save 15 percent of your yearly income.[33] But a more nuanced answer is that your optimal savings depend largely on your preferred lifestyle, reasonably anticipated earnings from investments and pension plans, and expected number of years without work. Various retirement calculators on the Internet can serve as a starting point for computing a ballpark amount of savings that you should have prior to retirement. For example, Moneychimp's "Simple

---

30. Herb Weisbaum, "Should You Save for Your Retirement or Your Kids' College? Here's the Math," NBC News, November 6, 2018, https://www.nbcnews.com/better/pop-culture/should-you-save-your-retirement-or-your-kids-college-here-ncna931431.

31. Bankrate, "Simple Savings Calculator," Bankrate.com, accessed December 20, 2020, http://www.bankrate.com/calculators/savings/simple-savings-calculator.aspx.

32. John Waggoner, "How Much Money Do I Need to Retire?" AARP, accessed December 20, 2020, https://www.aarp.org/work/retirement-planning/info-2015/nest-egg-retirement-amount.html.

33. Fidelity Viewpoints, "How Much Should I Save for Retirement?" Fidelity, July 21, 2020, https://www.fidelity.com/viewpoints/retirement/how-much-money-should-I-save.

Retirement Calculator" computes an annual retirement income based on three questions: (1) current principal; (2) pre-retirement annual additions, years to grow, and growth rate; and (3) post-retirement years to pay out and growth rate.[34]

Obtain professional financial advice

Relying on the Internet should not be the final step. You should consult a trustworthy financial professional at least periodically. Many workplaces offer employees opportunities to speak with retirement experts at no cost.

Low-income earners may also be able to obtain financial planning advice at no charge from professional volunteers. For example, most chapters of the Financial Planning Association (FPA) offer free help to underserved populations.[35] You can search on the Internet for an FPA chapter in your state and obtain contact information for pro bono services.[36] In addition, you can find a wealth of information on a website called Wife. org, run by a nonprofit organization that is "dedicated to providing an unbiased, financial education to women in their quest for financial independence."[37] Of course, you do not have to be a woman to read the information on this website!

If you will be hiring a financial adviser at your own expense, you should seek recommendations from knowledgeable

34. Moneychimp, "Simple Retirement Calculator," Moneychimp.com, accessed December 9, 2019, http://www.moneychimp.com/calculator/retirement_calculator.htm.

35. Financial Planning Association, "FPA Pro Bono Resources & Tools," Financial Planning Association, accessed December 20, 2020, http://www.onefpa.org/advocacy/Pages/ProBonoProgram.aspx.

36. Financial Planning Association, "FPA Chapters List," Financial Planning Association, accessed December 20, 2020, https://www.onefpa.org/community/Pages/FPA-Chapters-List.aspx.

37. Women's Institute for Financial Education, "A Man Is Not a Financial Plan," WIFE.org, accessed, December 20, 2020, http://www.wife.org.

acquaintances. You should also carefully interview potential advisers to determine their level of experience, fee structure, and whether they are committed to selling particular financial products to their clients because their companies require them to do so. You should look for a certified financial planner rather than an individual with no certification. You will also want to know if the individual charges a flat fee or an hourly fee or is compensated by commission only. Flat fees can take the form of a particular sum, such as $1,500 a year, or a percentage of your assets, typically 1 percent. Paying a fee equivalent to 1 percent of your assets may be daunting if you are fairly well off. On the other hand, advisers working on commission might be motivated to recommend that you make frequent changes that will yield a commission for them or that you purchase particular assets that will put more money in their pockets. You may want to ask candidates for the names of a couple of clients whom you can call as references to determine their level of satisfaction.[38]

Financial advisers can help clients develop savings plans, follow them, and diversify their portfolios to provide some degree of protection against market fluctuations. Competent advisers will formulate investment strategies based on how much financial risk their clients want to tolerate and what the clients' investment objectives are, as well as general rules of thumb.

A particularly important decision is that of asset allocation, that is, choosing the appropriate combination of stocks, bonds, and possibly other assets (e.g., real estate).[39] In a strong stock market, stocks can be very lucrative, but they can also quickly

---

38. *Wall Street Journal*, "How to Choose a Financial Planner," *Wall Street Journal*, accessed December 20, 2020, http://guides.wsj.com/personal-finance/managing-your-money/how-to-choose-a-financial-planner/tab/print/.

39. Richard Thaler and Cass Sunstein, *Nudge: Improving Decisions about Health, Wealth, and Happiness* (New York: Penguin Books, 2009), 120.

plummet in value when the market falls. By contrast, bonds pay a fixed interest rate for a designated period of time and are thus predictable and low-risk. However, bonds' interest rates provide less income than stocks with high dividends.

Some experts advise that the percentage of stocks in an individual's portfolio should be determined roughly by subtracting the investor's age from 100 or 120, with the remainder allocated to bonds. Thus, a 65-year-old should have 35–55 percent of her money in stocks and the remainder in bonds.[40] The exact allotment will depend on how risk-averse the investor is. To maintain the preferred asset allocation over time, the investor will periodically need to adjust the distribution of her money as earnings vary in the different asset categories.[41] Asset diversification lowers the risk of loss because if one sector, such as the stock market, has a downturn, the investor will still have a significant portion of her assets in other sectors that are not experiencing similar weakness.

Even those who are self-motivated to save will benefit from professional support. In 2020, the best savings account interest rates, typically offered by online banks, hovered around 2 percent, and many were as low as 0.01 percent.[42] You are unlikely to build robust savings with that modest growth rate. Today's economy requires more sophisticated investment choices than simply putting your money in a bank's savings account.

---

40. Robert Powell, "How to Use the 100-Minus-Your-Age Rule of Thumb When Investing in Your 401(k)," *USA Today*, February 16, 2018, https://www.usatoday.com/story/money/personalfinance/retirement/2018/02/16/how-use-100-minus-your-age-rule-thumb-when-investing-your-401-k/310338002/.

41. Thaler and Sunstein, *Nudge*, 125.

42. Lou Carlozo, "Best Savings Accounts—December 2020," *U.S. News & World Report*, updated December 2, 2020, https://money.usnews.com/banking/lt-savings-accounts.

It is difficult, even for an experienced investor, to avoid having a few (hopefully minimal) investment failures. To maintain a sense of perspective, develop realistic expectations, and know what questions to ask. It is prudent to remain updated about the market and to engage in some degree of self-education. Nevertheless, for me, at least, peace of mind depends on having a professional expert look after my savings.

Retiring with adequate savings will not guarantee a healthy and fulfilling aging experience because illness and misfortune can intervene regardless of the size of your bank account. However, the value of a comfortable monthly income in retirement cannot be ignored. If you are fortunate, it can enable you to move to a retirement community (discussed in the next chapter) if you wish to do so, pursue travel and other pleasures, and obtain the best available medical and personal care when necessary.

Obtain an interest-free loan if facing a financial crisis

If you are facing a crisis and cannot obtain a loan from a bank, you may be able to apply for an interest-free loan. The Hebrew Free Loan Association is a national organization that serves qualifying, low-income individuals of all faiths.[43] Some churches may offer similar programs.

I now turn to two financial products that you may consider in planning your fiscal future: long-term care insurance and reverse mortgages. In each case, there are potential benefits but also significant pitfalls.

LONG-TERM CARE INSURANCE

When I first began researching long-term care insurance, I thought purchasing such insurance would be an easy call.

---

43. See Hebrew Free Loan Association of Northeast Ohio, "About," Hebrew Free Loan Association of Northeast Ohio, accessed December 20, 2020, https://interestfree.org/hfla-of-northeast-ohio/.

I am generally risk-averse, and in the absence of children who could become unpaid caregivers, obtaining a policy would surely be prudent. It turns out that, as in the case of so many other matters related to eldercare, there is no clear and certain answer to the question of whether you should buy long-term care insurance.

Only 7.5 million Americans have long-term care insurance policies.[44] Long-term care insurance policies cover all or some of the following services: nursing home stays, assisted living, adult day care, and home care. If you end up needing long-term care for several years, you will likely benefit greatly from insurance, which will give you the freedom to choose services without worrying too much about costs. In her book, *Parenting Our Parents: Transforming the Challenge into a Journey of Love,* Jane Wolf Frances relates that her parents' long-term care policies were invaluable when they were in their 80s and could no longer manage without assistance. Consequently, she decided to buy her own policy at a relatively young age in order to pay lower premiums.[45]

Policy costs and limitations

Typical policies, however, have a variety of limitations that may give you pause. Coverage generally becomes available only when the policyholder needs significant assistance with a minimum of two activities of daily living (e.g., bathing and dressing) because of physical limitations that are expected to last at least ninety days or because of severe cognitive impairment.

---

44. American Association for Long-Term Care Insurance, *Long-Term Care Insurance Facts—Data—Statistics—2020 Reports,* accessed December 20, 2020, https://www.aaltci.org/long-term-care-insurance/learning-center/ltcfacts-2020.php#2020total.

45. Jane Wolf Frances, *Parenting Our Parents: Transforming the Challenge into a Journey of Love* (London: Rowman & Littlefield, 2019), 79.

Before this point of advanced disability, the insurer will not reimburse customers for expenses even if they obtain help from professional caregivers.[46] In addition, most policies exclude coverage for an initial period of time (called an "elimination period"), generally ranging from the first 30 to 90 days of long-term care.[47] Many policies provide benefits for only three years and have payment maximums, such as $160 per day for nursing home care.[48] If the designated top payment amount is fixed and a purchaser uses benefits decades after obtaining her policy, she may find that costs have risen significantly. Therefore, the policy will cover her for a smaller percentage of care expenditures than anticipated. Even if benefits grow over time under policy terms, the increases often do not fully adjust for inflation.[49]

What premiums can you expect to pay? According to the AARP, the average annual premium for a long-term care policy is $2,700. Generous discounts are often available if couples buy policies together, and the younger you are when you make the purchase, the lower the premium.[50] Thus, a 55-year-old couple

---

46. US Department of Health and Human Services, "Receiving Long-Term Care Insurance Benefits," *LongTermCare.gov*, updated October 15, 2020, https://longtermcare.acl.gov/costs-how-to-pay/what-is-long-term-care-insurance/receiving-long-term-care-insurance-benefits.html.

47. US Department of Health and Human Services, "Receiving Long-Term Care Insurance Benefits."

48. Stark, "5 Things You Should Know about Long-Term Care Insurance."

49. Jeffrey R. Brown and Amy Finkelstein, "Insuring Long-Term Care in the United States," *Journal of Economic Perspective* 25, no. 4 (2011): 119–42; Julia Kagan, "Insurance Inflation Protection," *Investopedia*, updated August 11, 2019, https://www.investopedia.com/terms/i/insurance-inflation-protection.asp.

50. Stark, "5 Things You Should Know about Long-Term Care Insurance"; American Association for Long-Term Care Insurance, *Long-Term Care Insurance Facts*.

may pay a total of $2,100 in premiums each year, while a couple buying policies at the age of 65 could pay $3,700 per year. Prices also depend on the number of years the policy covers, on the degree to which benefits grow to adjust for inflation, and on other policy terms.[51] You should also be aware that long-term care insurers often opt to raise premiums, so your costs could rise significantly during your lifetime.[52]

Another pitfall is that some consumers allow their policies to lapse because of the high costs of premiums and the uncertainty of deriving significant future benefits (since not everyone needs a prolonged period of long-term care). Individuals who become financially stressed may see the considerable expense of the annual premium as one they can easily eliminate without suffering any immediate adversity. In addition, people with cognitive decline may simply forget to pay their premiums.[53] However, it is critical to understand that if you let your policy lapse, you get no return whatsoever

---

51. American Association for Long-Term Care Insurance, "2020 National Long-Term Care Insurance Price Index," American Association for Long-Term Care Insurance, accessed December 20, 2020, https://www.aaltci.org/news/wp-content/uploads/2020/02/2020-Price-Index-LTC-Age-55-Trad-vs-LinkedBenefit.pdf.

52. Walecia Conrad, "The Ever-Rising Cost of Long-Term Care Insurance," CBS News, May 23, 2018, https://www.cbsnews.com/news/the-ever-rising-cost-of-long-term-care-insurance/; Maryalene LaPonsie, "Why No One Can Afford Long-Term Care Insurance (and What to Use Instead)," *U.S. News & World Report*, July 13, 2018, https://money.usnews.com/money/personal-finance/articles/2016-03-10/why-no-one-can-afford-long-term-care-insurance-and-what-to-use-instead.

53. Wenliang Hou, Wei Sun, and Anthony Webb, "Why Do People Lapse Their Long-Term Care Insurance?," Center for Retirement Research at Boston College, October 2015, http://crr.bc.edu/wp-content/uploads/2015/09/IB_15-17.pdf (finding that over a third of seniors let their policies lapse); Kathleen Ujvari, "Disrupting the Marketplace: The State of Private Long-Term Care Insurance, 2018 Update," AARP Public

on your investment of thousands upon thousands of premium dollars paid before you canceled the policy. Some insurers offer nonforfeiture benefits that allow you to get some value for your policy if you stop paying premiums, but these benefits add to your costs.[54]

Your financial circumstances

Medicaid is yet another factor that complicates the decision as to whether to buy a long-term care insurance policy. Individuals with few financial resources can obtain Medicaid coverage for nursing home care once they spend down their assets.[55] Detailed guidelines determine Medicaid eligibility, as discussed at greater length in Chapter 7. Typically, single people can keep their home, personal effects, and vehicle but must have no more than $2,000 in "countable resources" (cash, financial accounts, stocks, bonds, available assets in trust). In addition, in 2021, single Medicaid recipients' monthly income had to be under $2,382.[56] Medicaid pays for care only after long-term care insurance payments have been exhausted.

Policy Institute, August 6, 2018, https://www.aarp.org/content/dam/aarp/ppi/2018/08/disrupting-the-marketplace-the-state-of-private-long-term-care-insurance.pdf (asserting that "from 2008 through 2011, almost 11 percent of all buyers let their policies lapse during the first year of purchase but that the lapse rate dropped to 1.5 percent in later policy years.").

54. Erica Farrell, "LTC Policy Features: What Is Contingent Nonforfeiture?" LTC Consumer, January 16, 2019, https://ltcconsumer.com/ltc-policy-features-contingent-nonforfeiture/.

55. Geoff Williams, "How a Medicaid Spend Down Works," *U.S. News and World Report*, May 17, 2019, https://money.usnews.com/money/retirement/baby-boomers/articles/how-a-medicaid-spend-down-works.

56. American Council on Aging, "Medicaid Eligibility: 2021 Income, Asset & Care Requirements for Nursing Homes & Long-Term Care," American Council on Aging, updated December 4, 2020, https://www.medicaidplanningassistance.org/medicaid-eligibility/.

Some individuals do not feel that Medicaid coverage is a good option because it typically provides less choice as to nursing facilities and the type of long-term care you can receive. For example, Medicaid generally does not pay for assisted living facilities, and not all nursing homes are Medicaid certified.[57] Thus, if you prioritize having a lot of choices, you may opt for long-term care insurance even if premium payments stretch your budget. Nevertheless, in purely financial terms, long-term care insurance is not a prudent investment for individuals who are likely to qualify for Medicaid.

At the same time, people with significant income and assets may be wiser to save and invest the money that they would otherwise spend on premiums. Wealthy individuals can afford to take the gamble. If you are affluent and need long-term care, you can pay for it even without an insurance policy, and if you never need long-term care, you will have saved the considerable expenditure of paying for a policy of which you will never take advantage.

So, should you buy long-term care insurance? On the one hand, premium payments run in the thousands of dollars annually and will likely rise in the future.[58] Whether or not you will ever derive any plan benefits is uncertain because your long-term care needs will be unpredictable at the time of purchase. Because consumers often buy policies decades before they need benefits, another small risk is that your insurer will become insolvent before you

---

57. Fidelity Viewpoints, "Long-Term Care: Options and Considerations," Fidelity, February 8, 2019, https://www.fidelity.com/viewpoints/personal-finance/long-term-care-costs-options; LaPonsie, "No One Can Afford Long-Term Care Insurance"; Medicaid.gov, "Nursing Facilities," Medicaid.gov, accessed July 12, 2019, https://www.medicaid.gov/medicaid/ltss/institutional/nursing/index.html.

58. Greg Iacurci, "States Try to Beat Back Rate Increases on Long-Term-Care Policies," *Investment News*, September 13, 2018, https://www.investmentnews.com/article/20180913/FREE/180919958/states-try-to-beat-back-rate-increases-on-long-term-care-policies.

require long-term care, so your policy will not be honored. Yet another concern is that your policy will not be used when you need it because you are cognitively impaired and have forgotten about it, and those who care for you do not know that it exists.

On the other hand, research suggests that 15 percent of individuals who are 65 and older incur long-term care costs in excess of $250,000,[59] and for such patients, insurance could be invaluable. According to the American Association for Long-Term Care Insurance, the industry paid 11 billion in claims for 310,000 claimants in 2019.[60] There is simply no way to predict what your needs will be at the end of life.

Financial advisers' recommendations as to who should buy long-term care insurance vary. According to Christine Benz, an investment expert, retirees who pull less than 4 percent out of their savings each year for living expenses often do not need insurance.[61] Other experts recommend that you forego long-term care insurance if premiums will exceed 5 percent of your income.[62] According to George Kiraly, a certified financial planner, "if you have assets worth between $300,000 and $600,000 above and beyond the value of your home," you should seriously consider long-term care coverage.[63] He adds that those with assets worth

59. Benz, "75 Must Know Statistics"; Derek Guyton, Jennifer Leming, Stephen M. Weber, Jacklin Youssef, and Jean A. Young, "Planning for Health Care Costs in Retirement," *Vanguard*, June 2018, https://pressroom.vanguard.com/nonindexed/Research-Planning-for-healthcare-costs-in-retirement_061918.pdf.

60. American Association for Long-Term Care Insurance, *Long-Term Care Insurance Facts*.

61. Stark, "5 Things You Should Know about Long-Term Care Insurance."

62. National Association of Insurance Commissioners, "Long-Term Care Insurance," National Association of Insurance Commissioners, updated October 5, 2020, https://www.naic.org/cipr_topics/topic_long_term_care.htm.

63. Karin Price Mueller, "Is Long-Term Care Insurance Right for Me?," *NJMoneyHelp.com*, updated January 30, 2019, https://www.nj.com/business/2018/06/is_long-term_care_insurance_right_for_me.html.

$2 million or more can almost always pay for their own long-term care out of pocket and thus can forgo insurance.

Your age and health status

Insurers incentivize consumers to make the decision earlier rather than later in life by offering lower premiums for younger purchasers and establishing strict health-based eligibility rules. For example, those with memory loss, mobility limitations, a stroke history, or diabetes, may be screened out by insurers and deemed ineligible for coverage.[64] The average age of individuals who purchase policies is 56.[65] Keep in mind that the younger you are when you buy your policy, the lower the premium cost, but the more years you have to pay premiums.[66] The AARP suggests that the "optimal age to shop for a long-term care policy, assuming you're still in good health and eligible for coverage, is between 60 and 65."[67]

My husband became ineligible for long-term care insurance when he received his Parkinson's disease diagnosis at age 55,

---

64. American Association for Long-Term Care Insurance, "Long-Term Care Insurance Health Qualifications. Are You Even Insurable?" American Association for Long-Term Care Insurance, accessed December 20, 2020, http://www.aaltci.org/long-term-care-insurance/learning-center/are-you-even-insurable.php; Genworth, *TrueView Underwriting*[SM] *Guide*, Genworth, 2013, https://pinneyinsurance.com/underwriting-docs/Genworth-LTC-UW-Guide.pdf.

65. Howard Gleckman, "Sales of Traditional Long-Term Care Insurance Policies Continue to Fall," *Forbes*, July 3, 2019, https://www.forbes.com/sites/howardgleckman/2019/07/03/sales-of-traditional-long-term-care-insurance-policies-continue-to-fall/#5d48b9b1161d.

66. Mueller, "Is Long-Term Care Insurance Right for Me?"

67. Adam Shell, "Buy Long-Term Care Insurance at the Right Age to Get the Best Value," AARP, December 20, 2019, https://www.aarp.org/caregiving/financial-legal/info-2019/when-to-buy-long-term-care-insurance.html#:~:text=The%20optimal%20age%20to%20shop,a%20look%20five%20years%20earlier.

even though medications and exercise may enable him to continue taking care of himself without paid assistance for a couple of decades. Indeed, in 2019, long-term care insurers denied 19.4 percent of application from individuals under 50 and 46.2 percent of applications from individuals aged 70–74.[68] The fact that you could at any time find yourself disqualified by a diagnosis is the strongest argument for purchasing a policy at a younger rather than older age. Otherwise, you take the risk that you will eventually want such a policy but not be able to find an insurer who is willing to sell it to you.

Hybrid products

The market for stand-alone long-term care policies has shrunk in recent years. According to *Forbes*, only 60,000 policies were sold in 2018, compared to 750,000 in 2000.[69] Moreover, the number of insurers selling long-term care policies fell from 125 in 2000 to approximately 15 today.[70]

Instead, many people are opting for "hybrid" long-term care policies. A popular choice is a policy that combines life insurance with long-term care benefits.[71] Here is how it works: if you never need long-term care, your heirs will receive death benefit in an amount that is modestly higher than what you paid for the policy (with perhaps a 2 percent growth rate). If you do

68. American Association for Long-Term Care Insurance, *Long-Term Care Insurance Facts*.

69. Gleckman, "Sales of Traditional Long-Term Care Insurance"; Jamie Hopkins, "Hybrid Life Insurance Policies Increasingly Popular as Long-Term Care Funding Strategy," *Forbes*, October 10, 2018, https://www.forbes.com/sites/jamiehopkins/2018/10/10/hybrid-life-insurance-policies-increasingly-popular-as-long-term-care-funding-strategy/#5bf41ad1efaa.

70. Gleckman, "Sales of Traditional Long-Term Care Insurance".

71. Cameron Huddleston, "How to Use Life Insurance to Pay for Long-Term Care," *Forbes Advisor*, updated July 20, 2020, https://www.forbes.com/advisor/life-insurance/long-term-care-hybrid/.

need long-term care, you will have a much larger sum available, typically several times the cost of the policy.[72] A less common hybrid product is a hybrid long-term care annuity.[73] Both policies add a savings and investment component to insurance. One challenge posed by life insurance hybrids (and annuity hybrids) is that they require very large one-time premium payments, such as $50,000–$75,000 or more depending on coverage.[74] Nevertheless, those with financial means would be prudent to investigate these options.

REVERSE MORTGAGES

Reverse mortgages are heavily advertised on television by celebrities such as Henry Winkler and Tom Selleck. As tempting as these ads make reverse mortgages sound, they too require careful consideration and are not a prudent choice for many consumers.

Reverse mortgages are loans that allow borrowers who are at least 62 years old to convert part of the equity in their home into cash, so long as the home is their primary place of residence. Retirees who are homeowners but have limited incomes may rely on these loans to cover basic living expenses and to pay health care costs, though proceeds can be used for any purpose.

The term "reverse mortgage" is used to describe these loans because instead of making monthly payments to a bank, as in the case of traditional mortgages, borrowers receive payments

72. Bud Boland, "Does It Makes Sense to Buy Hybrid Long-Term Care Insurance?" *Kiplinger*, April 30, 2019, https://www.kiplinger.com/article/retirement/T036-C032-S014-should-you-buy-hybrid-long-term-care-insurance.html.

73. Fidelity Viewpoints, "Long-Term Care: Options and Considerations."

74. Boland, "Does It Makes Sense to Buy Hybrid Long-Term Care Insurance?"; Eleanor Laise, "Hybrid Insurance Policies Gaining Steam," *Kiplinger*, January 2017, https://www.kiplinger.com/article/insurance/T036-C000-S004-hybrid-policies-gaining-steam.html.

from lenders. Those who obtain reverse mortgages are not required to pay back their loans until the home is sold or otherwise vacated, for example, upon moving to a nursing home or upon death. You need only continue to pay property taxes, homeowners insurance, and condominium fees, if applicable, and to maintain the home in good repair.[75]

So far, so good. However, reverse mortgages come with significant drawbacks. Borrowers incur substantial upfront fees, including mortgage insurance premiums, loan origination fees, and closing costs, as well as ongoing fees such as high interest rates and service fees. *Forbes* has called reverse mortgages "one of the most expensive forms of credit you can get."[76] Also, because the loan must be paid off upon death, heirs may be left with little to inherit. Furthermore, if the reason for leaving the home is a move to a long-term care facility, the loan will become due at the same time that you must begin paying the very high cost of institutional care.[77] Worse yet, a surviving spouse or partner whose name is not on the loan will face foreclosure if he or she cannot pay off the reverse mortgage after the homeowner's death.[78] Foreclosure can also occur if the borrower fails to pay property taxes or homeowners' insurance or does not maintain the home in an acceptable condition.[79] Finally, those who choose a lump sum payment and obtain

---

75. National Reverse Mortgage Lenders Association, "Your Guide to Reverse Mortgages," National Reverse Mortgage Lenders Association, accessed December 9, 2019, http://www.reversemortgage.org/.

76. Carolyn Rosenblatt, "The Hidden Truths about Reverse Mortgages," *Forbes*, July 23, 2012, http://www.forbes.com/sites/carolynrosenblatt/2012/07/23/hidden-truths-about-reverse-mortgages/2/.

77. Tara Mastroeni, "5 Times Reverse Mortgages Are a Bad Idea," *Forbes*, October 15, 2018, https://www.forbes.com/sites/taramastroeni/2018/10/15/tk-times-reverse-mortgages-are-a-bad-idea/#640d53be43d6.

78. Mastroeni, "5 Times Reverse Mortgages Are a Bad Idea."

79. Nick Penzenstadler and Jeff Kelly Lowenstein, "Seniors Were Sold a Risk-Free Retirement with Reverse Mortgages. Now They Face Foreclosure,"

a reverse mortgage in their 60s may exhaust the money long before they need it most.

In some circumstances, reverse mortgages will serve borrowers well as a way to stay in a beloved home and pay living expenses. However, financial advisers often consider reverse mortgages to be a choice of last resort, and seniors should not make the decision to obtain such a loan lightly.[80]

LONG-TERM CARE COSTS AS A POLICY ISSUE

A comprehensive solution to our long-term care affordability problem would need to be spearheaded by the government. Government authorities have recognized the severity of the problem and the need to address it, but it remains intractable.

Most states have instituted partnership programs that reward people who purchase long-term care insurance with more lenient Medicaid eligibility criteria. These programs provide that if you buy a partnership-qualified long-term care insurance plan, you can retain a larger amount of assets[81] and still qualify for Medicaid if your insurance policy benefits run out.[82] The partnerships approach is a sound first step to tackling long-term care costs, but it helps only those who can afford to

---

USA Today, July 5, 2019, https://www.usatoday.com/in-depth/news/investigations/2019/06/11/seniors-face-foreclosure-retirement-after-failed-reverse-mortgage/1329043001/.

80. Marc Lichtenfeld, "Taking Out a Reverse Mortgage Is Almost Never a Good Idea—Here's Why," *Business Insider*, April 26, 2018, https://www.businessinsider.com/reverse-mortgage-what-it-is-and-why-its-a-bad-idea-2018-4.

81. Medicare will disregard assets in an amount that is equivalent to the sum that your long-term care policy paid. For example, if your policy paid out $150,000 of insurance claim benefits, Medicaid will allow you to keep an additional $150,000 over the asset level you would otherwise have to meet to qualify for Medicaid.

82. US Department of Health and Human Services, "Where to Look for Long-term Care Insurance," LongTermCare.gov, updated

purchase insurance policies and who will ultimately exhaust their policy benefits and become eligible for Medicaid.

One federal initiative to address the long-term care cost problem on a national scale seemed promising for a brief time. The Community Living Assistance Services and Supports (CLASS) Act was part of President Barack Obama's Patient Protection and Affordable Care Act of 2010. It would have enabled participants to pay a monthly premium in order to be eligible for modest benefits for their long-term care needs that would be available after five years of paying premiums. This program, however, was abandoned in 2011 because it was deemed not to be financially viable.[83]

It is unlikely that federal and state governments will undertake further ambitious initiatives to support long-term care insurance purchases in the near future. Yet, advocates continue to call for solutions, including sweeping reforms such as mandatory social insurance systems. They note that other countries, such as Germany, the Netherlands, and Japan, have successfully adopted such programs.[84] As the US population ages, the need for mechanisms to finance long-term care will only grow, and we must hope that policy-makers and voters become committed to tackling this critical challenge.

October 15, 2020, https://longtermcare.acl.gov/costs-how-to-pay/what-is-long-term-care-insurance/where-to-look-for-long-term-care-insurance.html; LTC Partner, "State Long Term Care Partnerships | Policies & Programs," LTC Partner, accessed December 20, 2020, https://longtermcareinsurancepartner.com/long-term-care-insurance/state-long-term-care-partnerships-policies-programs.

83. "Secretary Sebelius' Letter to Congress about CLASS," October 14, 2011, http://www.ltcconsultants.com/articles/2011/class-dismissed/Sebelius-CLASS-Letter.pdf.

84. Michael K. Gusmano and Irina B. Grafova, "Financing Long-Term Care," *American Affairs Journal* 2, no. 3 (2018): 32–40.

FINANCIAL PREPAREDNESS CHECKLIST

* Save as much as possible for retirement. Do not pass up an opportunity to participate in a 401(k) plan. Recognize that even small amounts of savings can add up over the years.

* Seek professional financial advice. You may be able to obtain advice at no cost through your employer or volunteers in your community. If you hire an adviser, research the candidates' credentials, experience, reputation, and fee structure carefully.

* Do not save less for retirement in order to pay a greater share of your children's college education. Remember that loans are widely available to finance college educations but not retirement, and you do not want to become a burden to your children later on.

* Seek a financial adviser's guidance regarding long-term care insurance and think carefully about whether this is a wise purchase for you. Consider the option of life insurance or annuity hybrids if you can afford the initial premium payments.

* Understand the limitations and potential pitfalls of reverse mortgages and consider other alternatives before opting for this financial product for yourself or your loved ones.

CHAPTER 2

THE BENEFITS OF
COMMUNITY LIVING

My late mother-in-law, Helen, was a 93-year-old woman who was widowed for decades and lived alone in Massachusetts in the house she had owned for over 50 years. For most of her life, Helen enjoyed the company of many family members who lived nearby, but she outlived almost all of them. A niece and a neighbor were the only people who still visited her regularly. She enjoyed restaurants, antique shows, and movies, but she was not comfortable going to these alone. Helen still drove, and her mental faculties were strong, but she suffered from debilitating back pain and found it increasingly difficult to manage on her own. We live in Ohio, as does Andy's sister, and for many years we had encouraged Helen to move to our city. She resisted doing so while she was content with the life she had, and then she became too frail to set up an independent life in a new location. Ultimately, Helen fell at home and broke her ankle, and she could never walk again. She spent several unhappy months in a nursing home and died at a hospice facility.

In many ways, my mother-in-law was among the lucky, because she was able to thrive independently until she was in her 90s. But during her last three years, she found it very challenging to maintain her autonomy, avoid social isolation, and live comfortably.

Until her fall, Helen adamantly rejected all forms of long-term care, including a nursing home, assisted living facility, and home care. She refused to enter an institutional setting and did not trust any stranger to provide assistance in her home while she was there alone. She also wanted to leave her money to her children rather than spend it on expensive care for herself. Helen would immediately change the subject if anyone began a conversation about her future, and we do not know to what extent she turned the matter over in her own mind. The fierce independence and self-sufficiency that served my mother-in-law so well during her first nine decades backfired at the end of her life.

Many Americans, like Helen, value their autonomy and cling to the hope of remaining in their own homes to the end of their days. A move to a residential setting that is especially designed for seniors may be perceived not only as costly but also as an admission of defeat, an acknowledgement of loss of vigor and self-reliance.

Yet, it is unwise to dismiss lightly the idea of living in a community setting. Retirement communities of all types offer the benefits of social interaction and often intellectual and civic engagement through a variety of planned activities and opportunities. Thus, middle-aged individuals who are beginning to plan for their later years or are pondering options for parents who are finding it difficult to manage in their homes should carefully consider retirement communities.

When my parents were in their mid- to late 70s, they realized that they could no longer safely climb stairs multiple times a day and needed to move out of their large, two-story home. However, our family never contemplated a retirement community and never initiated a conversation about it. Instead, my parents moved into a large condominium with rooms that were all on one floor and ample storage space in the basement that enabled them to keep most of their belongings and avoid the arduous task of culling through them. But this may have been a mistake. As a widower, my father became socially isolated and quite lonely, a problem that might have been less pronounced had he lived in a retirement community.

THE IMPORTANCE OF SOCIAL INTERACTION AND FEELING USEFUL

I cannot emphasize enough how important it is to maintain social contacts and a sense of purpose throughout life. In the words of Epicurus, "Of all the things that wisdom provides for living one's entire life in happiness, the greatest by far is the possession of friendship." In the words of Gretchen Rubin, a contemporary writer, "You need close long-term relationships, you need to be able to confide in others, you need to belong."[1]

Experts have determined that successful social integration is of great importance in the later decades of life.[2] Researchers are learning that social interaction has a significant impact on the health, welfare, and longevity of older adults.

Loneliness is associated with a decline in functioning and even death in individuals over 60.[3] It can have an adverse effect on cardiovascular health, gait speed, and ability to accomplish

---

1. Gretchen Rubin, *The Happiness Project: Or, Why I Spent a Year Trying to Sing in the Morning, Clean My Closets, Fight Right, Read Aristotle, and Generally Have More Fun* (New York: HarperCollins, 2009), 142.

2. Tina Ten Bruggencate, Katrien G. Luijkx, and Janienke Sturm, "Social Needs of Older People: A Systematic Literature Review," *Ageing & Society* 38, no. 9 (September 2018): 1746; Karl Pillemer and Nina Glasgow, "Social Integration and Aging," in *Social Integration in the Second Half of Life*, ed. Karl Pillemer, Phyllis Moen, Elaine Wethington, and Nina Glasgow (Baltimore, MD: Johns Hopkins University Press, 2000), 41; George E. Vaillant, *Aging Well: Surprising Guideposts to a Happier Life from the Landmark Harvard Study of Adult Development* (Boston, MA: Little Brown, 2002), 200; Jane E. Brody, "Social Interaction Is Critical for Mental and Physical Health," *New York Times*, June 12, 2017, https://www.nytimes.com/2017/06/12/well/live/having-friends-is-good-for-you.html.

3. Bruggencate, Luijkx, and Sturm, "Social Needs of Older People," 1746; Carla M. Perissinotto, Irena Stijacic Cenzer, and Kenneth E. Covinsky, "Loneliness in Older Persons: A Predictor of Functional Decline and Death," *Archives of Internal Medicine* 172, no. 44 (2012): 1078–83.

activities of daily living (e.g., bathing and dressing).[4] It can also cause elevated blood pressure and hormone levels and less sleep.[5]

Countless people of all ages experienced some degree of social isolation during the COVID-19 pandemic. We now know firsthand how difficult it can be. Indeed, experts worried a great deal about the mental and physical health impacts of the public health orders that had to be issued in 2020.[6]

On the flip side, social integration can delay memory decline and preserve cognitive functioning in seniors.[7] It can

4. National Institute on Aging, "Social Isolation, Loneliness in Older People Pose Health Risks," US Department of Health and Human Services, April 23, 2019, https://www.nia.nih.gov/news/social-isolation-loneliness-older-people-pose-health-risks; Anthony D. Ong, Jeremy D. Rothstein, and Bert N. Uchino, "Loneliness Accentuates Age Differences in Cardiovascular Responses to Social Evaluative Threat," *Psychology and Aging* 27, no. 1 (2012): 190–98; Aparna Shankar, Anne McMunn, Panayotes Demakakos, Mark Hamer, and Andrew Steptoe, "Social Isolation and Loneliness: Prospective Associations with Functional Status in Older Adults," *Health Psychology* 36, no. 2 (2017): 179–87.

5. Population Reference Bureau, "Social Support, Networks, and Happiness," *Today's Research on Aging*, no. 17 (2009): 1–6, at 2; National Institute on Aging, "Social Isolation, Loneliness in Older People Pose Health Risks."

6. Centers for Disease Control and Prevention, "Coping with Stress," Centers for Disease Control and Prevention, updated December 11, 2020, https://www.cdc.gov/coronavirus/2019-ncov/daily-life-coping/managing-stress-anxiety.html.

7. Maria Cohut, "What Are the Health Benefits of Being Social?" *MedicalNewsToday*, February 23, 2018, https://www.medicalnewstoday.com/articles/321019.php; Karen Ertel, Maria Glymour, and Lisa F. Berkman, "Effects of Social Integration on Preserving Memory Function in a Nationally Representative US Elderly Population," *American Journal of Public Health* 98, no. 7 (2008): 1215–20; Valerie C. Crooks, James Lubben, Diana B. Petitti, Deborah Little, and Vicki Chiu, "Social Network, Cognitive Function, and Dementia Incidence among Elderly Women," *American Journal of Public Health* 98, no. 7 (2008): 1221–27.

also promote more positive disease outcomes and lengthen life.[8] This is true both nationally and internationally. A study involving over three thousand Japanese seniors found that activities with family members and friends and a sense of belonging to a neighborhood are "significant predictors of 5-year survival among the seniors."[9] Similarly, a study of 300 elderly individuals in India confirmed that strong social support promotes successful aging in older adults and enhances their sense of control over their lives.[10] Deep friendships that provide people with a sense of self-worth and of being loved may be even more important than family relationships that are obligatory.[11]

---

8. Cohut, "What Are the Health Benefits of Being Social"; Julianne Holt-Lunstad, Timothy B. Smith, and J. Bradley Layton, "Social Relationships and Mortality Risk: A Meta-Analytic Review," *PLoS Medicine* 7, no. 7 (2010): e1000316; Joe Tomaka, Sharon Thompson, and Rebecca Palacios, "The Relation of Social Isolation, Loneliness, and Social Support to Disease Outcomes Among the Elderly," *Journal of Aging and Health* 18, no. 3 (2006): 359–84; Angela K. Troyer, "The Health Benefits of Socializing," *Psychology Today*, June 30, 2016, https://www.psychologytoday.com/us/blog/living-mild-cognitive-impairment/201606/the-health-benefits-socializing.

9. Ayako Morita, Takehito Takano, Keiko Nakamura, Masashi Kizuki, and Kaoruko Seino, "Contribution of Interaction with Family, Friends and Neighbours, and Sense of Neighbourhood attachment to Survival in Senior Citizens: 5-Year Follow-Up Study," *Social Science and Medicine* 70, no. 4 (2009): 543–49.

10. Sahab Sinha, P. Nayyar, and Surat P. Sinha, "Social Support and Self-Control as Variables in Attitude toward Life and Perceived Control among Older People in India," *Journal of Social Psychology* 142, no. 4 (2002): 527–40.

11. Karen L. Fingerman, Meng Huo, Susan T Charles, and Debra J. Umberson, "Variety Is the Spice of Late Life: Social Integration and Daily Activity," *Journal of Gerontology: Series B* 10, no. 10 (2019): 2; Katherine L. Fiori, Toni C. Antonucci, and Kai S. Cortina, "Social Network Typologies and Mental Health among Older Adults," *Journal of Gerontology: Series B* 61, no. 1 (2006): 25–32.

You need people with whom to celebrate happy occasions and successes. You also need people to whom you can reach out when you are distressed. Rabbi Harold Kushner is famous for writing the book *When Bad Things Happen to Good People* after his son died at the age of 14 from progeria—rapid aging syndrome. In a subsequent book, *Nine Essential Things I've Learned about Life*, he writes the following:

> One of the first pieces of advice I give to people going through a hard time—be it a death, a divorce, loss of a job, whatever shape misfortune may come in—is "Please don't try to handle this alone. I know you may be uncomfortable asking for help. [...] I know you don't like the idea of people seeing you at a time like this, when you are depressed and emotionally depleted. But a time like this is precisely when you need people to be with you."[12]

Social contact goes hand in hand with feeling useful to others, which is equally important to most people's well-being.[13] An extensive 2009 study published in the *Journal of Aging and Health* concluded that a persistently low perception of usefulness was associated with a shorter lifespan and a reduced sense of well-being, while elderly people with a high perception of social usefulness had better social and health outcomes.[14] Other

---

12. Harold S. Kushner, *Nine Essential Things I've Learned about Life* (New York: Anchor Books, 2015), 114–15.

13. Bruggencate, Luijkx, and Sturm, "Social Needs of Older People," 1767; Andrew Steptoe, Angus Deaton, and Arthur A. Stone, "Subjective Wellbeing, Health, and Ageing," *The Lancet* 385, no. 9968 (2015): 640–48.

14. Tara L. Gruenewald, Arun S. Karlamangla, Gail A. Greendale, Burton H. Singer, and Teresa E. Seeman, "Increased Mortality Risk in Older Adults with Persistently Low or Declining Feelings of Usefulness to Others," *Journal of Aging Health* 21, no. 2 (2009): 398–425. The study involved 1,189 adults who were 70–79 years old.

researchers have confirmed this result in subsequent studies.[15] Those who are retired and have few family obligations may suffer from "rolelessness" and need to find meaningful activities that enable them to maintain their identity as valued members of society.[16] Individuals who volunteer in their communities generally experience diminished depression, anxiety, loneliness, and social isolation.[17] For example, seniors who volunteered to help students in at-risk public schools scored better than others on tests measuring their health and happiness status.[18]

The importance of meaning and purposefulness does not escape older Americans. The Pathways to Encore Purpose Project surveyed nearly 1,200 adults aged 50–90 and conducted in-depth interviews with 102 of them to explore the role of "purpose" in their lives.[19] It found that "nearly a third of

15. Bruggencate, Luijkx, and Sturm, "Social Needs of Older People," 1767; Eric S. Kim, Ichiro Kawachi, Ying Chen, and Laura D. Kubzansky, "Association between Purpose in Life and Objective Measures of Physical Function in Older Adults," *JAMA Psychiatry* 74, no. 10 (2017): 1039–45; Shirley Musich, Shaohung S. Wang, Sandra Kraemer, Kevin Hawkins, and Ellen Wicker, "Purpose in Life and Positive Health Outcomes among Older Adults," *Population Health Management* 21, no. 2 (2018): 139–47.

16. Pillemer and Glasgow, "Social Integration in Aging," 37–38.

17. Kim Hayes, "Senior Volunteers Reap Health Benefits," *AARP*, July 27, 2017, https://www.aarp.org/health/healthy-living/info-2017/health-benefits-volunteering-seniors-fd.html; National & Community Service, "Volunteering Helps Keep Seniors Healthy, New Study Suggests," February 5, 2019, https://www.nationalservice.gov/newsroom/press-releases/2019/volunteering-helps-keep-seniors-healthy-new-study-suggests.

18. Judith Shulevitz, "Why Do Grandmothers Exist?" *New Republic*, January 29, 2013, http://www.newrepublic.com/article/112199/genetics-grandmothers-why-they-exist.

19. Anne Colby, Kathleen Remington, Matthew Bundick, Emily Morton, Heather Malin, and Elissa Hirsh, "Purpose in the Encore Years: Shaping Lives of Meaning and Contribution," Pathways to Encore Purpose Project (2018). The project is a collaboration between the Stanford Center on

older adults in the United States (31 percent) exhibit purpose beyond the self." Moreover, the researchers determined that "people who are purposeful have a positive outlook on life."[20] Dr. George E. Vaillant, who led a Harvard Medical School study of hundreds of individuals with diverse backgrounds, concluded the following in his book *Aging Well*:

> Play, create, learn new things and, most especially, make new friends. Do that and getting out of bed in the morning will seem a joy—even if you are no longer "important," even if your joints ache, and even if you no longer enjoy free access to the office Xerox machine.[21]

Planning for old age, therefore, should include planning to be socially engaged and active. Nurturing friendships and close ties to relatives is beneficial not only for the present but also for the future. The same is true for developing interests, hobbies, and volunteer work. Before retirement, it may often seem that you have little to no time for such pursuits, but engaging in them is worthwhile and necessary, if only as an investment for the future. After retirement, living in a good retirement community can be the key to a happy, social, and fulfilling life.

THE MANY FORMS OF INDEPENDENT RETIREMENT OR 55-PLUS COMMUNITIES

Retirement communities come in many forms and range widely in cost and structure. A variety of alternatives are worth considering.

Adolescence at Stanford University's Graduate School of Education and Encore.org.

20. Colby, "Purpose in the Encore Years," 2–3.
21. Vaillant, *Aging Well*, 248.

Independent living or 55-plus communities

Independent living communities (also known as planned retirement communities) are available in many cities and have amenities that foster social and intellectual engagement. They often offer community centers, activities, meals in a residents' dining hall, transportation services, and more. Some are called "over 55 communities" or "55-plus communities."[22] Retirees may own units or rent apartments, and generally, at least one resident must be 55 or older.

These communities do not offer medical or personal care services. However, they are frequently located near major medical and shopping centers and close to religious and cultural facilities. They have safety features such as guards and emergency buttons, and management handles all repairs. Planned retirement communities market themselves as providing independent seniors with security, convenience, and freedom from the burdens of home maintenance. Some also create a resort-like environment, emphasizing leisure and recreation. Websites such as SeniorHomes.com or A Place for Mom.com can facilitate searches for retirement communities.

Some of my friends whose parents moved to retirement communities in their 80s have reported that their parents were unhappy, especially if they selected the community simply based on its proximity to their children. They found themselves among people who "are not like them," were served food that was unpalatable, and were unprepared to meet the challenges of adjusting to a new environment.

But this does not have to be so. A move to a retirement community could be something to which we look forward. If it is financially feasible, people should move while they are still

22. "55+ Communities," SeniorHomes.com, accessed December 21, 2020, http://www.seniorhomes.com/p/55-communities/.

healthy enough to make friends and become active members of the community. Rather than being forced by frailty to move to the facility that is closest to children or siblings, retirees could research a variety of choices and select one that is truly a good fit. Under these more positive circumstances, seniors will hopefully find that friendships come easily because everyone is at the same stage in life and because those who opt for a particular community presumably share common preferences.

An added advantage of moving to a retirement community is that doing so enables seniors to leave homes that are now too large to take care of, have stairs that create a risk of falling, have icy driveways or sidewalks in the winter, or feature other hazards. Housing that is designed specifically for seniors may offer much safer and easier living environments.

Yet another benefit is that moving to a one- or two-bedroom apartment in an independent living community will require most seniors to downsize. Seniors who remain in their large homes rarely cull through their possessions and thoughtfully decide what is essential to keep and to whom to distribute the rest. All too often, elderly people or their families rush through this process when the senior must move to an institutional care setting because of a medical crisis or after death. Sadly, it can cause significant stress and family conflict. Downsizing on your own terms can save you and your loved ones much heartache later on.

Naturally occurring retirement communities

Seniors who seek a community environment are not limited to planned retirement communities. Instead, they may create retirement communities for themselves in their existing homes or in apartment buildings, condominiums, or townhomes to which they move after retirement. Such arrangements have been termed "elder/senior cohousing" or "naturally occurring retirement communities" (NORCs).[23] Those living in a self-created retirement community can check on one another, share caregivers and drivers in order to reduce costs, and carpool together. They can also socialize frequently and participate together in volunteer work, continuing education, and cultural programs.

This approach worked well for my two elderly relatives, Nettie and Mae, who lived to be 96 and 104, respectively. They spent several decades in an apartment complex in Cleveland that catered largely to seniors. Rent was reasonable, and a number of programs were offered each month in a community room, including bingo games and speakers. In addition, a van provided transportation to local destinations for a fee. Nettie and Mae lived in separate apartments "so they would continue to get along well," but they sustained each other through joint activities, daily visits, and many meals together.

Some NORCs have evolved to resemble more formal retirement communities with professional managers and financial support from outside sources, which enables residents to benefit from a variety of services. While seniors age in place and do not move to new homes, they can enjoy free or heavily discounted social programs and outings, home-delivered meals, assessments of their care needs, yard work and chore services, exercise and preventive health programs, caregiver support groups, classes, and more. At least 25 states have NORCS, and 35 exist in New York City alone.[24]

---

23. Dana Goldstein, "Cities of the Old," *Politico*, January 11, 2017, https://www.politico.com/agenda/story/2017/01/norcs-naturally-occurring-retirement-communities-000270; Tim Parker, "What Is a Naturally Occurring Retirement Community?" *The Balance*, updated October 21, 2020, https://www.thebalance.com/what-is-a-naturally-occurring-retirement-community-4585208.

24. Sally Abrahms, "Naturally Occurring Retirement Communities: A Creative Housing Option," *Hartford Extra Mile*, updated January 13, 2020,

Village networks

Closely related are "village networks," the first of which was Beacon Hill Village in Boston, launched in 2002. Today, there are 200 villages in the United States and 150 more in development.[25] Seniors create villages in their own communities, and these are nonprofit organizations, usually with a paid coordinator and a network of volunteers. Villages provide residents with transportation, social events, discounted medical and wellness services, referrals for various service providers, and volunteers that can help residents with a multitude of tasks, such as shopping, computer work, and moving furniture.[26] In the words of one advocate, a village is "a community that relies on the passion, talents, and expertise of the people in it."[27] They are thus consumer-driven, membership-based organizations designed and governed by those who use them. Members typically pay $250–$1,000 per person or household per year (with discounts available to those who cannot afford the fee), which covers basic transportation services and regular social events, and other services can be added for a fee.

https://extramile.thehartford.com/transitions/naturally-occurring-retirement-communities/.

25. Linda Abbit, "The Village Model: A Neighborly Way to Age in Place," Senior Planet, October 30, 2017, https://seniorplanet.org/the-village-model-a-neighborly-way-to-age-in-place/; Stuart M. Butler and Carmen Diaz, "How 'Villages' Help Seniors Age at Home," The Brookings Institution, October 19, 2015, https://www.brookings.edu/blog/usc-brookings-schaeffer-on-health-policy/2015/10/19/how-villages-help-seniors-age-at-home/; Tobi Elkin, "Can the Village Movement Scale to Support Aging in Place?" Stria, February 11, 2019, https://strianews.com/the-village-movement-supports-aging-in-place/; Andrew Scharlach, Carrie Graham, and Amanda Lehning, "The 'Village' Model: A Consumer-Driven Approach for Aging in Place," The Gerontologist 52, no. 3 (2011): 418–27.

26. Butler and Diaz, "'Villages' Help Seniors Age at Home"; Elkin, "Can the Village Movement Scale?."

27. Abbit, "The Village Model."

Fundraising efforts and grants often provide further financial support. A website called "Village to Village Network" provides information about locating, establishing, and supporting senior villages.[28]

Additional services available for independent living

Several other resources can help seniors continue to live independently. A number of them are described below.

Shared housing services

Baby boomers and retirees who are interested in shared housing but find it difficult to identify appropriate housemates might turn to "matchmaking" services. These are available through online vendors as well as through workshops and meetings that take place in local communities. For example, two well-known providers are the National Shared Housing Resource Center and the Golden Girls Network, which serves women only.[29] Financial pressures, a desire for close social ties, and concern about aging alone may all induce individuals (most commonly women) to seek home-sharing living arrangements.[30] You might want a housemate to move into a home you already own or you might want to purchase a new home that is a better fit for

---

28. "Village to Village Network," Village to Village Network, accessed December 21, 2020, https://www.vtvnetwork.org/content.aspx?page_id=0&club_id=691012&sl=1341055492.

29. Homepage, National Shared Housing Resource Center, accessed December 21, 2020, http://nationalsharedhousing.org/; "Golden Girls Network," ProgramsforElderly.com, accessed December 21, 2020, http://www.programsforelderly.com/housing-golden-girls-network-senior-home-sharing-cohousing-bonnie-moore.php.

30. Amy Blackstone, "Grow Old Like 'The Golden Girls,'" *New York Times*, June 7, 2019, https://www.nytimes.com/2019/06/07/opinion/retirement-aging-golden-girls.html.

elderly people and have one or more co-owners. Entrepreneurs are offering not only matchmaking services but also house-sharing coaching. Coaches counsel clients about financial arrangements, establishing house rules, allocating space, and attending to other logistics.[31]

Senior centers

Senior centers are not a form of retirement community, but they can provide social and intellectual enrichment and other forms of support for seniors who are living independently or in informal retirement communities. Approximately 11,400 senior centers serve 1 million older Americans each day.[32] Senior centers offer meals and nutritional programs; fitness and wellness classes; transportation services; counseling regarding public benefits and employment matters; volunteer opportunities; and social, recreational, educational, and arts activities. According to the National Council on Aging (NCOA), the average age of participants is 75, about 70 percent are women, and half live alone. Senior Centers receive funding from federal, state, and local government entities but also depend on grants, private donations, and modest fees charged for some activities. The NCOA states enthusiastically that senior center participants "can learn to manage and delay the onset of chronic disease and experience measurable improvements in their physical, social, spiritual, emotional, mental, and economic well-being."[33]

31. Kayla Laterman, "Getting a Roommate in Your Golden Years," *New York Times*, January 12, 2018, https://www.nytimes.com/2018/01/12/realestate/getting-a-roommate-in-your-golden-years.html.

32. National Council on Aging, "Senior Centers: Fact Sheet," National Council on Aging, accessed December 21, 2020, https://www.ncoa.org/resources/fact-sheet-senior-centers/.

33. National Council on Aging, "Senior Center Facts," National Council on Aging, accessed December 21, 2020, http://www.ncoa.org/press-room/fact-sheets/senior-centers-fact-sheet.html.

You can do a simple Google search for "senior centers in [your city]" in order to locate those that are nearest to you.

Meals on wheels

Meals on Wheels programs can provide support for economically disadvantaged seniors who do not otherwise have access to prepared meals. Approximately five thousand local Senior Nutrition Programs in the United States provide meals for almost 2.4 million seniors in need each year. Some operate at senior centers; some deliver meals directly to seniors who are homebound and have low incomes; and many programs do both. Programs may ask for modest contributions or provide food at no cost.[34] Home-delivered meals can enhance the nutritional intake of clients, reduce food insecurity, and even provide valuable social contact through the delivery person's brief visit.[35]

Faith-based and nonprofit organizations

You may find faith-based organizations in your community that provide a variety of services to seniors. For example, the Jewish Family Service Association (JFSA) provides care management and counseling, in-home care, and community programs

---

34. "Find a Meals on Wheels Provider near You," Meals on Wheels America, accessed December 21, 2020, https://www.mealsonwheelsamerica.org/find-meals.

35. Edward A. Frongillo and Wendy S. Wolfe, "Impact of Participation in Home-Delivered Meals on Nutrient Intake, Dietary Patterns, and Food Insecurity of Older Persons in New York State," *Journal of Nutrition for the Elderly* 29, no. 3 (2010): 293–310; Edward A. Frongillo, Tanushree D. Isaacman, Claire M. Horan, Elaine Wethington, and Karl Pillemer, "Adequacy of and Satisfaction with Delivery and Use of Home-Delivered Meals," *Journal of Nutrition for the Elderly* 29, no. 3 (2010): 211–26; Brian Polzner, "Research Review: The Powerful Impact of Meals on Wheels," *Today's Geriatric Medicine* 10, no. 4 (2017): 28.

for seniors at reasonable fees or at no cost.[36] Likewise, the Presbyterian SeniorCare Network in Pennsylvania provides "a continuum of care and service options, from at-home services and personal care and skilled nursing communities to affordable housing and premier retirement communities."[37]

In 2019, I helped a neighbor obtain a JFSA caseworker, and I attended his first meeting with her. The caseworker set him up with a cleaning service and a few hours of home care each week and promised to visit him at home every month to assess whether he had further needs. When my friend decided to move to an assisted living facility, the caseworker helped coordinate the move. She arranged for a relocation company (see Chapter 3), took him shopping for new clothes and supplies, and set him up with physical and occupational therapy at his new residence.

Nonprofit organizations that are not religiously affiliated may also offer resources and support for frail individuals and their caregivers. For example, in Cleveland, Ohio, the Benjamin Rose Institute on Aging helps older people and their families access resources to promote their physical and emotional health. Its mission is to assist seniors to "live independently with assistance at home, get involved to remain active and engaged, and navigate towards a more secure financial future."[38] Be sure to research all of the offerings that are available in your community.

---

36. Jewish Family Service, "Jay and Rose Phillips Aging Care & Connections," Jewish Family Service, accessed December 21, 2020, https://www.jewishfamilyservice.org/services/senior-solutions.

37. Presbyterian SeniorCare Network, "We Are all about Making Aging Easier®," Presbyterian SeniorCare Network, accessed December 21, 2020, https://www.srcare.org/.

38. Benjamin Rose Institute on Aging, "For Older People & Families," Benjamin Rose Institute on Aging, accessed December 21, 2020, https://www.benrose.org/home.

Programs of All-Inclusive Care for the Elderly (PACE)

PACE is a Medicare and Medicaid program that is available to individuals who

- are 55 or older,
- live in the service area of a **PACE** organization,
- are certified by their state as needing nursing home–level care,
- are able to live safely in the community with the help of PACE services at the time they join.

PACE can provide a wide array of medical, social, nutritional, counseling, and other services.[39] Most participants are frail, low-income seniors who are eligible for both Medicare and Medicaid. Interdisciplinary teams develop care plans and deliver services to participants.[40] You can search for a PACE Program near you on the *Medicare.gov* website.[41]

CONTINUING CARE RETIREMENT COMMUNITIES

For seniors who remain healthy, independent living facilities and self-created retirement communities can be an effective low-cost approach to fostering social engagement, intellectual activity, and a sense of usefulness and purpose. However, a

---

39. Department of Health and Human Services, "PACE," Medicare.gov, accessed December 21, 2020, https://www.medicare.gov/your-medicare-costs/get-help-paying-costs/pace.

40. Centers for Medicare and Medicaid Services, "Programs of All-Inclusive Care for the Elderly Benefits," Medicaid.gov, accessed December 21, 2020, https://www.medicaid.gov/medicaid/ltss/pace/pace-benefits/index.html.

41. Available at https://www.medicare.gov/find-a-plan/questions/pace-home.aspx.

different, more structured model, the continuing care retirement community (CCRC), merits serious consideration because it offers more services and guaranteed availability of higher levels of care as your medical needs change. A central feature of CCRCs is that they have independent living, assisted living, and nursing home care all in the same campus. CCRCs are not an option for low-income individuals because of their high entry and monthly fees. However, those with ample savings or considerable home equity should give CCRCs serious thought.

My own CCRC visits

While investigating options for my late father and researching this book, I visited several CCRCs. I provide the cost information I obtained at the time, in 2014, though prices are presumably higher today.

The first CCRC was in an urban setting with premier medical centers, a large university, and several cultural institutions nearby. It consisted of one multi-floor building that offered 100 independent living apartments and 30 assisted living units. Those needing temporary or permanent nursing care were referred to an affiliated facility located a mile away.

A tour of the CCRC revealed wood paneling, luxurious carpeting, two attractive dining rooms, several beautifully appointed common rooms, a rooftop terrace with a garden, an exercise room, a library, and an art studio. The independent living suites were spacious and airy with ample light and storage space, and many were newly renovated.

I had done extensive reading prior to my visits, so I was prepared for the very high initial entry fees and monthly charges that all of the facilities required. At this CCRC entry fees that were 75 percent refundable upon leaving the CCRC or upon death, ranged from $170,000 to $402,000, depending on the size and features of the apartment. As an alternative, residents could opt for lower entry fees that ranged from $75,000 to

$347,000 that were spread over 72 months. The lower entry fees were partially refundable only if the resident left or died before the end of 72 months. For example, if a resident died after 60 months, her estate would receive an amount representing payments for the last 12 months of the 72-month period, that is, one-sixth of the entry fee. In addition to paying an entry fee, CCRC residents pay monthly fees. At this CCRC, the lowest was $1,872 per month for an efficiency apartment, and the highest was $3,876 for a two-bedroom unit. If a second person shares the living quarters, both the entry fee and monthly fee are higher. Fees for assisted living and nursing care were even higher by considerable amounts.

A second CCRC was situated in a rural setting, featuring a beautiful campus of over one hundred acres that was home to just over three hundred residents. There were ponds, walking trails, an abundance of green space, and many gardens cultivated by residents. Independent housing was available in cottages or apartment buildings, and all activities and meetings took place in a large, central building so that community members would come together as often as possible. The building included a library, wood-working shop, several restaurants, a game room, a large swimming pool and fitness center, and a medical clinic, all of which were being used by many residents during my visit. The same building also included 48 attractive assisted living units and 48 nursing care rooms so that residents in these wings continued to be part of the community and could easily access activities. A child daycare center on the premises allowed elderly residents to help care for young children and contributed to the lively environment.

At this CCRC, the entry fee for a "platinum plan" that covered all levels of care a resident might need at no extra charge ranged from $92,000 to $423,500 for single occupancy, and singles' monthly fees ranged from $2,514 to $4,702. For double occupancy, platinum plan entry fees ranged from $210,500 to $472,000, and monthly fees ranged from $4,404 to $6,230. Residents could obtain less comprehensive plans that would require additional payments for assisted living or nursing care at reduced costs. These plans' entry fees started at $32,000, and monthly fees were as low as $1,408 for a studio apartment. Plans with partially refundable entry fees were somewhat more expensive.

I also visited two CCRCs in suburban settings, both of which had large, beautifully landscaped campuses. They offered independent living residents the option of either villas or apartments that were adjacent to the community building. One was a high-end CCRC, with an emphasis on luxury. Its entry fees for singles were 75 percent refundable, beginning at $251,000 and reaching as high as $603,000, and its monthly fees ranged from $2,707 to $4,763. Monthly fees rose if the resident moved to assisted living. The second suburban CCRC was more modest in terms of decor, architecture, and apartment sizes, but also had the most reasonable fees. The singles' entry fees for a life care plan were $73,000–$313,000 and monthly fees were $1,767 to $3,116. With a life care plan, a resident would not need to pay additional fees if he or she moved to the assisted living or nursing home sections of the CCRC.

The CCRCs had much in common. Their fees generally include weekly housekeeping service, most utilities, scheduled transportation, maintenance, a 24-hour emergency call system, 24-hour security, all activities, and a dining allowance. The meals covered by the fees ranged from whatever you could buy for $200 a month to one meal of your choice every day. Applicants for residency undergo a financial screening, but all CCRC officials assured me that if residents exhaust their money despite being responsible about their finances, they are allowed to stay, and their expenses are covered by a charitable foundation or fund.

The administrators with whom I spoke emphasized that the staff members know residents well, and everyone contributes to ensuring the members' well-being. The CCRCs I visited had large staffs and several mentioned that they employed 200–300 people, though many of them worked part-time. Because residents interact regularly with security officers, housekeepers, dining employees, and the CCRC's social workers and health-care staff, any difficulties or significant health changes were likely to be quickly detected. Those needing extra assistance while remaining in independent living may turn to an in-home care agency that is affiliated with the CCRC and hire an aide for an hourly fee.

Each CCRC had memory care services for nursing center residents living with dementia. In several cases, these individuals were fully integrated into the community and wore a bracelet or anklet that tracked their movements for their own safety. In other cases, they lived in a unit with locked doors so they would not wander away from the building.

The CCRCs had daily or weekly newsletters with lengthy activity lists, and this information was also available through their intranet. These included scheduled transportation to medical and shopping destinations, arts and crafts, exercise classes, games, movies, concerts, coffee and ice cream socials, and lectures. The facilities that were closest to institutions of higher learning benefitted from their cultural offerings, and residents could attend university events or even audit classes. All of the CCRCs allowed residents to enjoy significant self-governance, with residents' councils and numerous committees.

In each case, however, I left with at least one concern. In two of the CCRCs, the many common rooms, hallways, and lobbies were generally empty. This observation caused me to wonder about whether the CCRC in fact created a robust social environment for its residents. By contrast, the community buildings in the other two CCRCs were bustling with activity, and I saw people chatting and smiling wherever I went.

The low-point of a tour at one facility was the assisted living floor, which was shabby and had not been renovated in decades. My tour guide showed me the door to the "spa" room in which residents are bathed, but upon questioning, admitted that assistance with baths or showers was offered only twice a week for those who could not wash themselves. At another CCRC, I was told that the aide-to-patient ratio in the skilled nursing wing was nine or 10 to one, and nurses were responsible for 25 patients each, which seemed like an overwhelming patient load.

At the rural CCRC, those wishing to access the renowned medical facilities in the closest large city had to make special transportation arrangements, for which they paid separately, and they had to travel approximately thirty-five miles. When I asked about religious services at this facility, I was told that they were available for several religious groups. However, because only 15 of the 300 residents were Jewish, there were no Jewish services, and the closest synagogue was 30 minutes away. This would have clearly been a drawback for my father, a retired rabbi. The answer to this casual question emphasized to me how important it is to research all aspects of the community and to spend as much time as possible at CCRCs of interest.

CCRC benefits

There are approximately two thousand CCRCs in the United States.[42] High-quality CCRCs can constitute an excellent living alternative for seniors. CCRCs feature a continuum of care, ranging from independent living to assisted living to skilled nursing homes, generally all in the same campus. Residents who move into a CCRC live in apartments, cottages, townhouses, or single-family homes, depending on the choices available at the facility. Ideally, CCRCs offer a large variety of services. These can include meals; social, educational, and

---

42. Mary Kate Nelson, "Only 22% of CCRCs in the U.S. are For-Profit," *Senior Housing News,* May 24, 2018, https://seniorhousingnews.com/2018/05/24/only-22-of-ccrcs-in-the-u-s-are-for-profit/ (referring to 1955 CCRCs).

other recreational programs; scheduled transportation; exercise facilities and classes; resident health clinics with nursing, physician, pharmacy, and physical and occupational therapy services; beauty salons; religious services; libraries; restaurants; guest accommodations; and more.[43] Thus, residents do not have to leave campus for purposes of daily living. Moreover, scheduled transportation enables even those who do not drive to visit destinations such as nearby theaters, museums, shopping centers, medical specialists, and places of worship.

CCRCs often work hard to enable seniors to remain physically active and intellectually engaged and to retain a sense of meaning and purpose in their lives. Some are located near beaches or golf courses, and many are affiliated with religious groups or other social and community organizations.[44] A particularly creative trend is the establishment of CCRCs on or near university campuses. This arrangement allows seniors to take classes, attend cultural and sporting events, volunteer, and mentor students.[45]

---

43. Danny Szlauderbach, "Continuing Care Retirement Communities (CCRC): An All-in-One Senior Living Option," A Place for Mom, October 24, 2020, https://www.aplaceformom.com/planning-and-advice/articles/continuing-care-retirement-communities.

44. CARF International, "Consumer Guide to Understanding Financial Performance and Reporting in Continuing Care Retirement Communities," CARF International, June 2016, http://www.carf.org/FinancialPerformanceCCRCs/ ; National Continuing Care Residents Association, "Consumer's Guide to Continuing Care Retirement Communities," National Continuing Care Residents Association, May 2018, https://static1.squarespace.com/static/5898f6e4e6f2e17c07ec6bbf/t/5c6c406cb208fc363845c1cf/1550598265596/Consumer%E2%80%99s+Guide+to+CCRCs+%28NaCCRA%29.pdf.

45. Andrew Carle, "Can University Retirement Communities Reverse Aging?" *Forbes*, April 22, 2019, https://www.forbes.com/sites/andrewcarle/2019/04/22/can-university-retirement-communities-reverse-aging/#21ac83b82558; Lisa Morgenroth and Michael Hanley, "On Campus and in the Community: How Higher Education Can Inform Seniors Housing Models," *Seniors Housing & Care Journal*, 23, no. 1 (2015): 70–75.

A good CCRC can provide an ideal solution for seniors, especially those without family members who can frequently visit and care for them. Life can be active, rich, and fulfilling. In the words of one satisfied resident, "It's like being on a cruise. [...] You don't have to change the sheets, and there's always something to do."[46] A ready social circle is available, and in times of need, close friends in the community and professional staff members can provide care and support.

Studies have confirmed the benefits of CCRCs. The Mather Lifeways Institute on Aging administered surveys in 2018 to over five thousand CCRC residents in 80 facilities across 29 states. The Institute concluded that CCRC residents are generally happier and healthier than their counterparts with other living arrangements.[47] CCRC dwellers scored better in many aspects of emotional, social, physical, spiritual, intellectual, and vocational wellness.[48] Another study compared seniors attending adult day care programs to those living in CCRCs and found evidence that "CCRCs provide a better social outlet for older adults than" day care centers.[49]

---

46. Jane Gross, "Doctor Focuses on the Minds of the Elderly," *New York Times*, April 30, 2011, http://www.nytimes.com/2011/05/01/us/01elderly.html?pagewanted=all.

47. The researchers also studied a "sample of 1,000 community-at-large older adults [...] from a publicly available data set from the Health and Retirement Study."

48. Mather LifeWays Institute on Aging, "The Age Well Study," Mather LifeWays Institute on Aging, January 2019, 5–6, https://www.matherlifewaysinstituteonaging.com/wp-content/uploads/2019/01/Mather_AgeWell_FINAL.pdf; Brad Breeding, "New Study Shows CCRC Residents Are Happier and Healthier," MyLifeSite, December 10, 2018, https://www.mylifesite.net/blog/post/ccrc-residents-are-happier-and-healthier/.

49. Liat Ayalon, "Loneliness and Anxiety about Aging in Adult Day Care Centers and Continuing Care Retirement Communities," *Innovation in Aging*, 2, no. 2 (June 2018), https://www.ncbi.nlm.nih.gov/pmc/articles/PMC6177038/.

In theory, at least, seniors can feel far less anxiety about the future because the CCRC is home for life, even if you have to move among different components of the campus because of deteriorating health. Thus, seniors can avoid social isolation and maintain many of their friendships and support networks as they seek higher levels of care.[50] CCRCs may also spare couples the trauma of separation if one spouse's health deteriorates to the point of needing nursing home care, since that facility will be within easy reach of the other spouse's residence. Some CCRCs have special sections dedicated to dementia and Alzheimer's patients and offer state-of-the-art memory care.

Friends and staff members can encourage and support residents in making appropriate decisions about difficult matters such as giving up driving or seeking higher levels of care. By contrast, seniors who live independently without strong support networks may unwisely delay such steps and suffer adverse or even catastrophic consequences as a result. Furthermore, residents who need home care, assisted living, or nursing home services at the CCRC can still see on-campus friends, who can serve the roles of quality-of-care overseers and advocates.

The median age of new residents in CCRCs is 81.[51] This is likely because living in a CCRC is relatively expensive, and many people worry that their savings will run out if they spend too many years there. Among the four CCRCs that I visited,

---

50. AARP, "About Continuing Care Retirement Communities: What They Are and How They Work," AARP, updated October 24, 2019, http://www.aarp.org/relationships/caregiving-resource-center/info-09-2010/ho_continuing_care_retirement_communities.html.

51. Carla Fried, "Is a Continuing Care Retirement Community Right for You?" *Money*, December 22, 2016, http://money.com/money/4579934/continuing-care-retirement-communities-cost/; Scott James, "Boomers Create a Surge in Luxury Care Communities," *New York Times*, December 4, 2018, https://www.nytimes.com/2018/12/04/business/retirement/continuing-care-retirement-communities-baby-boomers.html.

new residents were slightly younger. An administrator at one told me that the average age at entry was 76 at her facility. Others were less specific and stated that the average move-in range was mid- to late 70s.

Moving to a high-quality CCRC can be the most comprehensive solution to the challenges of living well in old age. A national survey of 3,647 family members of CCRC residents revealed that 77 percent of them were "likely" or "very likely" to consider moving to a CCRC in the future.[52] Their interest in CCRCs was strongly influenced by their loved ones' positive experiences. Nevertheless, a move to a CCRC will be daunting or entirely impossible for many people because of its high cost.

CCRC costs and financial risk

Many CCRCs require residents to pay entrance fees, which averaged $329,900 in 2018.[53] Entrance fees depend in part on the size and type of living unit selected and the contract format. Some CCRCs, however, do not require entrance fees and have higher monthly fees.[54]

---

52. Mather LifeWays Institute on Aging, Ziegler, and Brecht Associates, Inc., "Final Report of National Survey of Family Members of Residents Living in Continuing Care Retirement Communities," Brecht Associates, Inc., December 2011, https://www.brechtassociates.com/wp-content/uploads/2016/01/National-Study-of-Adult-Children-of-CCRC-Residents.pdf; Brad Breeding, "Why Adult Children of CCRC Residents Opt for a CCRC Too," MyLifeSite, January 28, 2019, https://www.mylifesite.net/blog/post/why-adult-children-ccrc-residents-opt-for-ccrc-too/.

53. James, "Boomers Create a Surge in Luxury Care Communities," (noting that entrance fees average approximately $300,000, but for the highest-end units, they can reach $1 million); Tim Regan, "New Pricing Models, Unit Mixes Could Gain Favor With More CCRCs," *Senior Housing News*, July 15, 2018, https://seniorhousingnews.com/2018/07/15/new-pricing-models-unit-mixes-gain-favor/.

54. Regan, "New Pricing Models"; Brad Breeding, "Senior Living Pricing: Snapshot of Average Cost of Senior Living," MyLifeSite, February

Typically, the entrance fee is refundable in whole or in part if residents die or move out, but refunds may be granted only once the unit is occupied by someone else. CCRCs may establish policies of full refunds (minus a fixed charge), partial refunds, or declining scale refunds and may designate a period of time after which they will not provide refunds.[55]

In addition, residents must pay monthly charges that typically range from $2,000 to $4,000 but can reach $10,000 and beyond.[56] CCRCs may also impose additional fees for the various services they provide.[57] Residents can expect modest annual increases in their monthly fees that allow for building upkeep and renovation.[58] One CCRC administrator told me that any facility that does not review its fees regularly in order to adopt "cost of living" increases is suspect and likely is not well maintained. However, institutions that experience financial stress may raise their fees considerably or begin charging for amenities that were initially free. Seniors who are accustomed to living in a home that is paid off and to enjoying a relatively low cost of living may be particularly wary of incurring high monthly expenses.

16, 2016, https://www.mylifesite.net/blog/post/senior-living-pricing-snapshot-of-average-cost/.

55. CARF International, "Consumer Guide," 2; Eleanor Laise, "CCRCs Raise Financial Questions for Retirees," *Kiplinger's Retirement Report*, January 7, 2019, https://www.kiplinger.com/article/retirement/T037-C000-S004-ccrcs-raise-financial-questions-for-retirees.html.

56. Laise, "CCRCs Raise Financial Questions"; James, "Boomers Create a Surge in Luxury Care Communities."

57. Brad Breeding, "Number-Crunching: A Look at Differing CCRC Pricing Sheets," MyLifeSite, June 11, 2018, https://www.mylifesite.net/blog/post/number-crunching-look-differing-ccrc-pricing-sheets/.

58. CARF International, "Consumer Guide," 14.

Three or four different contract options are available for CCRCs. Some facilities offer only one option, and others offer multiple alternatives.

* A life care or extensive contract (type A) is the high-end option that includes all housing, residential services, and amenities and allows residents to enjoy the benefits of assisted living, medical treatment, and skilled nursing care without additional costs. Under this model, residents are entitled to lifetime services at all necessary levels of care without incurring monthly fee increases because of changes in their health status. Residents choosing type A contracts will have the advantage of predictable costs but may pay large sums of money for services they end up not using.
* Modified contracts (type B) include housing, residential services, amenities, and specified sets of health-care services (e.g., 30 or 60 days of assisted living or nursing care). Entrance and monthly fees are lower than under type A contracts, but the CCRC charges for extra services once those that are included are exhausted.
* Fee-for-service (type C) contracts typically feature even lower entrance and monthly fees and include housing, residential services, and amenities but no health-care services. The CCRC guarantees residents access to assisted living and skilled nursing but individuals must pay for them at market rates.
* Rental agreements (type D) allow seniors to rent housing on a monthly or annual basis and live in the CCRC. Residents pay for all services on a fee-for-services basis, and the CCRC may not guarantee access to assisted living or nursing care. Type D contracts may require no entrance fees, and lower monthly charges cover housing only.[59]

---

59. CARF International, "Consumer Guide," 14; Elaine K. Howley, "Top 5 Things to Know about Continuing Care Retirement Communities,"

In some cases, CCRCs offer equity agreements that enable individuals to own their CCRC house, condominium, or townhome. Residents or their heirs can then sell the property to age- and income-appropriate buyers.[60]

In many cases, the Internal Revenue Service will recognize a portion of the entrance fee and monthly fees as a prepaid health-care expense[61] that is tax-deductible as a medical cost.[62] Residents should consult tax or financial advisers concerning this potential deduction.

The financial and organizational structure of CCRCs varies. The majority are nonprofit, but for-profit entities operate 22 percent of facilities.[63] CCRCs may have endowment funds and extensive donor development programs.[64] Some are independent and are limited to one site. In other cases, a parent company owns and operates multiple CCRCs. Multisite organizations can benefit from economies of scale, have more opportunities to learn from experience, and can spread risk

---

U.S. News & World Report, September 17, 2018, https://health.usnews.com/wellness/aging-well/articles/2018-09-17/top-5-things-to-know-about-continuing-care-retirement-communities; Brookdale Senior Living, "Rental vs. Life Care," Brookdale Senior Living, accessed December 21, 2020, https://www.brookdale.com/en/our-services/continuing-care-retirement-communities/rental-vs-life-care.html.

60. CARF International, "Consumer Guide," 5; AARP, "About Continuing Care Retirement Communities."

61. The amount depends on the CCRC's aggregate medical expenditures compared to its overall expenditures or overall income from resident fees.

62. Brad Breeding, "You May Be Able to Deduct Some CCRC Costs from Your Taxes," MyLifeSite, August 24, 2020, https://www.mylifesite.net/blog/post/you-may-be-able-to-deduct-some-ccrc-costs-from-your-taxes/.

63. Nelson, "22% of CCRCs in the U.S. Are For-Profit."

64. Brad Breeding, "Differences between For-Profit and Not-For-Profit CCRCs," Kendal.org, October 5, 2018, https://www.kendal.org/news/differences-between-for-profit-and-not-for-profit-ccrcs/; CARF International, "Consumer Guide," 13.

among the different facilities. Thus, if one CCRC temporarily experiences financial difficulties, income from other facilities will subsidize it. However, multisite operations' disadvantages include increased bureaucracy, nonlocalized decisions about individual CCRCs, and multiple facilities competing for limited resources.[65]

As an increasing number of baby boomers seek out CCRCs, they may become somewhat more affordable due to economies of scale and high occupancy rates. At the end of 2019, the CCRC occupancy rate averaged 88 percent.[66]

According to some sources, CCRCs work hard to ensure that residents can stay even if they deplete their financial resources. Management may apply the refundable portion of the entrance fee toward monthly payments or may provide opportunities for other residents to make voluntary contributions that support those in need. Some are able to offer other forms of financial aid thanks to ambitious fundraising activities.[67]

So, are CCRCs unaffordable for people who are not wealthy? Not necessarily. Many seniors will be able to cover entry fees with proceeds from the sale of their homes. Furthermore, because monthly fees include a comprehensive set of services, CCRCs may minimize other living expenses. To illustrate, a single person's $3,000 fee for a one-bedroom apartment will include numerous activities, transportation, many meals, utilities, an emergency call system, and more. Thus, if you do not seek to travel extensively or engage in other expensive leisure activities,

65. National Continuing Care Residents Association, "Consumer's Guide to Continuing Care Retirement Communities," 19–20.

66. National Investment Center, "Senior Housing Occupancy Rises Nationwide in Fourth Quarter, 2019," NIC, January 9, 2020, https://www.nic.org/news-press/senior-housing-occupancy-rises-nationwide-in-fourth-quarter-2019/.

67. Breeding, "Differences between For-Profit and Not-for-Profit CCRCs"; CARF International, "Consumer Guide," 13.

ordinarily you may not need to spend much beyond the $3,000 fee each month.

During my own CCRC visits, I asked administrators to estimate the net worth of individuals who are good candidates for a CCRC, but they declined to provide any numbers. One, however, told me that a very rough rule of thumb is that residents' assets should be worth at least twice the entry fee, and their monthly income (from social security, pension, investments, etc.) should equal at least twice the monthly fee in order to cover living expenses, such as medical care and travel.

Other concerns

Seniors may find it very difficult to leave beloved homes and familiar surroundings in which they have lived for decades. Moving will be especially daunting if it means seeing dear friends and relatives much less frequently.

At the same time, those who are eager to live in a CCRC may find that their CCRC of choice has a waiting list that takes up to two years to clear. Consequently, it is important to begin researching CCRCs well in advance of being ready to move to one and to be prepared to delay the transition.

Consumers should also be aware that CCRCs are often under-regulated by government authorities. Although federal and state laws govern the nursing homes and assisted living facilities located within CCRCs,[68] CCRCs as entities in and of themselves are subject to inconsistent oversight. Indeed, states could go much further in regulating CCRCs in order to minimize the financial risk to residents and maximize the likelihood of the facilities' economic success.

---

68. Nursing Home Reform Act, 42 U.S.C §1396r (2008), 42 U.S.C. §1395i-3 (2014), 42 CFR §§ 483.15–483.75 (2020); "Assisted Living Laws by State: Know Your Rights," AssistedLiving.com, accessed December 21, 2020, https://www.assistedliving.com/laws-by-state/.

As of 2018, 12 states had no CCRC-specific regulations.[69] A 2010 government report found that the states that did regulate CCRCs established a range of requirements. The laws of different states featured some or all of the following:

- Licensing requirements, with varying degrees of financial disclosures and feasibility study standards;
- Annual submission of audited financial statements;
- Review of CCRC resident contracts;
- A mandated "cooling-off period" during which dissatisfied residents may cancel their contracts and receive a refund of their full entrance fee, from which only specified costs can be deducted (typically the period ranges from prior to occupancy to one year after occupancy);
- Protection of CCRC residents' financial interests through (1) requirements that fees and deposits be escrowed, (2) specified criteria for raising monthly fees, and (3) authority to place liens or grant preferred status to claims in order to provide residents with recourse in the event of the CCRC's bankruptcy;
- Disclosure requirements concerning CCRCs' past, present, and anticipated future financial circumstances;
- Disclosure obligations concerning nonfinancial matters such as what policies operate when residents experience financial difficulties or whether the CCRC can transfer residents involuntarily to assisted living or nursing home care;
- Regulatory provisions that allow and encourage CCRC residents to form groups or councils for purposes of communicating with management and representing the interests of the residents at large;

---

69. Brad Breeding, "Understanding the Regulatory Process for CCRCs," MyLifeSite, April 3, 2018, https://www.mylifesite.net/blog/post/understanding-regulatory-process-ccrcs/.

- Pre-approval of CCRC marketing and advertising material.[70]

Only one organization, the Commission on Accreditation of Rehabilitation Facilities (CARF), accredits CCRCs, and no states require this accreditation.[71] As of the end of 2019, CARF listed only 170 facilities as accredited on its website.[72] Therefore, the majority of CCRCs do not pursue accreditation, likely because it is costly, burdensome, and voluntary.

It is possible that the availability of assisted living and nursing homes on campus will ironically diminish residents' autonomy. Management may pressure or require residents to move to higher levels of care when their health deteriorates even if the resident is resistant to such a change. CCRCs represent (often in their contracts) that they will not make decisions about transfers without consulting the patient, family members, and health-care providers, but the facility retains the right to make the ultimate decision.[73] In many cases, assistance from a home aide will be adequate to allow a resident to stay in an independent living unit. Moreover, if higher levels of care are

---

70. US Government Accountability Office, "Older Americans: Continuing Care Retirement Communities Can Provide Benefits, but Not Without Some Risk," US Government Accountability Office (2010), 11–32.

71. Brad Breeding, "Leveling the Playing Field: CCRC Ratings and Rankings," MyLifeSite, September 11, 2017, https://www.mylifesite.net/blog/post/leveling-the-playing-field-ccrc-ratings-and-rankings/; National Continuing Care Residents Association, "Consumer's Guide to Continuing Care Retirement Communities," 16–17 (noting that only 15 percent of CCRCs are CARF accredited).

72. CARF International, "List of CARF-CCAC Accredited Continuing Care Retirement Communities," CARF International, accessed December 21, 2020, http://carf.org/ccrcListing.aspx.

73. Brad Breeding, "Will a CCRC Move Me to Assisted Living Too Soon?" MyLifeSite, October 30, 2017, https://www.mylifesite.net/blog/post/will-a-ccrc-move-me-to-assisted-living-too-soon/.

included in the resident's contract, the CCRC will lose money by providing more services and therefore will be motivated to avoid unnecessary accelerations of care.[74] Nevertheless, residents must understand the limits of their ability to decide where they will live within the CCRC.

CCRC without Walls

A CCRC alternative that appeals to some seniors is an emerging program called "CCRC without Walls."[75] This program, which is available through at least thirty CCRCs, allows clients to remain in their off campus homes while taking advantage of many CCRC services.[76] These include personal attention from a care coordinator, nonmedical home care, emergency response systems, in-home meals, transportation, health clubs, social events, therapy, and, when necessary, assisted living or nursing home care. Members pay entrance fees and monthly fees, but they are lower than those paid by full CCRC residents. One such program, Kendal at Home, offers a "platinum plan" with entrance fees of $50,000 and monthly fees of $400–$700.[77] Another, Judson at Home (JAH), has an entrance fee of only $9,500 for a single person and then annual fees that it does not disclose on its website. It states that "under certain

---

74. Breeding, "Will a CCRC Move Me."

75. Carlo Calma, "Providers Continue to Expand CCRC without Walls Model," *Senior Housing News*, September 4, 2017, https://seniorhousingnews.com/2017/09/04/senior-living-providers-love-ccrcs-without-walls/; Paula Span, "A Retirement Community That Comes to You," *New York Times*, November 8, 2019, https://www.nytimes.com/2019/11/08/health/retirement-home-ccrc.html.

76. Tim Mullaney, "Large Senior Housing Provider Kendal Expands At-Home Services," *Home Health Care News*, June 25, 2018, https://homehealthcarenews.com/2018/06/large-senior-housing-provider-kendal-expands-at-home-services/.

77. Mullaney, "Large Senior Housing Provider."

conditions 50 percent of your JAH Membership fee can be applied to the cost of moving into a Judson Community. It is also fully refundable if you move out of state."[78] According to one source, entrance fees are typically $20,000–$45,000, and monthly fees can be as low as $200.[79]

To maintain the financial viability of the program, CCRCs without Walls generally accept only individuals who are healthy, competent, and functioning independently so that they do not need immediate institutional or other intensive care. CCRCs without Walls may not fully combat the problem of social isolation if participants do not frequently go to the campus and become involved in activities. However, the programs may address many of the needs of aging individuals at a more reasonable cost than CCRC residency.

RETIREMENT COMMUNITY PREPAREDNESS CHECKLIST

* It is critical that you live in an environment that facilitates staying active physically, mentally, and socially for as long as possible. If you are at risk of becoming socially isolated or living in conditions that become hazardous as you age, investigate retirement communities, such as independent living residences, 55-plus communities, NORCs, and village networks. If finances allow, consider CCRCs and keep their costs in mind as you make financial spending and savings choices.

---

78. Judson, "Judson Membership—Overview and Pricing," Judson, accessed December 9, 2019, https://www.judsonsmartliving.org/judsonathome/overview-and-pricing/.

79. Irving Levin Associates, "Senior Living Business: 'At-Home' Programs Help Seniors Age in Place," Irving Levin Associates, accessed December 21, 2020, https://www.levinassociates.com/archives/seniorcare/1006slbhead2/.

* Explore nearby senior centers that can provide various forms of support, including socially and intellectually enriching activities.
* Keep the importance of having a robust social circle in mind. The transition to a retirement community can be eased by moving to a facility in your own city, moving with a group of friends, or selecting one in which friends are already living.
* If you are considering retirement communities for yourself or loved ones, ask about their waiting lists. The more popular and reputable retirement communities may require long waits. For example, during several CCRC visits, my hosts told me that it could take 18–24 months to obtain a living unit after making an initial deposit.
* Finding an appropriate retirement community should involve significant research. Once you identify a facility of interest, you should spend significant time there to determine whether it is a good fit. CCRCs often have guest suites that you can rent for a few nights, and an actual stay at the facility for at least two days is very helpful in the decision-making process. It is only by spending time at the retirement community and speaking with residents that you can get a real feel for the place.
* If you are considering a CCRC, be sure to visit its assisted living, nursing home, and memory care components and to speak with residents about them. How do residents fare in these units? To what extent do they remain integrated into the community? Are these attractive settings? Do those who move to them from independent living feel stigmatized?
* If you are considering moving to a CCRC or other type of community or facility, do your research and reading. I cite many illuminating articles in the footnotes to this chapter, and the websites on which they are posted provide a treasure trove of further information.
* Learn about the questions you should ask in the course of researching senior housing. For example, Brookdale Senior

Living provides a document entitled "Your Senior Living Search: Questions to Ask."[80] It recommends investigating the following topics (and offers detailed suggested inquiries about them):

- Staff
- Living and housing
- Meals and food
- Social life and recreation
- Personal services (e.g., banking, laundry, exercise)
- Medical services
- The community/residents
- Policies and procedures

* Once you select a retirement community and have a contract in hand, read it carefully. You would also be wise to consult a lawyer prior to signing the contract if it is complicated (as in the case of CCRCs) or if you have questions about it. You should also consult a financial or tax adviser to determine whether any tax deductions are available and whether moving to the facility requires you to change any of your financial practices.

---

80. Brookdale Senior Living, "What to Ask When Visiting a Senior Living Community," Brookdale Senior Living, accessed December 21, 2020, file:///C:/Users/User/Downloads/Question_List_Senior_Living_Visit. pdf (providing a list you can download).

CHAPTER 3

HELP WITH MONEY, CARE, AND HOME MANAGEMENT

During our phone conversations, my sister often told me how much time she spent paying my father's bills, filling his pill boxes, scheduling his medical appointments, accompanying him to doctors' offices, taking care of repairs, and much more. My sister's help enabled my father, who was in his late 80s, to continue residing in his house, with added assistance from paid caregivers. I still feel somewhat guilty about the disproportionate burden she bore because she was the one who lived close to our father, and I am grateful that he had her devoted assistance.

What about those of us who will not have loved ones available to offer daily or weekly support? Who might provide us help with these critical matters? Thankfully, professional services are increasingly becoming available to meet seniors' needs. These professionals can alleviate some of the burdens of caregiving if you are taking care of a loved one and be of help to you if you are a senior without adequate support systems.

DAILY MONEY MANAGERS

Daily money managers (DMMs) offer a range of services to seniors. These most commonly include the following:

- Bill paying, including calls to payees regarding incorrect bills;

- Balancing checkbooks and organizing bank records;
- Preparing and delivering bank deposits;
- Organizing tax documents and other paperwork;
- Negotiating with creditors;
- Providing referrals to and working with legal, tax, and investment professionals.[1]

DMMs generally visit the homes of elderly clients in order to assist them with financial tasks. They typically charge between $75 and $150 per hour, but some charge a flat monthly fee.[2] Some DMMs provide services on a volunteer or reduced-fee basis to economically disadvantaged clients. The American Association of Daily Money Managers (AADMM) website features a list of agencies that offer such DMM assistance in several states.[3]

Daily money management is an emerging profession, and the AADMM had approximately 800 members in the United States and Canada in 2020.[4] The AADMM website enables

1. American Association of Daily Money Managers, "Daily Money Management and You," American Association of Daily Money Managers, accessed December 22, 2020, https://secure.aadmm.com/dmms-and-you/.

2. Lynnette Khalfani-Cox, "Need Help Managing Day-to-Day Finances?" AARP, July 1, 2016, https://www.aarp.org/money/budgeting-saving/info-2016/money-management-on-a-budget.html; Jeff Brown, "Do Investors Need a Daily Money Manager?" *U.S. News and World Report*, November 26, 2018, https://money.usnews.com/investing/investing-101/articles/do-investors-need-a-daily-money-manager.

3. American Association of Daily Money Managers, "Volunteer Outreach State Agency Information," American Association of Daily Money Managers, accessed December 22, 2020, https://secure.aadmm.com/state-agencies/.

4. American Association of Daily Money Managers, "History of AADMM," American Association of Daily Money Managers, accessed December 22, 2020, https://secure.aadmm.com/about-aadmm/history-of-aadmm/.

users to search for DMMs by geographic location.[5] However, because the AADMM has relatively few members, you may need to turn to other sources to locate a DMM near you. Estate lawyers, accountants, and agencies that assist seniors may be able to provide referrals.

The daily money management field is not regulated by state or federal authorities.[6] This is of concern because DMMs have access to clients' checkbooks, financial information, and other sensitive materials, and thus dishonest individuals would have ample opportunities to exploit the elderly. The AADMM publishes a code of ethics, but there is no enforcement mechanism that can ensure compliance.[7]

It is therefore very important to employ trustworthy individuals. Recommendations from people who are familiar with the DMM you are considering can be particularly valuable. DMM certification is another quality indicator and is available through the AADMM. Applicants for certification must have completed 1,500 hours of paid DMM work[8] over the prior three years. They must also undergo a background check and pass a test consisting of 100 multiple-choice questions.[9] At the end of 2020, however, the list of certified DMMs published on the AADMM website was short, including only

5. American Association of Daily Money Managers, "Find a DMM," American Association of Daily Money Managers, accessed December 22, 2020, https://secure.aadmm.com/find-a-dmm/.

6. Khalfani-Cox, "Day-to-Day Finances"; Brown, "Do Investors Need Daily Money Manager."

7. American Association of Daily Money Managers, "Code of Ethics," American Association of Daily Money Managers, accessed December 22, 2020, https://secure.aadmm.com/code-of-ethics/.

8. The minimum 1,500 hours of experience must include at least 1,250 of paid work and 250 of eligible pro bono work.

9. American Association of Daily Money Managers, "The Certified Daily Money Manager® (CDMM®)" American Association of Daily Money Managers, accessed December 22, 2020, https://secure.aadmm.com/certification/.

82 professionals.[10] It appears that most DMMs currently do not consider certification to be a worthwhile credential.

Another safeguard is to ensure that the DMM is bonded and employed by an organization with an insurance policy that will provide appropriate compensation for theft, fraud, and other forms of malpractice.[11] Elderly people who use DMMs can also take the following precautions: limit the money available in the checking account that the DMM will use, sign all checks themselves, and review all financial statements or ask a trusted friend or relative to do so.[12] Automating as many payments as possible will also reduce the DMM's workload, decrease charges, and limit opportunities for errors or dishonesty.

GERIATRIC CARE MANAGERS

Geriatric care managers (GCMs) provide an array of services that can be invaluable for seniors who lack sufficient family support. GCMs are generally social workers, nurses, gerontologists, psychologists, or other human service professionals who focus on assessment, monitoring, planning, problem-solving, and advocacy for elderly clients and their caregivers.[13] More

---

10. American Association of Daily Money Managers, "List of Certified Professional Daily Money Managers," American Association of Daily Money Managers, accessed December 22, 2020, https://secure.aadmm.com/certified-pdmms/.

11. Anne Tergesen, "A Little Help with the Bills," *Wall Street Journal*, July 27, 2012, http://online.wsj.com/articles/SB10000872396390444484010 4577550910299244458; Brown, "Do Investors Need Daily Money Manager."

12. Valerie Keene, "Daily Money Management Programs for Seniors," *Nolo*, accessed December 22, 2020, https://www.nolo.com/legal-encyclopedia/daily-money-management-programs-seniors-32269.html.

13. Aging Life Care Association, "What You Need to Know," Aging Life Care Association, accessed December 22, 2020, https://www.aginglifecare.org/ALCA/About_Aging_Life_Care/What_you_need_to_know/ALCA/About_Aging_Life_Care/What_you_need_to_know.aspx?hkey=e3b15907-97b1-4a4a-acac-cc1d515bd311.

specifically, geriatric care management can be defined as "a service that assesses an individual's medical and social service needs, then coordinates assistance from paid service providers and unpaid help from family and friends to enable persons with disabilities to live with as much independence as possible."[14]

The first encounter with a GCM involves a comprehensive assessment, after which a variety of services can be provided. The Aging Life Care Association (ALCA) website asserts that GCMs can do all of the following:

- Assist in selecting appropriate housing or residential settings;
- Determine what home care services are necessary and assist in monitoring them;
- Attend doctor appointments with clients, facilitate communication with doctors, and monitor the client's compliance with medical instructions;
- Provide referrals to elder law attorneys or consult with them;
- Provide expert opinions for purposes of court proceedings;
- Oversee bill paying and review financial affairs in consultation with accountants or the client's power of attorney;
- Help clients obtain federal and state entitlements and benefits;
- Assess the home environment and offer recommendations to enhance clients' safety and general welfare.[15]

ALCA members can choose among a variety of certifications. They can become certified care managers, certified case managers, certified social work case managers, and certified

14. Lisa M. Scott and Candace Sharkey, "Putting the Pieces Together: Private-Duty Home Healthcare and Geriatric Care Management: One Home Health Agency's Model," *Home Healthcare Nurse* 25, no. 3 (2007): 167–72.

15. Aging Life Care Association, "What You Need to Know."

advanced social work case managers.[16] ALCA's website enables users to search for local GCMs.[17] GCMs typically charge $50–$200 per hour for their services, and these costs are not covered by health insurance.[18]

GCM use has been associated with a number of benefits for the elderly and for caregivers. These include fewer emergency department visits, hospitalizations, and falls; increased ability to follow instructions concerning medications; decreased depression, and a greater probability of delaying or avoiding a move to assisted living or a nursing home.[19] For family members, GCMs can be invaluable resources and relieve a considerable amount of stress. They can undertake many challenging eldercare tasks and serve as "onsite eyes and ears."[20]

---

16. Aging Life Care Association, "Certification Bodies," Aging Life Care Association, accessed December 22, 2020, https://www.aginglifecare.org/ALCA/Join_Us/Certification_Bodies/ALCA/Join_Us/Certification_Bodies.aspx.

17. Aging Life Care Association, "Find an Aging Life Care Expert Search," Aging Life Care Association, accessed December 22, 2020, https://www.aginglifecare.org/ALCA/About_Aging_Life_Care/Find_an_Aging_Life_Care_Expert/ALCA/About_Aging_Life_Care/Search/Find_an_Expert.aspx?hkey=78a6cb03-e912-4993-9b68-df1573e9d8af.

18. Paying for Senior Care, "Find a Geriatric Care Manager to Develop a Senior Care Plan by State or Zip," Paying for Senior Care, accessed December 22, 2020, https://www.payingforseniorcare.com/longtermcare/find_geriatric_care_managers.html.

19. Marilyn Wideman, "Geriatric Care Management: Role, Need, and Benefits," *Home Healthcare Nurse* 30, no. 9 (2012): 556; Susan Valoff, "What Is a Geriatric Care Manager? And Do I Need One?" *San Diego Union-Tribune*, September 20, 2018, https://www.sandiegouniontribune.com/caregiver/caregiving-essentials/resources/sd-me-geriatric-care-manager-20180514-story.html.

20. Jane Wolf Frances, *Parenting Our Parents: Transforming the Challenge into a Journey of Love* (Lanham, MD: Rowman & Littlefield, 2019), 76–80; Carol Bradley Bursack, "Geriatric Care Managers Can Help Busy Caregivers,"

ELDER LAW ATTORNEYS

Elder law attorneys can assist not only the elderly themselves but also those who are wise enough to want to plan ahead of time for old age. In the words of one lawyer, they can steer clients away from being "geriatric gamblers" and "planning procrastinators" to being "pragmatic planners."[21]

Elder law attorneys may provide both legal assistance and general care coordination for aging clients. The legal matters that an elder law attorney can address include the following:

- Health and personal care planning, including advance directives;
- Financial planning, housing matters, and tax issues (income, estate, and gift tax);
- Planning for a well spouse when the other requires long-term care, including asset protection and the attainment of public benefits such as Medicaid and veterans' benefits;
- Medicare payments;
- Obtaining a court-appointed guardian for a person who has lost decision-making ability;
- Avoiding the need for a guardian by naming a substitute decision maker in a power of attorney document so the named person can assume decision-making responsibilities if the need arises;
- Defending residents' rights in residential facilities such as nursing homes;

AgingCare, updated April 22, 2020, https://www.agingcare.com/articles/geriatric-care-managers-help-for-elders-needs-138976.htm; Susan M. Enguidanos and Paula M. Jamison, "Moving from Tacit Knowledge to Evidence-Based Practice: The Kaiser Permanente Community Partners Study," *Home Health Care Service Quarterly* 25, nos. 1–2 (2006): 13–31.

21. Robert Abrams, "Are You a Planner or a Gambler?," *New York State Bar Association Journal* (July/August 2011), 6–7.

- Handling employment and retirement concerns;
- Drafting wills and trusts and assisting with estate planning and probate;
- All other legal planning for aging, illness, and incapacity.[22]

The National Academy of Elder Law Attorneys and National Elder Law Foundation websites allow users to search for certified elder law attorneys in their own state.[23] The American Bar Association has accredited the National Elder Law Foundation to certify lawyers as elder law attorneys. As of 2021, there were over five hundred certified elder law attorneys in the United States.[24] Those certified must demonstrate that they have practiced law for the preceding five years and handled at least 60 elder law matters on which they spent a minimum of 16 hours per week on average during the past three years. They also must have at least 45 hours of continuing legal education in elder law during the preceding three years. Certification further involves an examination and must be renewed every five years.[25]

Chapter 4 provides an extensive discussion of the legal documents you should have to be prepared for your later years

22. Care.com, "What an Elder Law Attorney Does—and Why You Might Need One," Care.com, September 19, 2018, https://www.care.com/c/stories/5460/elder-care-attorney-questions/; FindLaw, "What Does an Elder Law Attorney Do?" FindLaw, updated July 2, 2019, https://elder.findlaw.com/what-is-elder-law/what-does-an-elder-law-attorney-do-.html; Rebecca C. Morgan, "The Future of Elder Law Practice," *William Mitchell Law Review* 37, no. 1 (2010): 1–48.

23. Homepage, National Academy of Elder Law Attorneys, accessed December 22, 2020, https://www.naela.org/; "Welcome," National Elder Law Foundation, accessed December 22, 2020, www.nelf.org.

24. National Elder Law Foundation, "Welcome."

25. National Elder Law Foundation, "Program for the Certification of Elder Law Attorneys," National Elder Law Foundation, accessed December 22, 2020, https://nelf.org/page/NELFRulesandRegulations.

or for potential loss of decision-making capacity at any point in life.

ORGANIZING, ADAPTING, AND SELLING YOUR HOME

As my parents reached their mid-70s, my sisters and I became increasingly concerned about their ability to stay in their large, two-story home. Occasionally, they seemed unsteady on their feet, and a few times, they fell. We worried about their ability to maneuver up or down the stairs and to manage a big house. Yet, they resisted moving to a smaller, one-story residence because it seemed like an overwhelming task. They had accumulated decades' worth of possessions and papers, and they lacked the energy to cull through them. It took us years to convince them to move, and then it took a long time to sell their house. It turns out that there were plenty of professionals who could have helped them organize their home, prepare it for sale, and adapt it to their needs while they waited to make their decision and purchase a condominium. If only we had known!

Adapting your home

People who wish to remain in their homes but have mobility or other impairments can modify their residences to better suit their needs. For example, you might make the following changes:

- Install grab bars for support in the shower, over the tub, and by the toilet;
- Buy a raised toilet seat;
- Widen doorways and passageways to accommodate a walker or wheelchair;
- Install a chair lift for the stairs;

- Install a ramp to avoid using steps to enter the house;
- Buy specialized furniture, such as adjustable beds and recliners.

Such changes can make the home significantly safer and reduce the likelihood of falls and trips to the emergency room. For advice about modifying your home, you can consult an occupational therapist. The website Healthgrades. com allows users to search for local occupational therapists online. Individuals who cannot afford home modifications may be able to receive financial assistance through a variety of organizations, such as the US Department of Veterans Affairs, the American Red Cross, the American Parkinson Disease Association, and many others. A website called HomeAdvisor. com provides a useful resource guide entitled "Grants for Home Modification: 16 Resources for Homeowners with Disabilities."

Personal emergency response and detection systems

A particularly valuable addition to the home of a frail individual is a personal emergency response system. These devices allow elderly people to contact a special dispatcher, 911, or family members by pushing a button on a bracelet or pendant. If an emergency occurs in the house or immediately outside of it, such as a fall, the client need only push the button to send a signal to a console that automatically dials an emergency number.[26]

Some advanced models operate through cellular service and will work anywhere (not just at home). In addition, some systems have fall detection capabilities, designed to protect people who cannot push a button because of a disability or

---

26. AgingInPlace, "A Complete Guide to Medical Alert Systems," AgingInPlace, updated December 2020, https://www.aginginplace.org/a-complete-guide-to-medical-alert-systems/.

the severity of the fall.[27] The technology, however, is imperfect and can be excessively sensitive. One annoyed customer told me that his alarm was triggered when he pounded his fist on a lectern for emphasis while delivering a lecture to a large audience, causing him no end of embarrassment. *Consumer Reports* provides helpful tips and comparisons among leading products in an article entitled "How to Choose a Medical Alert System."[28]

Be aware that you will have to pay for your emergency response system out of pocket because health insurance does not cover it.[29] Nevertheless, these devices can be cost-effective. They can reduce the need for in-home care aides because they enable elderly people to obtain help quickly and easily even if they are alone at home.

Unfortunately, some people who have personal emergency response and detection systems rarely wear them or do not activate them when appropriate. Most commonly, they underutilize them because they do not believe they need them, do not want to admit that they are vulnerable, are worried about scaring family members whom the company will notify whenever they activate the device, or wish to avoid hospital visits at all costs. Automated systems can be particularly helpful for such individuals.

---

27. AgingInPlace, "A Complete Guide to Medical Alert Systems."

28. Catherine Roberts, "How to Choose a Medical Alert System," Consumer Reports, updated October 19, 2020, https://www.consumerreports.org/medical-alert-systems/how-to-choose-a-medical-alert-system/; Amy Goyer, "How to Choose a Medical Alert System," AARP, updated November 11, 2019, https://www.aarp.org/caregiving/home-care/info-2017/medic-alert-systems-options.html.

29. Harry Wang, "Tech Advances Will Give Aging Baby Boomers More Independence," *E-Commerce Times*, October 1, 2014, http://www.ecommercetimes.com/story/81128.html; Goyer, "How to Choose a Medical Alert System."

Seniors may worry that having a personal emergency response and detection system will reduce their social contact because family and friends will check on them less often. This may be a valid concern in some cases, but overall, the devices have been found to be effective when used, and users are most often satisfied with them. They enhance seniors' sense of security, allow them to remain independent longer, and even shorten hospital stays because patients receive immediate attention when they are injured.[30]

Professional organizers

Professional organizers will help you organize just about anything. Some specialize in serving seniors.

Organizing can be useful at any time, especially prior to moving out of your home. A professional could help you downsize and discard possessions and paperwork that have been accumulated over decades. Your friends and relatives will be very grateful to you if you spare them the stress and agony of having to do this work themselves after you move to a long-term care facility or pass away.

According to the National Association of Productivity and Organizing Professionals' website (yes, they have their own national association),

Professional Organizers and Productivity Consultants assist clients with home office organization, time management,

30. Virginia Hessels, Glenn S. Le Prell, and William C. Mann, "Advances in Personal Emergency Response and Detection Systems," *Assistive Technology* 23, no. 3 (2011): 152–61; Colin Grubb, "Is a Medical Alert Worth the Cost?," Consumersadvocate.org, April 27, 2015, https://www.consumersadvocate.org/medical-alerts/is-medical-alert-worth-it; Morgan Haefner, "Humana Partners with Philips on 2 Remote Monitoring Initiatives," *Becker's Payer Issues*, December 4, 2019, https://www.beckershospitalreview.com/payer-issues/humana-partners-with-philips-on-2-remote-monitoring-initiatives.html.

corporate efficiency, specialty projects (from organizing photos to cataloging inventories), writing (whether blogs, books or lectures), virtual organizing [...] downsizing, and moving and relocation.[31]

The association has over 3,500 members worldwide and offers certification, an annual conference, a blog, and educational online classes. Its website features a directory that makes it easy for users to locate nearby professional organizers.[32] A quick search reveals that many organizers have a knack for clever names. For example, who could resist employing a service named "Leff's Last Re-Sort" or "Can the Clutter"?

Relocation specialists

Once you are ready to sell your home or the home of an elderly loved one, you might want to consult additional experts. Relocation experts can help you downsize, sell your home, and find a new one, and some specialize in serving seniors.

When my neighbor, a widower, moved from his large home to an assisted living facility, he benefitted greatly from the services of a relocation specialist. She was experienced in working with seniors and was patient, sensitive, and responsive to his needs. The relocation specialist and her team helped my friend go through all of his possessions and select the relatively few that would accompany him to his new one-bedroom apartment, having carefully measured it and determined how much it could contain.

---

31. National Association of Productivity & Organizing Professionals, "A Guide to Getting Started in the Organizing & Productivity Profession," National Association of Productivity & Organizing Professionals, accessed December 22, 2020, https://cdn.ymaws.com/www.napo.net/resource/resmgr/website_update/getting_started_guide_final.pdf.
32. Homepage, National Association of Productivity & Organizing Professionals, accessed December 22, 2020, https://www.napo.net/.

They donated the remainder to good causes and disposed of things that were unusable. They also did all the packing, moving, and unpacking. When my friend arrived at the residence, he found everything in place, with nothing left to do but relax and enjoy his new home.

The National Association of Senior Move Managers trains and supports its members.[33] You can search for a senior move manager in your area on the association's website.[34] Information about "senior friendly" real estate agents is also available on the National Care Planning Council's website.[35]

Home staging

If you just need help selling your home, you might consult a home stager, especially if you have not recently updated your residence. Home stagers assist customers by "accentuating positive architectural features, opening up spaces, neutralizing colors, and conveying comfort […] [to] present your property in its best light."[36]

As my parents learned after initially having difficulty selling their house, stripping off old wallpaper, applying fresh, light-colored paint, and replacing dark appliances with white or stainless steel ones can make a big difference. The Real Estate Staging Association enables users to search for nearby stagers through its

---

33. Homepage, National Association of Senior Move Managers, accessed December 22, 2020, https://www.nasmm.org/.

34. National Association of Senior Move Managers, "Find a Senior Move Manager," National Association of Senior Move Managers, accessed December 22, 2020, https://www.nasmm.org/find/index.cfm.

35. National Care Planning Council, "Find Real Estate or Senior Relocation Services," National Care Planning Council, accessed December 22, 2020, https://www.longtermcarelink.net/a7seniorrelocation_SRES.htm.

36. Define by Redesign, "The Basics of Home Staging," Define by Redesign, accessed December 10, 2019, http://www.definebyredesign.com/services/homestaging.php.

website.[37] If you do not want to use a stager or cannot afford one, you can ask your real estate agent for suggestions as to how to make the home more appealing to buyers and hope that he or she has a good eye. Cosmetic changes can make the home sell more quickly and help you get a higher price for it.

EMPLOYING ELDER CARE SERVICE PROFESSIONALS

The benefits of employing reliable DMMs, GCMs, elder law attorneys, and experts who can assist elderly people manage at home can be considerable. These professionals can help seniors maintain their independence and avoid having to move to assisted living or nursing facilities.

One 2012 study estimated that seniors who lived at home until death with the help of DMMs and GCMs saved an average of $60,000 in total costs by avoiding nursing homes. The lifetime cost of care management averaged $108,810, and that of DMM services was $8,656.[38] Admittedly, these expenses are unaffordable for many seniors. In some cases, adult children who have the means hire and pay for service professionals for their parents in order to reduce their own workload and enjoy peace of mind.

Hired assistants may be a good financial investment for a variety of reasons (in addition to enabling seniors to avoid or postpone nursing home care). They may save clients' money by paying clients' bills so they avoid costly errors, late fees, and interest. They may also assist them with applying

---

37. Homepage, Real Estate Staging Association, accessed December 22, 2020, https://www.realestatestagingassociation.com.

38. Debra Sacks, Dhiman Das, Raquel Romanick, Matt Caron, Carmen Morano, and Marianne C. Fahs, "The Value of Daily Money Management: An Analysis of Outcomes and Costs," *Journal of Evidence-Base Social Work* 9, no. 5 (2012): 498–511.

for government benefits and identifying free or inexpensive community resources.

In addition, DMMs can potentially combat elder financial abuse. Women over 80 who are widowed, lonely, and in poor health are particularly vulnerable.[39] Elders may be deceived by strangers who call or e-mail them or knock on their doors, caregivers who demand loans or gifts, and even family members who take advantage of a relative's frailty. Seniors who use computers but are naive about spam and financial swindles may be victimized by electronic scams. Skilled professionals who oversee elderly individuals' financial affairs should be able to save their clients from being duped by exploiters.[40]

Those without children or other dedicated, unpaid helpers need not manage their affairs completely on their own or fail to manage them altogether. DMMs, GCMs, organizers, and other specialists can provide much-needed assistance to elderly individuals with physical ailments that limit their functionality, such as arthritis or deteriorating vision, and to those who simply no longer wish to take care of certain mundane tasks. Unfortunately, however, elderly people whose cognitive abilities

---

39. Sacks, Das, Romanick, Caron, Morano, and Fahs, "Value of Daily Money Management," 509–10; Jean A. Teresi et al., "State of the Science on Prevention of Elder Abuse and Lessons Learned from Child Abuse and Domestic Violence Prevention: Toward a Conceptual Framework for Research," *Journal of Elder Abuse & Neglect* 28, nos. 4–5 (August–December 2016): 263–300; Stephen Deane, "Elder Financial Exploitation: Why It Is a Concern, What Regulators Are Doing about It, and Looking Ahead," US Securities and Exchange Commission: Office of the Investor Advocate (June 2018), 5, https://www.sec.gov/files/elder-financial-exploitation.pdf.

40. Kenn Beam Tacchino, "Preventing Financial Elder Abuse," *Journal of Personal Finance* 16, no. 1 (2017): 78–89; Catherine Schnaubelt, "Financial Elder Abuse: The Dark Side of Aging and Finances," *Forbes*, July 5, 2018, https://www.forbes.com/sites/catherineschnaubelt/2018/07/05/financial-elder-abuse-the-dark-side-of-aging-and-finances/#6990a3a311f7.

decline will likely be unable to hire, work with, and supervise professionals on their own.

When the client is mentally impaired, the success of professionals' services generally depends on the availability of children or others who can explain the client's needs, offer access to documents and accounts, and provide some degree of oversight. For the childless, this role could be filled by trusted friends or more distant relatives. Paid professionals can relieve much of the burden that would otherwise be borne by unpaid caregivers so that the latter need not attend to the elderly person's affairs on a day-to-day basis. Planned retirement communities, discussed in Chapter 2, or elder law attorneys may have DMMs and GCMs on staff or be able to provide reliable referrals.

For individuals who live alone without a close-knit social circle, the challenge is to recognize that their mental capacity is declining and that they need the aid of service professionals. Consequently, it is all the more important for older adults to maintain social bonds and frequent contact with trusted friends or relatives. Living in a retirement community or otherwise in close proximity to loved ones can be critical to seniors' welfare. In addition, seniors would be wise to form a relationship with an elder law attorney and/or a GCM while their full faculties are intact so that a skilled expert will know them well, monitor them, and suggest interventions when appropriate.

In fact, consulting an elder law attorney would be a responsible step for every working person to take long before retirement. As discussed in Chapter 4, every individual should have a detailed will, living will, durable power of attorney for health care, and durable power of attorney for property and finances. Of particular relevance here, properly designated agents can coordinate the work of DMMs and GCMs for incapacitated persons.

As baby boomers age, we are likely to see growth in the emerging professions of DMMs, GCMs, elder law attorneys, and others who specialize in helping seniors. At the same time, let us hope that professional organizations and state governments will implement uniform and stringent certification and oversight requirements. DMMs and GCMs in particular have seniors' financial, physical, and emotional health in their hands. Clients should not have to gamble when hiring them and be left to guess about their quality and integrity.

HELP WITH MONEY, CARE, AND HOME MANAGEMENT PREPAREDNESS CHECKLIST

* If you or a loved one has trouble managing fiscal matters, consider hiring a DMM.
* Seniors without strong family support systems should consider hiring GCMs.
* Consult an elder law attorney to ensure that you are legally prepared for your later years, as discussed more fully in Chapter 4.
* If you or a loved one is having trouble adapting, organizing, or selling a home or managing a move to a new residence, consider hiring professionals who can assist with these tasks: occupational therapists, organizers, relocation experts, and home stagers.
* When hiring professionals, opt for those who are members of their professional organizations, have undertaken relevant educational programs, and, if possible, are certified in their specialty.
* Have a personal emergency response and detection system installed in the home to ensure that you or your loved one can get immediate assistance in an emergency.

CHAPTER 4

ESSENTIAL LEGAL PLANNING

In Chapter 1, I discussed the woefully inadequate retirement savings that many Americans accrue during their working lives. Are we any better at legal preparedness for old age? Unfortunately, the answer is no.

I remember a phone call I received from a friend who was in her 70s and was suffering a recurrence of an aggressive cancer. "I'm thinking I should have a will," she said and asked me to recommend a lawyer. I was shocked that this highly educated woman had not previously executed a will, especially given her age and medical history, but she is not alone. An alarming number of Americans do not have wills. According to 2019 statistics, only 40 percent of US adults have wills, and among those who are 55 or older, only 55 percent have wills.[1]

---

1. Caring.com, "2019 Survey Finds That Most People Believe Having a Will Is Important, but Less Than Half Have One," Caring.com, accessed December 10, 2019, https://www.caring.com/caregivers/estate-planning/wills-survey/; Merrill Lynch and Age Wave, "Leaving a Legacy: A Lasting Gift to Loved Ones," Merrill Lynch, 2019, https://mlaem.fs.ml.com/content/dam/ML/Articles/pdf/ml_LegacyStudy_Final.pdf. See also Stacy Francis, "Op-ed: More People Are Creating Wills amid the Pandemic," CNBC, October 5, 2020, https://www.cnbc.com/2020/10/05/op-ed-more-people-are-creating-wills-amid-the-pandemic.html (stating that a LegalZoom.com survey found that 62 percent of Americans still do not have wills).

The COVID-19 pandemic vividly demonstrated how unpredictable life is. You can be healthy one day and in the intensive care unit, needing a ventilator a few days later. No one, at any age, can count on having years ahead of good health and mental acuity. The information in this chapter, therefore, is vital for everyone, regardless of age and circumstances.

Thorough planning must include contemplation of worst-case scenarios, such as a temporary or permanent loss of mental faculties. Eleven percent of individuals 65 and older suffer from dementia, as do about one-third of those 85 and older.[2] Many others experience temporary incapacity resulting from illness or surgery. Therefore, it is prudent to consider this possibility and to formulate contingency plans. It is also wise to ensure that your assets will be distributed in accordance with your wishes after you die. Legal documents can accomplish all of these goals.

ADVANCE DIRECTIVES FOR HEALTH CARE

I am a member of the ethics committee of University Hospitals in Cleveland, Ohio. In one meeting several years ago, we learned of a case in which a man needed to undergo surgery to remove his very painful kidney stones. His daughter accompanied him to an appointment with a surgeon. Based on the conversation, the physician determined that the man had dementia and was not capable of providing informed consent to the procedure. The daughter volunteered to consent in place of her father but admitted that her father had not executed an advance directive

---

2. Alzheimer's Association, "2021 Alzheimer's Disease Facts and Figures," Alzheimer's Association, 2021, https://www.alz.org/media/Documents/alzheimers-facts-and-figures.pdf; National Institutes of Health, "Dealing with Dementia," *NIH News in Health*, December 2017, https://newsinhealth.nih.gov/special-issues/seniors/dealing-dementia#:~:text=By%20some%20estimates%2C%20about%20one,isn't%20a%20disease%20itself.

naming her as his agent and that she had not been appointed as her father's guardian by an Ohio court. Consequently, the surgeon could not obtain informed consent to the procedure from any authorized party and refused to perform the surgery. He told the daughter that because her father's dementia would prevent him from executing a valid advance directive, he could not have this nonemergency operation until she obtained guardianship and thus legal authority to consent to his care. Appointment of a guardian, however, involves court proceedings and can take several months, during which time the man would not receive treatment and could potentially suffer excruciating pain.[3] Although some states designate default surrogates (typically close relatives) to make medical decisions in such circumstances,[4] my home state of Ohio is not one of them.

The patient could have avoided this unfortunate outcome if he had an advance directive. An advance directive is a set of documents that allow you to appoint a decision maker and provide legally valid instructions concerning your health care that take effect if you become incapacitated.[5] An advance directive should include the following components: (1) a living

---

3. Lawrence A. Frolik and Linda S. Whitton, *Everyday Law for Seniors* (Boulder, CO: Paradigm, 2012), 138–53; Amber R. Comer, Margaret Gaffney, Cynthia Stone, and Alexia Torke, "The Effect of a State Health Care Consent Law on Patient Care in Hospitals: A Survey of Physicians," *Journal of Hospital Administration*, 7, no. 2 (2018): 31–35.

4. Erin S. DeMartino et al., "Who Decides When a Patient Can't? Statutes on Alternate Decision Makers," *New England Journal of Medicine*, 376, no. 15 (2017): 1478–82; Shana Wynn, "Decisions by Surrogates: An Overview of Surrogate Consent Laws in the United States," American Bar Association, republished online October 15, 2018, https://www.americanbar.org/groups/law_aging/publications/bifocal/vol_36/issue_1_october2014/default_surrogate_consent_statutes/.

5. American Cancer Society, "Types of Advance Directives," American Cancer Society, updated May 13, 2019, https://www.cancer.org/content/cancer/en/treatment/finding-and-paying-for-treatment/understanding-financial-and-legal-matters/advance-directives/types-of-advance-health-care-directives.html;

will, (2) a durable power of attorney for health care, and (3) an organ donation form (if you wish to be a donor). States generally provide all three in one packet. I will discuss each of these documents separately below.

Adults with decision-making capacity have the ability to consent to medical treatment and a right to refuse health-care interventions even if doing so will shorten their lives. On the other hand, incapacity is an inability to make and communicate informed decisions, so that mentally incapacitated patients by definition cannot make choices for themselves. Determinations of incapacity are made by physicians.[6]

Researchers have found that 45–70 percent of elderly patients are unable to make end-of-life decision themselves.[7] Before losing capacity, individuals may have strong views about the care they want and do not want to receive in particular circumstances, and the prospect of having those wishes ignored can be heartbreaking. If you want to make sure that your doctors follow your wishes even if you can no longer express them, you need an advance directive. As the story above illustrates, in some circumstances, it may be difficult, if not impossible, to obtain nonemergency care without this document.

All 50 states and the District of Columbia recognize advance directives, although the state laws differ in their particulars.[8] For example, the states vary as to their instructions for completing

US National Library of Medicine, "Advance Directives," *MedlinePlus*, updated December 17, 2020, https://medlineplus.gov/advancedirectives.html.

6. Christopher Libby and Gary Gillette, "Competency and Capacity," in StatPearls [online] (Treasure Island, FL: StatPearls, 2019), https://www.ncbi.nlm.nih.gov/books/NBK532862/.

7. Deborah Carr and Elizabeth A. Luth, "Advance Care Planning: Contemporary Issues and Future Directions," *Innovation in Aging*, 1, no. 1 (March 2017): 2.

8. Charles P. Sabatino, "Overcoming the Balkanization of State Advance Directive Laws," *Journal of Law, Medicine & Ethics* 46, no. 4 (2018): 985.

an advance directive, in some cases requiring notarization, and in others asking for the signature of one or two witnesses.[9]

The Patient Self-Determination Act of 1990 requires that all hospitals, long- term care facilities, home health agencies, hospice programs, and health maintenance organizations receiving Medicare and Medicaid payments recognize patient advance directives. They must also do the following:

- Ask patients at the time of admission if they have advance directives;
- Give patients written information about advance directives;
- Document patients' advance directives in their medical records;
- Comply with state law requirements concerning advance directives;
- Avoid discrimination against individuals based on their having or not having advance directives;
- Educate staff and the community about advance directives.[10]

Nevertheless, by now you probably will not be surprised to learn that relatively few Americans have taken advantage of this opportunity to plan for the future. Experts estimate that only one-quarter to one-third of American adults have medical advance directives.[11]

Admittedly, it is not easy to think about being very sick and incapacitated. It also may not be easy to decide who your

---

9. Sabatino, "Overcoming the Balkanization," 978–87.

10. 42 U.S.C. § 1395cc(f) (2010).

11. Asim Alshanberi et al., "Advance Directives in Patients over 60 Years Old: Assessment of Perceived Value and Need for Education in the Outpatient Setting," *Archives of Medicine* 10, no. 4 (2018): 1; Kuldeep N. Yadav et al., "Approximately One in Three US Adults Completes Any Type of Advance Directive for End-of-Life Care," *Health Affairs* 36, no. 7 (2017): 1244–51.

decision maker should be. In 2019, Andrea Useem published an article in the *Washington Post* titled, "I'm an ICU nurse. I know I need an end-of-life directive. So why can't I bring myself to write it?" The task can be all the more challenging for people who are not health-care professionals.

Ms. Useem ultimately did fill out an advance directive. Her primary reason for doing so was that she knew how difficult decision-making is for families when they have no guidance from the patient. Advance planning is thus an act of great kindness for your loved ones who will have to make treatment decisions in the future whether or not you tell them what you want.[12]

If you or your loved one is a nursing home resident, you may be tempted to rely on staff members to fill out an advance directive for you, but this may be inadvisable. Staff members will likely be rushed and may have limited expertise regarding the matter.[13] Elder law or estate planning attorneys are a far better choice and may include an advance directive in an estate planning package that also includes your will or trust. A simple package (without a living trust) can cost under $1,000.[14]

In the alternative, you may turn to web-based tools that you can download for a nominal fee or at no cost. For example, Aging with Dignity's Five Wishes offers a form on its website that costs $5.00. It contains many helpful explanations and

---

12. Andrea Useem, "I'm an ICU Nurse. I Know I Need an End-of-Life Directive. So Why Can't I Bring Myself to Write It?," *Washington Post*, August 12, 2019.

13. Jessica Nutik Zitter, *Extreme Measures: Finding a Better Path to the End of Life* (New York: Avery, 2017).

14. Martindale-Nolo Research, "How Much Lawyers Charge to Prepare Estate Planning Documents," Lawyers.com, updated May 21, 2019, https://www.lawyers.com/legal-info/trusts-estates/cost-of-creating-an-estate-plan-and-administering-an-estate/how-much-lawyers-charge-to-prepare-estate-planning-documents.html.

allows you to provide detailed instructions. The form is valid in 42 states (that it lists) and the District of Columbia.[15] AARP offers a second option, enabling users to download state-specific advance directive forms from its website without charge.[16]

I now turn to a detailed discussion of each of the documents that make up the advance directive. They are a living will, durable power of attorney for health care, and anatomical gift form.

Living wills

One important component of the advanced directive is the living will. Living wills allow individuals to specify the kinds of treatment they would wish to have if they are terminally ill,[17] permanently unconscious, or severely injured. Living wills apply "to situations in which the decision to use life-sustaining treatments may prolong an individual's life for a limited period

---

15. Available at https://fivewishes.org/shop/order/product/five-wishes. You can also find a free sample form at http://www.agingwithdignity.org/forms/5wishes.pdf.

16. Available at "https://www.aarp.org/caregiving/financial-legal/free-printable-advance-directives/.

17. According to the American Cancer Society,

A terminal condition or illness is one that is life-limiting. In the near future it is expected the illness will result in permanent unconsciousness from which the person is unlikely to recover or death. Examples of terminal conditions may include but are not limited to advanced cancers, multiple organ failure, or some massive heart attacks and strokes. Definitions of terminal illness can be different from state to state.

American Cancer Society, *Frequently Asked Questions about Advance Directives*, American Cancer Society, updated May 13, 2019, https://www.cancer.org/treatment/finding-and-paying-for-treatment/understanding-financial-and-legal-matters/advance-directives/faqs.html.

of time and not obtaining such treatment would result in death."[18]

Because I live in Ohio, I will use the state's advance directive documents as examples in this chapter, but they are similar to the forms that many other states have adopted. Ohio's Living Will Declaration enables individuals to assert the following:

> If I am in a **TERMINAL CONDITION** and unable to make my own health care decisions, OR if I am in a **PERMANENTLY UNCONSCIOUS STATE** and there is no reasonable possibility that I will regain the capacity to make informed decisions, then I direct my physician to let me die naturally, providing me only with **comfort care**.

For the purpose of providing comfort care, I authorize my physician to

1. Administer no life-sustaining treatment, including CPR;
2. Withhold or withdraw artificially or technologically supplied nutrition or hydration, provided that, if I am in a permanently unconscious state, I have authorized such withholding or withdrawal under Special Instructions below and the other conditions have been met;
3. Issue a DNR Order; and
4. Take no action to postpone my death, providing me with only the care necessary to make me comfortable and to relieve pain.[19]

---

18. US Government Accountability Office, "Report to Congress, Advance Care Planning: Selected States' Efforts to Educate and Address Access Challenges," US Government Accountability Office, February 2019, https://www.gao.gov/assets/700/696985.pdf.

19. Caring Connections, "OHIO Advance Directive Planning for Important Health Care Decisions," National Hospice and Palliative Care Organization, revised 2020, https://www.nhpco.org/wp-content/uploads/Ohio.pdf. CPR is cardiopulmonary resuscitation, and DNR stands for "do not resuscitate."

Notably, the standard form in Ohio and some other states includes only instructions for withholding care. By contrast, Maine allows you to check a box beside the statement "**I Choose to Prolong Life**: I want my life to be prolonged as long as possible within the limits of generally accepted health-care standards."[20] If you prefer that doctors do everything to prolong your life under all reasonable circumstances and your state's form does not provide that choice, you should work with an attorney to create a living will that is different from the standard form. If you cannot afford an attorney, cross out the standard language and take advantage of the blank space provided in the living will form for additional instructions and limitations to express your wishes.

It is essential to realize that living wills apply only in limited circumstances, generally at the end of life. However, sadly, many people suffer from dementia for many years, and they become unable to make decisions about their health care long before they die. Consequently, it is essential to appoint a medical decision maker who is familiar with your wishes and can be trusted to implement them when the time comes. To that end, you must have a durable power of attorney for health care (also called a health care power of attorney) in addition to your living will.

Durable power of attorney for health care

A durable power of attorney for health care names an agent (also called a proxy) who will serve as your decision maker anytime you are unable to make decisions for yourself, not just at the end of life. It is also important to name one or more alternative decision makers in case your original proxy is herself incapacitated or unavailable when needed.

---

20. Caring Connections, "MAINE Advance Directive Planning for Important Health Care Decisions," National Hospice and Palliative Care Organization, revised 2020, https://www.nhpco.org/wp-content/uploads/Maine.pdf.

The Ohio Health Care Power of Attorney document lists a large number of decisions that are within the power of the agent but allows you to cross items off the list or to provide additional details concerning your wishes. For example, you can indicate that you want your agent to have authority to do the following:

- To consent to the administration of pain-relieving drugs, treatments, or procedures, including surgery, that aim to alleviate discomfort, even if they might hasten your death.
- To consent or refuse to consent to life-sustaining treatment, including nutrition and hydration if you are terminally ill.
- To consent or refuse to consent to any medical treatment.
- To request and review medical information regarding your mental or physical health.
- To consent to the disclosure of your medical information to other people, such as family members.
- To select, hire, and fire health-care providers and service providers such as in-home care aides.
- To have you admitted or discharged from medical institutions such as a hospital, nursing home, assisted living facility, or hospice.[21]

As is typical in many states,[22] Ohio limits the authority of the agent in several ways, and you cannot override these limitations:

- Your agent cannot order the withdrawal of any treatment that is necessary to make you more comfortable or to relieve pain.

---

21. Caring Connections, "OHIO Advance Directive Planning," 11–12.

22. Diana Anderson, "Review of Advance Health Care Directive Laws in the United States, the Portability of Documents, and the Surrogate Decision Maker when No Document Is Executed," *National Academy of Elder Law Attorneys Journal* 8, no. 2 (2012): 183–203.

- If you are pregnant, your agent cannot refuse treatment if withholding treatment would end your pregnancy, unless the pregnancy or therapy would substantially endanger your life or two physicians determine that the fetus would not be born alive even with treatment.
- Your agent cannot order the withdrawal of life-sustaining treatment unless you are in a terminal condition or a permanently unconscious state and two physicians determine that the treatment would not promote your comfort.
- Your agent cannot order the withdrawal of any treatment to which you previously consented unless your condition has significantly changed so that the treatment is far less beneficial to you or has failed to achieve its purpose.[23]

While your downloadable state form may provide boilerplate language (with blank space for additional instructions), more creative advance directive forms can provide very detailed guidance for health-care proxies. A sample published in the *American Journal of Bioethics* addresses a variety of serious conditions separately and lists treatments that the principal may or may not want to receive. For example, one section addresses "moderate/severe dementia" that renders the person unable to care for herself or "remember things clearly." You can check boxes as to whether, if you had such dementia, you would want to have kidney dialysis, mechanical ventilation, and/or a feeding tube for various lengths of time as well as cardiopulmonary resuscitation, medicines, surgery, and blood transfusions.[24]

---

23. Caring Connections, "OHIO Advance Directive Planning," 13.

24. Benjamin H. Levi and Michael J. Green, "Too Soon to Give Up: Re-Examining the Value of Advance Directives," *American Journal of Bioethics* 10, no. 4 (2010): 3–22; Aarti Gupta and Romika Dhar, "Advance Healthcare

You should think carefully about whom to select as your medical decision maker. The person should be someone who knows you well and with whom you are comfortable discussing your treatment preferences. You should be able to trust your agent to follow your wishes even if she would make different decisions for herself. She should be a capable advocate who will do everything possible to follow your wishes even if faced with unresponsive health-care providers or family conflict about the treatment plan that you prefer. Your agent should be easily reachable and available when needed and willing to serve in this capacity for many years to come.[25]

My friend Naomi (not her real name) is an observant Jewish woman. Her mother, who is in her 80s, appointed her as her health-care proxy but does not share Naomi's religious views. My friend told me that her mother brings up medical decision-making a couple of times a year. She asks Naomi for reassurance that she will follow her wishes to limit care at the end of life even if doing so conflicts with Naomi's own religious beliefs. She is wise to have repeated conversations with Naomi and is comforted each time Naomi reiterates that she understands and will implement her mother's preferences.

I am often asked whether people who have multiple children should appoint all of them as simultaneous health-care proxies. I do not think that this is a prudent approach. Children often disagree about treatment plans—some wanting to prolong life at all costs, and others believing their parent would want comfort care only. Select one person, the person whom you trust most to serve as an effective and devoted decision maker.

Planning," in *Psychiatric Ethics in Late-Life Patients*, ed. Meera Balasubramaniam, Aarti Gupta, and Rajesh R. Tampi (Switzerland: Springer, 2019), 133–35.

25. ABA Commission on Law and Aging, "Tool #1: How to Select Your Health Care Agent or Proxy," American Bar Association, accessed December 23, 2020, https://www.americanbar.org/content/dam/aba/administrative/law_aging/tool1.pdf.

It is also very important to name an alternate health-care proxy, and your legal form will prompt you to do so. This is critical because your original agent might be unavailable or is herself incapacitated or deceased when she is needed.

If you do not name a decision maker, are incapacitated, and are hospitalized, the hospital will likely make every effort to locate your next of kin. It will attempt to follow your state's default surrogate consent law that spells out which relatives can make decisions in the absence of an advance directive.[26] However, the person or persons they reach may not make decisions that are compatible with your wishes. Worse yet, if multiple people are contacted, they may disagree about a course of action, causing treatment delays, family strife, and distress for the medical team.

Some individuals are ineligible to serve as proxies. Most commonly, states exclude (1) anyone younger than 18; (2) your health-care providers including the owners or operators of health, residential, or community care facilities that serve you; and (3) employees of your health-care providers, unless they are your spouse or close relative (in which case you can name them as your agent).[27]

I will discuss decision makers for property and finances below. If you have different agents for health-care and financial decisions, you should ensure that the two know each other, can communicate with each other, and fully understand your wishes. The health-care proxy will need the cooperation of the financial proxy in order to pay for whatever care is selected. You should also inform your family members as soon as you have appointed your agent(s) and alternate(s) in order to reduce the likelihood that others will later try to assert themselves as decision makers and create friction or conflict.

---

26. Wynn, "Decisions by Surrogates."
27. ABA Commission on Law and Aging, "Tool #1."

Anatomical gift form

According to the US Department of Health and Human Services, as of May 2021, 106,710 people were waiting for an organ. In 2020, 39,000 transplants were performed, but because of persistent organ shortages, 17 people die each day while waiting for organs. One donor can save as many as eight lives[28] by donating her kidneys, lungs, heart, liver, small bowel, and pancreas.[29] If you also donate tissue, including your eyes, heart valves, bone, skin, veins, and tendons, you can potentially help more than 75 people.[30]

Many people believe that making anatomical gifts will render their lives (and deaths) more meaningful, but only 60 percent of US adults have signed up to be organ donors.[31] You can become an organ donor when you apply for or renew your driver's license, and an icon on your license will indicate that you are a donor.

If you wish to be a donor, you should also fill out an organ donation form as part of your advance directive and discuss your donation preferences with your health-care agent. The

---

28. However, only 3 in 1,000 people die in a way that enables organ donation. Generally, the organs must be in good condition and donors must die in a hospital and have been on life support. Artificial support is also used immediately after death to preserve the organs in transplant-ready condition. In addition, the donor must be a match for a patient in need. Health Resources & Services Administration, "How Donation Works," Organdonor.gov, last reviewed April 2021, https://www.organdonor.gov/learn/process.

29. Health Resources & Services Administration, "Organ Donation Statistics," Organdonor.gov, last reviewed May 2021, https://www.organdonor.gov/statistics-stories/statistics.html#glance.

30. Donate Life America, "Tissue Donation," Donatelife.net, accessed December 24, 2020, https://www.donatelife.net/types-of-donation/tissue-donation/.

31. Health Resources & Services Administration, "Organ Donation Statistics."

form will document your wishes for your decision maker and any health-care providers that access it. Ohio's form allows you to make very specific choices, which you are not able to do when you indicate your general donor status on your driver's license. You can choose the types of organs and tissue you want to donate and the purposes for which they can be used (e.g., transplantation, research, or education).[32]

You can also donate your entire body to science for research purposes. The United Tissue Network provides instructions on its website.[33]

All states have organ and tissue donor registries. If you indicate that you are a donor on your driver's license, your state's motor vehicle office will automatically enter you in the registry.[34] If you want to include more specific information about your preferences, you can register online.[35] Some states also allow you to mail in the anatomical gift form that is included in your advance directive.[36]

Some people have religious or other reasons for not becoming organ donors. However, many people have no objection to being organ donors or even affirmatively want to do so, but they do not take the trouble to fill out the form and do not want to make a hasty decision when asked by a clerk while renewing their driver's licenses. This inaction can cost lives. If you want to donate your organs after death (I promise, you will not need them anymore), please take a few minutes to do the paperwork. If you are creating other legal documents to prepare for possible incapacity

---

32. Caring Connections, "OHIO Advance Directive Planning," 32.

33. Available at https://unitedtissue.org/donate-my-body-to-science/.

34. Health Resources & Services Administration, "Organ Donation FAQs," Organdonor.gov, accessed December 24, 2020, https://www.organdonor.gov/about/facts-terms/donation-faqs.html.

35. You can access all state registries through the following link: https://www.everplans.com/articles/state-by-state-organ-donation-registries.

36. Caring Connections, "OHIO Advance Directive Planning," 35.

and death, this is the perfect time to consider filling out an organ donation form as well. Doing so can be of great benefit to your loved ones who could be spared the trauma of having to decide whether to make you a donor without any guidance from you.

Advance directive for mental health treatment

Individuals with a history of mental illness may choose to prepare an advance directive that is specific to mental health treatments. People with capacity can designate agents who will make mental health-care decisions for them if they lose capacity, and they can provide specific instructions concerning wanted and unwanted therapies. If you wish, you can select one agent for mental health care and a different person to be in charge of all other care. If the agents are different, you should execute separate directives.[37] According to the National Resource Center on Psychiatric Advance Directives,[38] 25 states have enacted psychiatric advance directive statutes.[39]

An advance directive for mental health treatment should address matters such as

- which medications are acceptable and unacceptable to you;
- facilities at which treatment can be provided;

---

37. National Alliance on Mental Illness, "Psychiatric Advance Directives (PAD)," National Alliance on Mental Illness, accessed December 24, 2020, https://www.nami.org/Learn-More/Mental-Health-Public-Policy/Psychiatric-Advance-Directives-(PAD).

38. National Resource Center on Psychiatric Advance Directives, "Do All States Specifically Have PAD Statutes?" National Resource Center on Psychiatric Advance Directives, accessed December 24, 2020, https://www.nrc-pad.org/faqs/.

39. As of 2020, the states were Arizona, Hawaii, Idaho, Illinois, Indiana, Kentucky, Louisiana, Maine, Maryland, Michigan, Minnesota, Montana, New Jersey, New Mexico, North Carolina, Oregon, Ohio, Oklahoma, Pennsylvania, South Dakota, Tennessee, Texas, Utah, Washington, and Wyoming.

- which types of treatment you are willing to undergo (e.g., electroconvulsive treatment?);
- instructions concerning the temporary care of children or loved ones during your incapacity.

Mental health advance directives may be especially useful because they are tailored to a particular condition or conditions with which you have experience. The course of treatment is predictable and you can be specific in your instructions.[40]

Nevertheless, only a small fraction of patients with mental illness have a psychiatric advance directive. This may be because most people are unaware of this advance directive option, and few educational initiatives focus on this matter.[41]

Patients should also know that many state statutes allow physicians to override treatment requests with which they disagree in some circumstances.[42] For example, Ohio's statute governing declarations for mental health treatment permits an override if the patient is committed and a court "orders treatment in a manner contrary to the declaration" or if an "emergency situation endangers the life or health of the declarant or others."[43]

---

40. Lisa Brodoff, "Planning for Alzheimer's Disease with Mental Health Advance Directives," *Elder Law Journal* 17, no. 2 (2010): 239–308; Naomi M. Weinstein and Michael L. Perlin, " 'Who's Pretending to Care for Him?' How the Endless Jail-to-Hospital-to-Street-Repeat Cycle Deprives Persons with Mental Disabilities the Right to Continuity of Care," *Wake Forest Journal of Law & Policy* 8, no. 2 (2018): 455–502.

41. Brodoff, "Planning for Alzheimer's," 256; Substance Abuse and Mental Health Services Administration, "A Practical Guide to Psychiatric Advance Directives," Substance Abuse and Mental Health Services Administration, 2019, 5, https://www.samhsa.gov/sites/default/files/a_practical_guide_to_psychiatric_advance_directives.pdf.

42. Brodoff, "Planning for Alzheimer's," 256; Substance Abuse and Mental Health Services Administration, "Practical Guide to Psychiatric Advance Directives," 7.

43. Ohio Rev. Code § 2135.07(B).

Barriers to advance directive implementation

Unfortunately, the mere execution of an advance directive does not guarantee that your wishes will be honored in the event of incapacity. Several barriers may prevent health-care providers from following advance directives.

Portability

Individuals may complete an advance directive in one state and then move to another state and forget to prepare a new directive. Whether or not your advance directive is valid in the new state will depend on state law. Many states provide for recognition of out-of-state directives, but others do not.[44]

In addition, patients may give their advance directive to one physician or hospital but be treated at multiple unrelated facilities, as often occurs late in life. If a patient becomes incapacitated because of a medical crisis, but the clinicians providing care at the time do not have a copy of the advance directive, they may not be able to identify the patient's health-care proxy and determine what the patient's treatment preferences are.[45]

Ideally, if one doctor enters your advance directive into your electronic health record, it should be accessible to all health-care providers. Unfortunately, that is not the case. Contemporary electronic health record systems often are not interoperable, so that systems at different facilities often cannot communicate with each other.[46] Another pitfall is that some clinicians will ask

---

44. Sabatino, "Overcoming the Balkanization," 985.

45. Charles Sabatino, "Top Ten Myths and Facts about Health Care Advance Directives," *Bifocal* 37, no. 1 (2015): 6–9 (stating that "there is no guarantee that your directive will follow you in your medical record, especially if you are transferred from one facility to another"); Gupta and Dhar, "Advance Healthcare Planning," 134–35.

46. Shefali Luthra, "Electronic Records Offer a Chance to Ensure Patients' End-of-Life Plans Aren't Lost in Critical Moments," *Kaiser Health News,*

if you have an advance directive, and if you say yes, they will simply check a box on the electronic form. They will not ask you for a copy, so they do not actually obtain the information they need!

Seventeen states have state registries for advance directives, and if you live in one of them, you should file your documents with the registry. The states are Arizona, California, Colorado, Delaware, Idaho, Illinois, Louisiana, Maryland, Michigan, Montana, Nevada, North Carolina, Oklahoma, Oregon, Vermont, Virginia, and Washington.[47] Unfortunately, it is not known how often health-care providers check these registries or whether they know about them.[48] In addition, you should have a wallet card indicating that you have an advance directive,[49] and you can upload your advance directive to your iPhone using apps such as MyDirectives MOBILE™ or My Health Care Wishes.[50] Most importantly, however, you should be sure to

March 23, 2016, https://khn.org/news/electronic-records-offer-a-chance-to-ensure-patients-end-of-life-plans-arent-lost-in-critical-moments/; Kate Monica, "Lack of EHR Interoperability, API Use Hinder Value-Based Care," *EHR Intelligence*, September 17, 2018, https://ehrintelligence.com/news/lack-of-ehr-interoperability-api-use-hinder-value-based-care.

47. Preston Holmes, "Commission on Law & Aging Research A Tour of State Advance Directive Registries," *Bifocal* 37, no. 6 (2016): 122–27, https://www.americanbar.org/content/dam/aba/publications/bifocal/bifocaljuly-august2016.pdf; Anne L. Moody, "Summary of Health Care Decision Statutes Enacted in 2019," American Bar Association, accessed December 16, 2019, https://www.americanbar.org/content/dam/aba/administrative/law_aging/2019-hcpa-legis-update.pdf.

48. Alberto B. Lopez and Fredrick E. Vars, "Wrongful Living," *Iowa Law Review* 104, no. 5 (2019): 1921–76 (calling for a national advance directive registry).

49. It can be downloaded from https://www.americanbar.org/content/dam/aba/images/law_aging/app_walletcard.pdf.

50. American Bar Association Commission on Law and Aging, "My Health Care Wishes App Wallet Cards," American Bar Association, accessed

provide copies of your advance directive to all of your doctors and bring a copy with you whenever you undergo a procedure or go to the hospital.

Quality and specificity of instructions

According to one study, "directives often provide abstract guidance not easily translated to the nuanced contingencies of real-world patient care."[51] Many instructions are worded using medical terminology that patients do not fully understand. For example, laypeople may believe that the word "coma" means any non-responsive state, but in medicine it is characterized by precise criteria. Furthermore, some advance directives contain conditional instructions that depend on prognosis. You might have choices that apply "if I am in a coma that would resolve within a year."[52] But disease trajectory is often impossible to predict with any degree of certainty, and doctors can provide no specific timetable for recovery.[53]

Yet another problem is that living wills often express wishes in absolute terms, such as a refusal to accept dialysis or a ventilator. However, doctors may be convinced that a particular

---

December 24, 2020, https://www.americanbar.org/content/dam/aba/images/law_aging/app_walletcard.pdf.

51. Susan P. Shapiro, "Advance Directives: The Elusive Goal of Having the Last Word," *Journal of the National Academy of Elder Law Attorneys* 8, no. 2 (2012): 205–32; Useem, "I'm an ICU Nurse"; Brian L. Block, Alexander K. Smith, and Rebecca L. Sudore, "Universal Advance Directives— Necessary but Not Sufficient," *Journal of Law, Medicine, and Ethics* 46 (Winter 2018), 988–89.

52. Benjamin H. Levi and Michael J. Green, "Too Soon to Give Up: Re-Examining the Value of Advance Directives," *American Journal of Bioethics* 10, no. 4 (2010): 3–22.

53. Shapiro, "Advance Directives: The Elusive Goal," 220; Useem, "I'm an ICU Nurse."

intervention for a brief time will enable the patient to overcome a crisis and regain capacity along with a good quality of life. For this reason, some experts advise against articulating very specific preferences in advance directives. Instead, they recommend appointing an agent who will be familiar with your general wishes but maintain broad discretion to make decisions on a case-by-case basis.[54]

Precedent autonomy

Some clinicians may assert philosophical objections to following advance directive instructions for care limitation if you have developed dementia but seem to be living a contented life in this condition. Many people living with dementia seem happy and enjoy pleasures such as eating, watching television, and visiting with loved ones. The key question in the precedent autonomy debate is "Does an individual's request that simple life-sustaining treatment be avoided if he becomes demented remain valid into that dementia, when he may show apparent preferences to the contrary?"[55] In other words, do we defer to the autonomy of a pre-incapacity "then self," or do we instead focus on the altered "now self" in determining a person's wishes?

Consider the following example. A woman has an advance directive that instructs that if she is diagnosed with Alzheimer's disease or some other form of dementia, she should no longer

---

54. Shapiro, "Advance Directives: The Elusive Goal," 221–22; Smith and Sudore, "Universal Advance Directives," 988–89.

55. Michael J. Newton, "Precedent Autonomy: Life-Sustaining Intervention and the Demented Patient," *Cambridge Quarterly of Healthcare Ethics* 8, no. 2 (1999): 189–99; Andrea Lavazza and Massimo Reichlin, "Of Meatballs, Autonomy, and Human Dignity: Neuroethics and the Boundaries of Decision Making among Persons with Dementia," *AJOB Neuroscience* 9, no. 2 (2018): 88.

be given treatment for any serious or life-threatening condition. Specifically, she states,

> Should I become severely demented, I do not wish to have my life extended by technological means unless as the unintended result of palliative measures. I refuse any artificial feeding and hydration, since forgetting how to swallow provides an opportunity to die in dignity. Further, I refuse dialysis, mechanical ventilation, resuscitation, and any and all efforts to apply these technologies. Likewise, I refuse antibiotics since pneumonia is a friend. The moral challenge for loved ones is only to be present with me, and to pray for me. In the event that I am in pain, keep me comfortable as needed.[56]

After being diagnosed with Alzheimer's disease, the patient develops pneumonia and needs antibiotics. What complicates matters is that she is generally cheerful and appears to enjoy her meals and activities. Her doctors feel extremely uncomfortable about foregoing therapy and allowing her to die of a very treatable condition.

Scholars have engaged in vigorous debate as to whether it is ethical to follow a person's advance directive in these circumstances. Bioethicist Rebecca Dresser argues that if patients are able to enjoy and participate in their lives, it is not necessarily unethical to ignore their prior directives.[57] Treatment decisions should focus on the patient's "experiential reality." Indeed, memory loss and significant psychological changes may create a new person whose connection to the prior self is attenuated. By contrast, Professor Ronald Dworkin

56. Stephen G. Post, "Alzheimer Disease and the 'Then' Self," *Kennedy Institute of Ethics Journal* 5, no. 4 (1995): 307–21.

57. Rebecca Dresser, "Dworkin on Dementia: Elegant Theory, Questionable Policy," *Hastings Center Report* 25, no. 6 (1995): 32–38; Rebecca Dresser, "Missing Persons: Legal Perceptions of Incompetent Patients," *Rutgers Law Review* 46, no. 2 (1994): 609–719.

steadfastly defends precedent autonomy and an individual's right to maintain a coherent life narrative, including his or her end-of-life directive.[58]

It is thus possible that hospital authorities will refuse to follow the advance directive of a dementia patient who appears to enjoy daily pleasures. This may be particularly true if family members disagree with the wishes articulated in the document and argue passionately for continued care. It may also be true if no loved ones are present to insist that doctors adhere to the document's instructions.

Default surrogates

If you have not filled out a health care power of attorney and designated an agent, you will still be able to have someone close to you make decisions for you. State law designates who your default decision makers are and establishes their order of priority.[59] In most states, physicians will turn to the following individuals in the following order:

1. Spouse (unless legally separated)
2. Adult child
3. Parent
4. Adult sibling
5. If none of the above is available, in some states, physicians may rely on a close friend.[60]

---

58. Ronald Dworkin, *Life's Dominion: An Argument about Abortion, Euthanasia, and Individual Freedom* (New York: Vintage, 1994), 222–29; Newton, "Precedent Autonomy," 192–93.

59. Barry R. Furrow et al., Bioethics (St. Paul, MN: West Academic Publishing, 2018), 367–68.

60. American Bar Association, "Default State Surrogate Consent Statutes," American Bar Association, 2019, https://www.americanbar.org/content/dam/aba/administrative/law_aging/2019-sept-default-surrogate-consent-statutes.pdf (summarizing each state's law).

The problem is that the person who will end up making your decisions may not be the person you would have chosen for this task. Therefore, it is far better to take the initiative and formally appoint a health-care agent in a legal document, as detailed above.

Hospital ethics committees

What about people who have no one who can serve as a decision maker when they become incapacitated? In such cases it is likely that an ethics committee will step in. Ethics committees exist at most hospitals and some long-term care organizations.[61] They are composed of diverse stakeholders, including clinicians (doctors, nurses, pharmacists) with various areas of expertise, social workers, chaplains, ethicists, lawyers, and community representatives. Ethics committees are available for consultation in individual patient cases at the request of medical staff members. Consultations can involve one professional ethicist or a subcommittee of several committee members. The committees are called upon to make decisions for patients who have neither a decision maker nor a living will. They also mediate among family members with conflicting views in the absence of a formally named health-care proxy.[62]

---

61. Fatemeh Hajibabaee, Soodabeh Joolaee, Mohammad Ali Cheraghi, Pooneh Salari, and Patricia Rodney, "Hospital/Clinical Ethics Committees' Notion: An Overview," *Journal of Medical Ethics and History of Medicine* 9, no. 17 (2016):2; ABA Commission on Law & Aging, "Pathways to Health Care Decision-Making," American Bar Association, 2018, https://www.americanbar.org/content/dam/aba/administrative/law_aging/2019-pathways-hcdm.pdf.

62. Mark P. Aulisio and Robert M. Arnold, "Role of the Ethics Committee: Helping to Address Value Conflicts or Uncertainties," *Chest* 134, no. 2 (2008): 41–24; American Medical Association, "Ethics Committees in Health Care Institutions, Code of Medical Ethics Opinion 10.7," American Medical Association, accessed December 24, 2020,

I have served as a member of a hospital ethics committee for many years and am impressed by its work. The monthly meetings include thoughtful debates about important hospital policy matters and particularly challenging patient cases. I have also participated in ethics consults, most often regarding approval of medical procedures for incapacitated patients without proxies and termination of treatment for the dying. The subcommittee meets at length with the treating physicians and nurses and is serious, compassionate, thorough, and committed to making the best decision possible under the circumstances.

POWER OF ATTORNEY FOR PROPERTY AND FINANCES

Medical treatment choices are not the only decisions that need to be made for individuals who become cognitively incapacitated. Financial decisions can be equally difficult and important. I now turn to a discussion of safeguards that you can implement to ensure that your wishes concerning money and finances will be carried out if you lose capacity.

All states have power of attorney laws that enable an adult with decision-making capacity (called a principal) to delegate authority to handle financial and property matters to another person (called the agent, proxy, or attorney-in-fact). You likely want a "springing" power of attorney that will take effect only if you lose decision-making capacity.[63] You need to be very clear about the type of circumstances that will activate your

---

https://www.ama-assn.org/delivering-care/ethics/ethics-committees-health-care-institutions.

63. Frolik and Whitton, *Everyday Law for Seniors*, 160–61; Marlo Sollitto, "What Is the Difference between Durable and Springing Power of Attorney?" AgingCare, revised March 4, 2020, https://www.agingcare.com/articles/what-is-durable-power-of-attorney-140233.htm.

agent's power. For example, you might state that two physicians must certify your incapacity.

In the absence of a durable power of attorney, individuals who have lost capacity and cannot manage their own financial affairs may need to have a guardian (also called a conservator) appointed by a court. Concerned parties such as family members or state agencies can initiate guardianship proceedings, but the process can be long and expensive, often lasting several months. Furthermore, the court may appoint a guardian who would not be your first choice. Judges will likely opt for close family members, but you may have previously experienced conflict with the designated guardian or may have a friend or domestic partner whom you would prefer as a guardian.[64] If an individual has no relatives, the court may appoint a professional guardian.[65]

The law does not require that a lawyer prepare the power of attorney, and many states have forms available on the Internet. However, consulting a lawyer is advisable because a legal professional can help you tailor the document to your needs and preferences.[66] States have varying execution requirements that range from only a signature to notarization with witnesses.

Powers of attorney generally give the agent (the person taking over) authority over all financial matters, including receiving, depositing, and writing checks; paying bills; managing bank

---

64. Eric Widera, Veronika Steenpass, Daniel Marson, and Rebecca Sudore, "Finances in the Older Patient with Cognitive Impairment: 'He Didn't Want Me to Take Over'," *JAMA* 305, no. 7 (2011): 698–706.

65. Florida State Guardianship Association, "Guardianship FAQ," Florida State Guardianship, accessed December 24, 2020, https://www.floridaguardians.com/guardianship-faq/.

66. Widera, Steenpass, Marson, and Sudore, "Finances in the Older Patient," 701; "Why Not Just Use an Off-the-Shelf Power of Attorney Form," ElderLawAnswers.com, August 2, 2019, https://www.elderlawanswers.com/why-not-just-use-an-off-the-shelf-power-of-attorney-form-6760.

accounts, CDs, stocks, bonds, and other investments; and taking possession or selling any real estate or personal property. In addition, you can empower the agent to make gifts, to establish a trust, to have access to safe deposit boxes, to pay taxes, and to engage in litigation on your behalf.[67]

Many people worry about agents taking advantage of their position, and those worries are legitimate. The elderly are particularly vulnerable to financial abuse. Experts estimate that fraud costs seniors between \$2.9 billion and \$36.5 billion annually. Abuse instances are thought to be woefully underreported, perhaps in part because at least one-third of them are perpetrated by people well known to the victim: relatives, friends, neighbors, and paid caregivers.[68] A dishonest or unreliable agent with broad powers will have ample opportunity to engage in wrongdoing,[69] perhaps even

---

67. Ohio State Bar Association, "Law Facts: Financial Powers of Attorney," Ohio State Bar Association, May 17, 2018, https://www.ohiobar.org/public-resources/commonly-asked-law-questions-results/law-facts/law-facts-financial-powers-of-attorney/; Steve Weisman, *A Guide to Elder Planning: Everything You Need to Know to Protect Your Loved Ones and Yourself* (Upper Saddle River, NJ: FT Press, 2013), 27.

68. National Council on Aging, "What Is Elder Abuse?" National Council on Aging, accessed December 24, 2020, https://www.ncoa.org/public-policy-action/elder-justice/elder-abuse-facts/.

69. The law affords a degree of protection in some states. The Uniform Power of Attorney Act (UPOAA) is a model law (a proposed law that states should consider) that seeks to promote durable power of attorney use while deterring agent misconduct, and it was adopted (with some variation) by 25 states as of 2019. Under the law, there are consequences for a party's unreasonable refusal to honor a power of attorney. In addition, the statute articulates the agent's duties, including (1) acting in good faith within his or her granted scope of authority and consistent with the principal's expectations or best interest, (2) preserving the principal's estate plan, and (3) cooperating with the principal's health-care power of attorney. In addition, the law includes liability provisions applicable to agents guilty of wrongdoing, and it authorizes judicial review of agents'

compromising your financial future or that of your family members.[70]

You should carefully choose not only the person you name as your agent but also the degree of power the agent will have. In addition, it is wise to name an alternate agent who can take over if the first individual becomes unable or unwilling to serve. Experts also recommend that you establish some oversight mechanisms. You can instruct that the agent provide periodic reports and copies of financial statements to an attorney or financial adviser to ensure the agent's good-faith conduct.[71]

WILLS, TRUSTS, TRANSFER ON DEATH, AND OTHER ASSET DISTRIBUTION INSTRUCTIONS

Finally, you should think about what will happen to your money and valuables after your death. Will they be distributed in accordance with your intentions? How difficult will it be

---

conduct. Finally, the law requires that if you wish to grant agents authority to make decisions that could dissipate your property or alter your estate plan (such as by gifting large sums or creating trusts), you do so explicitly in the power of attorney document. National Conference of Commissioners on Uniform State Laws, "Uniform Power of Attorney Act (2006)," National Conference of Commissioners on Uniform State Laws, accessed December 24, 2020, https://www.uniformlaws.org/viewdocument/final-act-no-comments-52?CommunityKey=b1975254-8370-4a7c-947f-e5af0d6cb07c&tab=librarydocuments; Ann-Marie Botek, "Things You Can and Can't Do with Power of Attorney," AgingCare, updated November 12, 2020, https://www.agingcare.com/articles/things-you-can-and-cant-do-with-poa-152673.htm.

70. Frolik and Whitton, *Everyday Law for Seniors*, 162–63; Bob Carlson, "Why Your Power of Attorney Probably Is an Accident Waiting to Happen," *Forbes*, August 24, 2018, https://www.forbes.com/sites/bobcarlson/2018/08/24/why-your-power-of-attorney-probably-is-an-accident-waiting-to-happen/#7ea48197ac82.

71. Carlson, "Why Your Power of Attorney Probably Is an Accident Waiting to Happen."

for your loved ones to inherit your assets? A variety of legal instruments and instructions can help ensure that your wishes are fulfilled and that your survivors face as few hurdles as possible during the estate distribution process.

Wills

Preparing a will should be on every middle-aged person's agenda, including those who are not wealthy. Without a will you will have no input as to how your assets will be divided after your death, and your estate's distribution will be governed entirely by state law. Generally, under state intestate succession laws, only spouses, registered domestic partners, and blood relatives inherit. If the deceased person was married and is survived by his or her spouse, the spouse usually receives the largest portion of the estate, and if there are no children, the surviving spouse often receives all the property. Other parties such as unmarried partners, friends, and charities get nothing, and more distant relatives inherit only if there is no surviving spouse or children. If no relatives can be found, the state will take all of the assets.[72] If this is not how you would want your assets distributed after your death, you should be sure to have a will. For example, if there are charities about which you care deeply, you might want to leave them money or property, and you need a will in order to do so.

In your will, you should name a trusted person (such as an adult son or daughter) as executor of the estate. You should also name an alternate executor who can serve if the first individual becomes unable or unwilling to do so.

Individuals with uncomplicated finances may opt to use an online service such as LegalZoom or USLegal[73] in order

---

72. See, e.g., *Statute of Descent and Distribution*, Ohio Rev. Code § 2105.06 (2015).

73. Respectively, at Homepage, LegalZoom, accessed December 11, 2019, http://www.legalzoom.com and "Last Will and Testament Form

to prepare their wills. These websites charge very modest fees (under $100) for simple wills.

Attorneys, however, generally advise against using an online service for a document that is as important as a will. Attorneys may charge hourly or flat fees for basic wills, and the cost for a will may range from $300 to $1,200.[74] Online wills may not be sufficiently customized for individual needs, especially for those with children from prior marriages, children with special needs, spouses with dementia, and any number of other complicated personal circumstances. Furthermore, in the absence of professional oversight, you might make mistakes with "do-it-yourself" wills, such as clicking the wrong box. Decisions made without an expert's assistance can have serious adverse consequences in both personal and financial terms. An article in *Forbes* magazine describes the following "common trap":

> Mom wants to provide equally for her three children. Shares in GE constitute a third of her estate. So she leaves the stock to one child and the rest of her assets to the other two. Several months before she dies, she sells the stock. The child who was supposed to get it receives nothing.[75]

My friend Daniella (not her real name) told me about another type of mistake that her father made. She and her siblings have different income levels, and her father wanted to take this into account in dividing up his estate. He asked Daniella to agree in writing that he would allocate only 10 percent of the assets to

---

Templates" USLegalForms.com, accessed December 11, 2019, http://www.uslegalforms.com/wills/?auslf=buildawill.

74. Mary Randolph, "How Much Will a Lawyer Charge to Write Your Will?," *Nolo*, accessed December 24, 2020, https://www.nolo.com/legal-encyclopedia/how-much-will-lawyer-charge-write-your-will.html.

75. Deborah L. Jacobs, "How to Do Estate Planning on the Cheap," *Forbes*, November 19, 2010, http://www.forbes.com/forbes/2010/1206/investment-guide-living-will-software-cheap-estate-planning.html.

her so that her three siblings, whose incomes were somewhat lower than hers, could receive more. Daniella thought hard about this and consulted several friends. Although she understood her father's rationale, she felt deeply hurt. None of her siblings is disabled, and they all chose professions that made them happy and enabled them to support themselves. She worried that when the time came, she would not only mourn the loss of her father, but also feel jealous and resentful as her siblings enjoyed more generous inheritances than she received. Daniella decided against agreeing to the proposed estate plan and reassured her father that if any of her siblings ever faced real financial distress, she would help them as much as she could. Consequently, the siblings received equal shares of the modest estate and remain a close-knit family. I told this story to an experienced estate planning lawyer, and he confirmed that under the circumstances, Daniella's father had made a mistake that could have caused serious familial strife.

Trusts

Some people may also benefit from establishing a trust and should consult an attorney to explore this option. Trusts are complicated legal instruments, and you should not try to create one without the help of an experienced lawyer.

Professor Leon Gabinet, who is a colleague and an expert in trusts and estates, told me that he would advise anyone who owns a house and has a few hundred thousand dollars in additional assets (e.g., mutual funds or property) to establish a trust. There are different types of trusts, but a common choice is a revocable living trust, which allows your heirs to avoid proceedings of probate[76] for assets in the trust.

---

76. According to the American Bar Association, probate is "the formal legal process that gives recognition to a will and appoints the executor or personal representative who will administer the estate and distribute assets to the intended beneficiaries." American Bar Association, "The Probate

Other experts posit that if your only purpose is to avoid probate, you can use other tools, such as transfer on death (TOD) (discussed below). They recommend a trust only for people with particular life circumstances or needs. For example, a special needs trust is useful if you have a disabled child or another disabled person to whom you want to leave a bequest. It allows the disabled person to have an inheritance without losing Medicaid eligibility because the trustee has sole authority to disburse funds for things for which Medicaid does not pay. Trusts are also useful for those who wish to keep control over the finances of a child (or other beneficiary) beyond the grave. If you are worried that your children will squander their inheritance, you can create a trust that will dole out money sporadically and terminate only when the youngest child turns 50.

Property in a trust is titled in the name of the trustee and is managed by the trustee in accordance with instructions in the trust document. The trustee can be the person who created the trust. However, if you will manage your own trust during your lifetime, you should name a successor trustee and alternate successor trustee to take over in case you become incapacitated or die. An alternate is necessary to ensure that someone can take over if the original person you named dies, becomes incapacitated, or is otherwise unavailable.

Wealthy individuals can use professional trust companies to serve as trustees, although the fees for such services can be high. You can revise or revoke your trust at any time as long as you have mental capacity. In order to avoid probate completely, you must transfer all of your property to the trust, and if this is done, the trust will substitute for a will. However, you should still have a will just in case you forget to transfer something into the trust.

Process?" American Bar Association, accessed December 24, 2020, https://www.americanbar.org/groups/real_property_trust_estate/resources/estate_planning/the_probate_process/.

Another advantage of a trust is that it can help families avoid guardianship proceedings. If the person who established the trust becomes incapacitated, a named trustee will manage the trust, and no other individual needs to be appointed by the court to serve as guardian to take care of financial matters.

When you establish your trust, you can provide very detailed instructions. For example, you can include a directive that allows payment for long-term care at home but not for permanent care in a nursing home if you wish to avoid being moved to a nursing facility as long as your money lasts.[77]

Transfer on death

Property that is not included in a trust can be protected from probate through TOD designation. TOD allows you to name beneficiaries who will receive your assets upon your death without needing to go through probate.[78] You will need to check your state's laws as to which assets are eligible for TOD.

Generally, bank accounts can be set up as payable on death, and brokerage accounts can be registered as TOD. In some states, motor vehicles can also be registered as TOD. You will need to fill out forms that you obtain from the appropriate financial institutions and the Department of Motor Vehicles. You can also obtain a TOD deed for your home and other real estate in many states.[79] As with your other legal documents,

77. Frolik and Whitton, *Everyday Law for Seniors*, 163–65; Patrick Hicks, "An In-Depth Look at The Different Types of Trusts," *Trust & Will*, accessed August 17, 2021, https://trustandwill.com/learn/types-of-trusts.

78. Mary Randolph, "Avoiding Probate with Transfer-on-Death Accounts and Registrations," *Nolo*, accessed December 24, 2020, https://www.nolo.com/legal-encyclopedia/avoid-probate-transfer-on-death-accounts-29544.html.

79. Legal Counsel for the Elderly, "Transfer on Death Deed (TODD)," Legal Counsel for the Elderly, accessed December 24, 2020, https://www.aarp.org/content/dam/aarp/lce/resources/dc-transfer-on-death-deed.pdf; Mary Randolph, "States That Allow Transfer-On-Death Deeds

it is prudent to name alternate beneficiaries. Also, make sure that your forms are accurate and filed with the appropriate authorities (e.g., the Department of Motor Vehicles, Office of the Recorder of Deeds, your bank).

Other instructions

In order to help your family handle your affairs after your death, you should prepare several other documents as well. In addition to a will, it is wise to create a list of all valuables that are not mentioned in the will, such as jewelry and cars, with instructions as to who should inherit them. Forgetting to do this can cause tension, bitterness, and rivalries among children or siblings who all covet the same items.

In addition, you should create a memorandum that explains where important financial documents and items can be found (e.g., drawers at home, a home safe, a bank safe deposit box). You should give this memo to your agent for financial matters and to his or her alternate.

Your family will also need instructions about your wishes for funeral and burial or cremation arrangements. Do not assume that your loved ones will want to decide what to do with your remains. In many cases, they will appreciate clear guidance at a time that is chaotic and traumatic for them.

I first asked my parents where they wanted to be buried after my mother's breast cancer diagnosis in 1994. My mother said she wanted to be buried in Israel, near her parents, and my father said he wanted to be buried in California, near his family members. Puzzled, I asked them, "so, you don't want to be buried together?" They replied, "no, of course we want to be buried together—that is our first priority." It was clear that we would need many family discussions to work this out, and

---

for Real Estate," *Nolo*, accessed December 24, 2020, https://www.nolo.com/legal-encyclopedia/free-books/avoid-probate-book/chapter5-1.html.

happily, we had almost 20 years in which to do so. Ultimately, they decided to be buried in Michigan, where they had resided during their last three decades.

The average funeral cost was $9,000 in 2020,[80] but costs can vary widely.[81] For example, a high-end casket alone can cost $10,000,[82] whereas cremation can cost between $1,600 and $3,000.[83]

Some people feel strongly about how their bodies should be handled or what they want included in or excluded from their funeral ceremony (prayers, music, poems). Others prioritize saving their families money, especially if they have no life insurance policy. You may feel that you do not want to burden your family with demands about your funeral because you do not have strong preferences and will not be around to see it. However, I believe that most often your loved ones will appreciate having detailed guidance about a matter that will be difficult under the best of circumstances and can cause significant turmoil and tension.

STORING, DISSEMINATING, AND UPDATING YOUR LEGAL DOCUMENTS

A colleague at work whom I will call Brenda had an experience that emphasized to me the importance of having securely

---

80. This includes a casket, embalming, flowers, basic services, a grave marker, clothes or a shroud, a plot, a vault, and a hearse.

81. Secure Senior Life Insurance, "How Much Does the Average Funeral Cost in 2020?" Secure Senior Life Insurance, accessed December 24, 2020, https://secureseniorlifeinsurance.com/average-funeral-cost/.

82. Federal Trade Commission, "Funeral Costs and Pricing Checklist," Federal Trade Commission, July 2012, http://www.consumer.ftc.gov/articles/0301-funeral-costs-and-pricing-checklist#Calculating.

83. Parting.com, "Funeral Costs: How Much Does an Average Direct Cremation Cost?" Parting.com, September 6, 2020, https://www.parting.com/blog/cost-considerations-when-choosing-direct-cremation/.

stored financial documents and a trusted power of attorney for property and finances. Brenda's parents were in their 80s and lived independently in a house. When Brenda and her siblings tried to speak with their father about his finances and about appointing a decision maker, he always became agitated. He would accuse them of wanting to get their hands on his money and told them he was fine handling matters on his own.

One day, Brenda's parents suffered a catastrophic fire at their home. Her mother escaped unharmed, but she had dementia and knew nothing about the family finances. Brenda's father died of his wounds. Neither the computer nor any paperwork survived the fire, and so the adult children were left with absolutely no information about their parents' financial resources. It took them many months to figure out what insurance policies, bank accounts, and other assets their parents had, and the emotional stress compounded their tragedy.

It is critical that you appoint a trusted person or persons to serve as your health-care power of attorney and financial power of attorney. You must be willing to be transparent with them about your preferences and your financial resources. The individual(s) must have copies of all relevant documents so that they can properly fulfill their duties.

You should have multiple copies of important documents (e.g., your will, powers of attorney, list of professionals who handle your money and taxes). You should have a copy at home and a backup copy elsewhere, such as at work or in a safe deposit box. In addition, you should give copies of your legal documents to your decision makers and perhaps to other loved ones who are likely to be involved in your care.

Finally, it is not enough to create your documents and store them properly. It is important to revisit them occasionally to make sure you do not need to revise them. The American Bar Association's Commission on Law and Aging recommends that you recheck your documents whenever one of the "Five Ds" occurs:

1. Decade—when you start each new decade of your life.
2. Death—whenever you experience the death of a loved one.
3. Divorce—when you experience a divorce or other major family change.
4. Diagnosis—when you are diagnosed with a serious health condition.
5. Decline—when you experience a significant decline or deterioration of an existing health condition, especially when it diminishes your ability to live independently.[84]

Does legal preparedness make a difference? The answer is yes. According to a large study published in the *New England Journal of Medicine*, patients with advance directives generally received end-of-life care that was consistent with their treatment preferences.[85] Thus, if competently prepared and appropriately distributed, living wills and durable power of attorney for health-care documents significantly impact decision-making outcomes and help promote treatment plans that reflect patients' wishes. Likewise, properly prepared wills, powers of attorney, and other financial documents can provide your loved ones with much-needed guidance and help them avoid family conflicts. If you care about what medical care you will receive if you are incapacitated and what happens to your money in the event of your incapacity or death, then preparing

---

84. American Bar Association Commission on Law and Aging, "What to Do after Signing Your Health Care Advance Directive," American Bar Association, accessed December 24, 2020, https://www.americanbar.org/content/dam/aba/administrative/law_aging/tool8.pdf.

85. Maria J. Silveira, Scott Y.H. Kim, and Kenneth M. Langa, "Advance Directives and Outcomes of Surrogate Decision Making before Death," *New England Journal of Medicine* 362, no. 13 (2010): 1216–18; Mayo Clinic Staff, "Living Wills and Advance Directives for Medical Decisions," Mayo Clinic, August 22, 2020, https://www.mayoclinic.org/healthy-lifestyle/consumer-health/in-depth/living-wills/art-20046303.

the documents described in this chapter is well worth the time, cost, and effort.

LEGAL PREPAREDNESS CHECKLIST

All individuals who want to have a say in how they will be treated if they become incapacitated and what will happen to their assets in case of incapacity or death should implement multiple levels of legal protection. What follows is a legal preparedness checklist.

* No single document is sufficient. You should have a will (and possibly a trust), a power of attorney for property and finances, a living will, a durable power of attorney for health care, and if desired, an anatomical gift form. The latter three forms may be combined into a single advance directive for health care if permitted under state law. Those with a history of mental illness should also consider executing a separate advance directive for mental health treatment.
* If you do not have a trust, consider designating property as "transfer on death," so it can be kept out of probate.
* If an attorney will not be helping you prepare your documents, consult other sources. The websites LegalZoom and USLegal provide users with various legal forms that you can fill in. Likewise, the American Bar Association Commission on Law and Aging provides a useful resource for those interested in preparing advance directives. It is called *Tool Kit for Health Care Advance Planning* and is available on the Internet.[86]

---

86. American Bar Association Commission on Law and Aging, "Tool Kit for Health Care Advance Planning," American Bar Association, November 11, 2020, http://www.americanbar.org/groups/law_aging/resources/health_care_decision_making/consumer_s_toolkit_for_health_care_advance_planning.html.

* Recheck all personal legal documents at least once a decade and anytime a life-changing event occurs. Ensure that the documents continue to be accurate and reflect your wishes.
* If you move to a different state, execute a new advance directive that conforms to the new state's laws. Similarly, if you spend significant time in more than one state, for example, you winter in Florida or Arizona but live elsewhere the rest of the year, you should have advance directives for each of the states in which you live.
* Remain in close touch with your decision makers for health care and property to ensure that they continue to be available, trustworthy, and willing to follow your instructions. Verify that they fully understand your wishes and have no moral objections to your preferences regarding medical care. Repeated conversations will also help your agents advocate for you and prove that you had clear wishes if family members or doctors question them.
* Make sure that your proxies have copies of all your key legal documents and instructions.
* Be sure to name alternate decision makers for health care and property in case your original agent is unavailable or herself incapacitated or deceased when she is needed.
* Make sure that your health-care providers have copies of your advance directive (including your living will, health-care power of attorney, and organ donation form, if applicable). Ask all your doctors to verify that your advance directive is part of your electronic health record, and remember that they may use different computer systems, so they each need a copy.
* Take other measures to ensure that your loved ones and care providers can easily find your advance directive. Keep a copy of it on your smart phone and carry an advance

directive wallet card. If your state has an advance directive registry, make sure to enter your documents there as well.

* If you will receive care at a hospital, either as an inpatient or an outpatient, take your advance directive with you and make sure it is entered into the hospital's electronic health record system.

CHAPTER 5

DRIVING WHILE ELDERLY

In January 2019, Great Britain's Prince Phillip caused a car accident that left two women with minor injuries. He was 97 years old at the time. The incident shined an international spotlight on the topic of the elderly and driving.[1]

Accidents involving the elderly are not just something you read about in newspapers. My own neighborhood in Cleveland is home to many seniors. In the past few years, three of the businesses that my husband and I frequent suddenly had their front windows boarded up. In each instance, we were told that an elderly driver had hit the accelerator rather than the brakes when trying to park directly in front of the store or restaurant. In one case, a few days after the accident, the large dumpster into which the owners threw items damaged in the accident was also hit. It turned out that the culprit was the very same driver.

A good friend told me her own family's story. Her mother, whom I will call Ruth, died in her mid-80s and never gave up driving. A few months before she died, Ruth hit another car as she was very slowly exiting a Walgreen's parking lot. This was not even a fender-bender—Ruth's car had only a scratch on it, and no injuries were reported on the scene when the police arrived. Nevertheless, a year later, the other driver sued the

---

1. *New York Times*, "The Elderly and Driving: When Is It Time to Hit the Brakes?" *New York Times*, January 18, 2019, https://www.nytimes.com/2019/01/18/health/elderly-driving-cars-safety.html.

estate. She had undergone neck surgery and could no longer work in her physically challenging job, and she claimed it was all a result of the accident. Because the plaintiff sued for more than the value of Ruth's insurance policy, the family had to lawyer up, and the money in the estate could not be distributed. The case ultimately settled, and the insurer paid in full, but the family suffered considerable stress and anxiety while also mourning Ruth's death.

Many people with disabilities, including those who are elderly, reach a point at which they should voluntarily refrain from getting behind the wheel because of physical or cognitive impairments. Refusing to stop driving at the appropriate time is socially irresponsible and potentially catastrophic. At worst, it can injure or kill the elderly driver or someone else.

Admittedly, however, the end of driving can lead to a demoralizing loss of autonomy, a diminishing sense of self-worth, and a need for major lifestyle adjustments. It can also inhibit social interaction and cause a significant deterioration in quality of life.[2] Adequate transportation may be essential to continued social engagement; participation in cultural, religious, and recreational activities; access to goods and services including medical care; and a sense of belonging to your community.[3] In many locations, public transportation is poor to nonexistent. According to one report, "The majority of

---

2. Weidi Qin, Xiaoling Xiang, and Harry Taylor, "Driving Cessation and Social Isolation in Older Adults," *Journal of Aging and Health* (2019), https://doi.org/10.1177%2F0898264319870400.

3. National Aging and Disability Transportation Center, "Needs and Assessment: Survey of Older Adults, People with Disabilities, and Caregivers," KRC Research, 12, December 2018, http://www.krcresearch.com/wp-content/uploads/2018/12/KRC-nadtc-Survey-Report-120718-FINAL_ for-web.pdf ("Close to 9 in 10 who stopped driving have been negatively impacted—from being isolated to dependent. This limits them living their lives to the fullest and makes them feel frustrated.").

older Americans—79 percent—tend to live in car-dependent suburban and rural communities, which typically require frequent, longer distance trips by automobile."[4]

Seniors' reluctance to stop driving is thus often understandable and can become a major source of conflict for families. Learning how to assess driving ability, to have constructive conversations about when to stop driving, and to find transportation alternatives, is an important part of planning for aging and caregiving.

DRIVING AND COLLISION STATISTICS

To what extent do we really need to worry that elderly drivers are a hazard on the road? The data are more reassuring than I expected, though there is still cause for worry.

The Federal Highway Administration estimated that approximately 29.3 million individuals 70 and older had licenses in 2017, including more than 4 million who were 85 and older. Thus, approximately 83 percent of those who are 70 and above, including 62.1 percent of those who are 85 and over, still have licenses. Approximately 12.9 percent of all drivers are now 70 or older.[5]

Drivers who are 70 and older have higher rates of fatal crashes per mile driven than middle-aged drivers.[6] In 2019,

---

4. TRIP, "Preserving the Mobility and Safety of Older Americans," TRIP, March 2018, https://tripnet.org/wp-content/uploads/2018/08/Older_Americans_Mobility_TRIP_Report_2018.pdf.

5. Federal Highway Administration, "Distribution of Licensed Drivers—2018: By Sex and Percentage in Each Age Group and Relation to Population," Federal Highway Administration, January 2020, https://www.fhwa.dot.gov/policyinformation/statistics/2018/dl20.cfm; Insurance Institute for Highway Safety and Highway Loss Data Institute, "Older Drivers," updated September 2020, https://www.iihs.org/topics/older-drivers.

6. Insurance Institute for Highway Safety, "Older Drivers."

5,195 people aged 70 and older died in auto accidents.[7] Per mile traveled, fatal accident rates increase beginning at age 70–74, and the rate accelerates after age 80, with those 85 and older facing the highest risk of dying while behind the wheel.[8] However, the fact that deaths are more common among older drivers who have accidents is largely attributable to their frailty.[9] People who are frail are more likely to die of accident-related injuries than younger, more robust individuals. Consequently, these fatal accidents are fatal mostly for the older drivers themselves and their elderly passengers.

Regardless of the statistics, if you live to be old enough, there may well come a time when you have to stop driving. Will the government tell you when that time has come? Do state authorities offer clear guidance?

STATE REGULATION

When my mother-in-law went to the Massachusetts Department of Motor Vehicles to renew her driver's license at age 92, we were sure that she would be declined. She relied heavily on a walker, and when she walked in with one, state officials should have concluded that she had problems with her legs and may not be able to control car pedals. Yet, that evening, she called us and triumphantly announced that she had gotten a new driver's license without any problem. Once she passed her vision test, nobody asked her any further questions or brought up her use of a walker.

---

7. Insurance Institute for Highway Safety and Highway Loss Data Institute, "Fatality Facts 2019: Older People," Insurance Institute for Highway Safety and Highway Loss Data Institute, March 2021, https://www.iihs.org/topics/fatality-statistics/detail/older-people.

8. Insurance Institute for Highway Safety, "Fatality Facts 2018."

9. Insurance Institute for Highway Safety, "Fatality Facts 2018."

When I began conducting research for this chapter, I assumed that the states had implemented regulatory safeguards designed to keep unsafe elderly drivers off the roads. These would be a logical parallel to the prohibition on driving by those who are too young and on the requirement of road tests before issuance of the first license.

I knew that there were some regulatory gaps because of my mother-in-law's experience and because several other elderly acquaintances received no more than a traffic ticket after driving their cars into fire hydrants or parked vehicles, sometimes more than once. Nevertheless, I had imagined that regulation in this area was more extensive than it is, and I was surprised by how little certainty there is about what interventions are effective.

Special provisions for older drivers exist in 31 states and the District of Columbia, but these are generally limited to increased renewal frequency, renewal in person, and vision tests. Only the District of Columbia and Nevada require a medical certification after age 70, and only Illinois requires a road test for those 75 or older. To check the state license renewal requirements for older drivers in your state, you may refer to a chart compiled by the Insurance Institute for Highway Safety, which can be found on its website.[10]

The absence of more aggressive regulation may be due in part to concerns about age discrimination. If states implemented a

10. Insurance Institute for Highway Safety and Highway Loss Data Institute, Safety, "License Renewal Procedures by State," Insurance Institute for Highway Safety and Highway Loss Data Institute, December 2020, https://www.iihs.org/topics/older-drivers/license-renewal-laws-table; AAA, "State Laws," SeniorDriving.AAA.com, accessed December 24, 2020, https://seniordriving.aaa.com/states/(allowing users to click on a map and obtain information about their state laws); Valerie Keene, "D.C. Driving Laws for Seniors and Older Drivers," NOLO, accessed December 24, 2020, https://www.nolo.com/legal-encyclopedia/washington-dc-driving-laws-seniors-older-drivers.html.

rule that made renewal much more difficult after a certain age, they could be accused of violating the constitutional principle of equal protection of the law. Opponents could argue that younger people are not subject to the same requirements even if they have disabilities that could potentially affect their driving ability, but older individuals face automatic renewal hurdles regardless of their health status.

In truth, there is little evidence that strict regulations that would limit driving by the elderly would make the roads safer. California pilot tested a three-tier evaluation for driver's license renewal by all applicants, which required that those who failed the first two tiers take an on-road test. The first-tier screening consisted of a brief memory recall test, two vision tests, and the tester's observation of any visible physical limitations. The second tier consisted of a written test of driving knowledge and a perceptual response test designed to identify limitations in perception and cognition that are relevant to driving.[11] The state found only weak indications that the program reduced at-fault collisions with injuries or fatalities. A study in Maryland, however, concluded that individuals who were 78 and older and who performed poorly on certain cognitive tests were twice as likely as other drivers to cause crashes.[12] Although some literature supports the implementation of vision tests and in-person renewal for older license applicants, the efficacy of road tests remains very much in question.[13] Researchers have

---

11. Bayliss Camp, "California's Three-Tier Driving-Centered Assessment System: Outcome Analysis," State of California Department of Motor Vehicles (November 2011), vi, https://www.researchgate.net/publication/315815295_California's_Three-Tier_Driving-Centered_Assessment_System_Outcome_Analysis.

12. Karlene K. Ball et al., "Can High-Risk Older Drivers Be Identified through Performance-Based Measures in a Department of Motor Vehicles Setting?" *Journal of the American Geriatrics Society* 54, no. 1 (2006): 77–84.

13. Yll Agimi, Steven M Albert, Ada O. Youk, Patricia I. Documet, and Claudia A. Steiner, "Mandatory Physician Reporting of at-Risk

a limited ability to assess mandatory road tests because only Illinois requires them, and such tests generally face resistance, as they are costly and would require increased staffing. Thus, no clear methodology for identifying unsafe elderly drivers emerges from the literature.[14]

The efficacy of driver education courses is equally unclear. Although the AAA, AARP, and others offer educational courses for older drivers, there is no evidence that such courses reduce accident rates for seniors.[15] This is perhaps because the classes are voluntary and consequently attract a self-selected group of seniors who are especially conscientious. Nevertheless, such courses can increase seniors' awareness of their own impairments and improve driving behavior, including

---

Drivers: The Older Driver Example," *Gerontologist* 58, no. 3 (2018): 578–87 ("the requirement of undergoing vision testing at in-person license renewal was a significant predictor of a lower crash hospitalization rate" but "road testing, showed no consistent effect on crash hospitalization rates"); Insurance Institute for Highway Safety, "Older Drivers" ("Regulations requiring in-person renewal or vision testing are the only policies that are associated with lower fatality rates among older drivers, and only among drivers ages 85 and older."). Ediriweera Desapriya et al., "Vision Screening of Older Drivers for Preventing Road Traffic Injuries and Fatalities," *Cochrane Database of Systematic Reviews*, 2, 2014, https://www.cochranelibrary.com/cdsr/doi/10.1002/14651858.CD006252.pub4/epdf/full ("There is [...] lack of methodologically sound studies to assess the effects of vision screening tests on subsequent motor vehicle crash reduction.").

14. Emily Morgan, "Driving Dilemmas: A Guide to Driving Assessment in Primary Care," *Clinical Geriatric. Medicine* 34, no. 1 (2018): 107–15 ("There is no single validated screening instrument for driver safety.").

15. Gila Albert, "The Challenge of Safe Driving among Elderly Drivers," *Healthcare Technology Letters* 5, no. 1 (2018): 45–48; Cynthia Owsley, Gerald McGwin Jr, Janice M. Phillips, Sandre F. McNeal, and Beth T. Stalvey, "Impact of an Educational Program on the Safety of High-Risk, Visually Impaired, Older Drivers," *American Journal of Preventive Medicine* 26, no. 3 (2004): 222–29; Glenyth E. Nasvadi and John Vavrik, "Crash Risk of Older Drivers after Attending a Mature Driver Education Program," *Accident Analysis & Prevention* 39, no. 6 (2007): 1073–79.

encouraging self-imposed restrictions on when and where to drive. In addition, some experts argue that classroom education combined with on-road training significantly improves driving safety.[16]

Perhaps most troubling is the lack of structured reporting mechanisms for identifying at-risk drivers and for addressing the dangers they pose. Only six states[17] mandate that physicians report at-risk drivers to state authorities,[18] although all states permit doctors to do so. The states vary as to whether they accept reports from family members, friends, or anonymous sources and as to how such reports are to be submitted (e.g., by letter, form, or e-mail).[19] In addition, states do not consistently and effectively train law enforcement officers to identify and report medically at-risk drivers.[20] This training gap is particularly disturbing. A police officer at the scene of an accident who simply tickets an elderly driver who seems confused or has a

---

16. Sylvain Gagnon, "Driving Safety Improves after Individualized Training: An RCT Involving Older Drivers in an Urban Area," *Traffic Injury Prevention* 20, no. 6 (2019): 595–600.

17. The states are California, Delaware, Nevada, New Jersey, Oregon, and Pennsylvania.

18. American Geriatric Society, *Clinician's Guide to Assessing and Counseling Older Drivers*, 4th ed. (New York: American Geriatrics Society, 2019), 99; Michael Tortorello, "How Seniors Are Driving Safer, Driving Longer," Consumer Reports, June 1, 2017, https://www.consumerreports.org/elderly-driving/how-seniors-are-driving-safer-driving-longer/.

19. National Highway Traffic Safety Administration, "State Policy Affecting Community Mobility: Variability across the Country," National Highway Traffic Safety Administration, accessed December 24, 2020, https://one.nhtsa.gov/people/injury/olddrive/CommMobilityDementia/pages/CurrentScr-StatePolicy.htm.

20. Linda L. Hill, Jill Rybar, James Stowe, and Jana Jahns, "Development of a Curriculum and Roadside Screening Tool for Law Enforcement Identification of Medical Impairment in Aging Drivers," *Injury Epidemiology* 3, no. 13 (2016): 2.

history of multiple recent collisions may endanger public safety by failing to alert state authorities and to request follow-up action.

Reliance on family and friends as the primary source of information about seniors who should not be driving is dubious at best. Those who are close to the elderly individual may not be willing to jeopardize their relationship with the person by informing authorities of their concerns. Many states do not provide confidentiality protection for such reports. At the same time, many elderly people would know who contacted the authorities because they likely had prior confrontations about driving with the same individual. Several of my acquaintances have tried threatening their loved ones with a report to authorities and have promptly been told they would never be spoken to again if that happened.

If the state is notified of an at-risk driver, it may intervene in a variety of ways. State authorities will likely first consult the state's medical advisory board (if one exists), the driver's own physician, or another health-care provider. Short of revoking the elderly person's license, the state may impose driving restrictions, such as prohibiting driving on high-speed roads, at night, or outside a certain area.[21] Although older drivers may initially feel resentful, these limitations can actually enable seniors to remain independent and continue driving safely for a significant period of time.[22]

One encouraging research finding is that older drivers engage in some degree of self-regulation, even without state-imposed constraints. They are more likely than others to wear

---

21. J. Joyce, K. H. Lococo, K. W. Gish, T. Mastromatto, J. Stutts, D. Thomas, and R. Blomberg et al., "Older Driver Compliance with License Restrictions," National Highway Traffic Safety Administration, 3, April 2018, https://www.nhtsa.gov/sites/nhtsa.dot.gov/files/documents/older_driver_compliance_with_license_restrictions.pdf.
22. Joyce et al., "Older Driver Compliance," 2.

seatbelts, to limit driving in bad weather and after dark, to drive short distances, and to drive sober.[23] In 2017, drivers who were 70 and older drove an average of 43 percent fewer miles than drivers in the 35–54 age group.[24] As the population ages, researchers should undertake additional studies to determine which, if any, government interventions are most effective in promoting driver safety.

KNOWING WHEN TO STOP DRIVING AND MAKING IT HAPPEN

Everyone must accept that there may come a time when driving will no longer be a safe activity. It may become too dangerous because of physical disabilities, mental impairments, or the use of prescription drugs whose side effects diminish wakefulness, mental acuity, and response capacity. AAA offers an Internet resource called Roadwise Rx[25] that allows you to search for medication interactions, food interactions, and driver warnings. Seniors should also discuss the impact of new medications on driving with their prescribing physicians.

The signs of danger

How do you know when you or a loved one should consider turning in your driver's license? The AARP lists the following signs:

---

23. AAA, "Facts & Research," SeniorDriving.AAA.com, accessed December 24, 2020, https://seniordriving.aaa.com/resources-family-friends/conversations-about-driving/facts-research/; Centers for Disease Control and Prevention, "Older Adult Drivers: How Can Older Driver Deaths and Injuries Be Prevented?" Centers for Disease Control and Prevention, reviewed December 7, 2020, https://www.cdc.gov/motorvehiclesafety/older_adult_drivers/index.html.

24. Insurance Institute for Highway Safety, "Older Drivers".

25. Available at http://www.roadwiserx.com/.

- Delayed response to unexpected situations
- Becoming easily distracted while driving
- Decrease in confidence while driving
- Having difficulty moving into or maintaining the correct lane of traffic
- Hitting curbs when making right turns or backing up
- Getting scrapes or dents on your car, garage or mailbox
- Having frequent close calls
- Driving too fast or too slow for road conditions.[26]

If you are unsure about whether you or a loved one can continue to drive safely, you can get a comprehensive driving evaluation from an occupational therapist. These evaluations are available at rehabilitation centers, hospitals, and Veterans Administration Medical Centers and generally cost $200–$400.[27] Evaluators will not only determine whether it is appropriate for the individual to drive, but will provide advice regarding limitations (e.g., nighttime driving) or equipment (e.g., wide range mirrors) that should be adopted to promote safe driving.

Having the conversation

Confronting elderly loved ones who are not inclined to stop driving despite danger signs can be excruciatingly difficult. In my own family, such conversations have been painful. "You have been a generous, kind, hard-working person your entire life. Why are you courting tragedy now? How would you like

---

26. Kyle Rakow, "We Need to Talk: The Difficult Driving Conversation," AARP, accessed December 24, 2020, https://www.aarp.org/auto/driver-safety/info-2016/when-to-stop-driving-in-older-age.html.

27. "Professional Assessment," SeniorDriving.AAA.com, accessed December 24, 2020, https://seniordriving.aaa.com/evaluate-your-driving-ability/professional-assessment/.

to live your remaining years knowing that you have injured or even killed another human being because you won't face reality about your driving abilities?" Apparently, this is not an ideal approach!

If the older driver has a good relationship with his or her primary care physician, you may want to involve the doctor in the discussion. Numerous websites provide suggestions about having "the talk" with a loved one whose driving future is in question.[28] Here are a few good suggestions:

- Find a few opportunities to ride as a passenger in the older driver's car to observe his or her driving.
- Build consensus among family and friends that your loved one's driving is a problem before deciding to broach the topic with her.
- Think carefully and choose the right person to be the messenger.
- Pick the right time. Having upsetting conversations while the elderly person is behind the wheel is definitely not a good idea.
- Be prepared to have more than one discussion about driving. Progress from casual chats to more serious, action-oriented conversations.
- During each conversation, listen to the elderly driver, inquire about her feelings, and validate her concerns about what not driving anymore will mean.
- Ask the elderly driver what she herself thinks about her driving ability.

---

28. AARP, "We Need to Talk" AARP, accessed December 24, 2020, http://www.aarp.org/home-garden/transportation/we_need_to_talk/ ?cmp=RDRCT-WNTT; Medicare.org, "How to Talk with Seniors About Their Unsafe Driving," Medicare.org, accessed December 24, 2020, https://www.medicare.org/articles/how-to-talk-with-seniors-about-their-unsafe-driving/.

- Emphasize that you care deeply about the driver and that you are concerned about her safety and that of others.
- Present concrete examples of driving mistakes you have actually observed. Do not base the conversation on assumptions regarding older drivers or complaints you have heard from others.

FINDING TRANSPORTATION RESOURCES

Living in a retirement community (as discussed in Chapter 2) is one way to minimize the impact of surrendering your driver's license. Such communities may provide many on-campus amenities that reduce the need for a car. They may also offer routine and individually arranged transportation to various off-campus destinations, such as medical offices, grocery stores, and cultural events. Those living in other residential settings may be able to ask nearby friends or relatives to carpool for errands and entertainment and to assist with other transportation needs.

Many communities have supplemental transportation programs for the elderly. These programs use volunteers or charge a minimal fee per ride. Your city hall or local Area Agency on Aging can help you find convenient services.[29] Advocates have urged that government offices and aging-oriented organizations develop hotlines, directories, marketing information, and educational programs to inform the public about local transportation options. Unfortunately, today the available choices are generally limited because of financial and staffing constraints, and seniors may find them inadequate in terms of convenience and responsiveness to their needs.[30]

---

29. To locate a nearby Area Agency on Aging, call 1-800-677-1116 or go to https://eldercare.acl.gov.

30. Howard Gleckman, "Why Can't We Expand Access to Transportation for Older Adults?" *Forbes*, February 18, 2019, https://www.forbes.com/sites/howardgleckman/2019/02/18/why-cant-we-expand-access-to-transportation-for-older-adults/#7f91ac305c84; Joshua

Rideshare services such as Uber and Lyft make it easy to order and pay for transportation through your smartphone. However, older adults have not embraced the concept of "e-hail." A survey of over eight hundred older adults published in 2018 revealed that 74 percent did not know about rideshare services, and only 1.7 percent had actually arranged rides through them.[31] Seniors may not trust drivers who use private vehicles (rather than a car clearly marked as a taxi) or may not use apps on their smartphones. A service called GoGo Grandparent allows registered users to call a hotline number and order rideshare transportation through it.[32] Seniors may feel more comfortable with this more traditional method of ordering rides through a phone call.

Another option is to hire aides who will do the driving or run errands for you. You can retain such individuals by contacting local home care agencies or searching online. For example, an Internet resource called Care.com contains listings of individuals offering a variety of services, ranging from babysitting to elder care. Care.com verifies the identity of those advertising their services and can be asked to conduct full background checks. My family posted an ad on Craigslist when we needed someone to help my father with driving and other tasks. We then used an Internet service called Intelius to conduct a background check on the successful applicant prior to hiring him. Those who are

J. Turner, Carolyn E. Adams-Price, and Lesley Strawderman, "Formal Alternative Transportation Options for Older Adults: An Assessment of Need," *Journal of Gerontological Social Work* 60, no. 8 (2017): 619–46.

31. Jonathan M. Vivoda, Annie C. Harmon, Ganesh M. Babulal, and Brian J. Zikmund-Fisher, "E-hail (Rideshare) Knowledge, Use, Reliance, and Future Expectations among Older Adults," *Transportation Research Part F* 55 (2018): 426–34.

32. Brett Helling, "GoGoGrandparent Guide: Help Seniors Request Food and Rides with This App," updated December 3, 2020, https://www.ridester.com/gogograndparent-app-guidelines/.

active in a religious community may also ask their clergy if they can recommend responsible individuals who would like to work as occasional drivers for elderly community members.

In addition, there are a variety of ways to reduce the number of errands you have to run. Grocery stores and restaurants routinely offer delivery services, and many of us already took advantage of these during the COVID-19 pandemic. A great deal of shopping can also be accomplished at home through the Internet. Thus, seniors can balance the psychological benefits of leaving the house and mingling with others against the need for convenience and reduced access to transportation.

THE AID OF TECHNOLOGY

With emerging improvements in technology, older drivers may be able to extend their safe driving years. Many driver assistance systems have already been deployed and are increasingly common in contemporary vehicles. These include navigation systems, park distance information, lane departure warnings, automated emergency braking, automated headlights, and pedestrian detection.[33] Backup cameras provide drivers with a view of what is behind the car when it is in reverse and help them judge distances and back up safely. A feature called "adaptive cruise control" automatically adjusts the speed of a car on cruise control when the speed of the car ahead of it changes in order to maintain a specified distance between the two vehicles.[34] Traffic jam assist uses sensors and software that

33. National Highway Traffic Safety Administration, "Driver Assistance Technologies," United States Department of Transportation, accessed December 24, 2020, https://www.nhtsa.gov/equipment/driver-assistance-technologies.

34. Consumer Reports, "Guide to Adaptive Cruise Control: How This Convenience Feature Works to Reduce Your Stress on Long Drives," Consumer Reports, updated August 5, 2019, https://www.consumerreports.org/car-safety/adaptive-cruise-control-guide/.

adjust speed and handle braking and steering in heavy traffic that moves at up to 37 miles per hour.[35] Automatic emergency braking causes the car to stop if the system detects a pedestrian or an imminent collision and the driver fails to step on the brake pedal.

In the future, we will likely have autonomous vehicles in which all driving functions are automated.[36] Such technology, however, still faces significant technological barriers and may be hindered by concerns about legal liability, insurance regulation, and public acceptance.[37]

Older car buyers should carefully investigate vehicle safety features and consider them central to their purchasing decisions.[38] More importantly, as baby boomers age, we cannot ignore the likelihood that we will have to stop driving altogether in our later years. The availability of convenient and affordable transportation alternatives should be a factor in selecting retirement homes and communities.

---

35. John Markoff and Somini Sengupta, "Drivers with Hands Full Get a Backup: The Car," *New York Times*, January 12, 2013, http://www.nytimes.com/2013/01/12/science/drivers-with-hands-full-get-a-backup-the-car.html?pagewanted=all; "Traffic Jam Assist," Bosch Mobility Solutions.com, accessed December 24, 2020, https://www.bosch-mobility-solutions.com/en/products-and-services/passenger-cars-and-light-commercial-vehicles/automated-driving/traffic-jam-assist/.

36. Neal E. Boudette, "Despite High Hopes, Self-Driving Cars Are 'Way in the Future,'" *New York Times*, July 17, 2019, https://www.nytimes.com/2019/07/17/business/self-driving-autonomous-cars.html.

37. Ashley Nunes, Bryan Reimer, and Joseph F. Coughlin, "People Must Retain Control of Autonomous Vehicles," *Nature* 556 (April 6, 2018), https://www.nature.com/articles/d41586-018-04158-5/.

38. See the AAA's "Find the Right Vehicle for You." This website allows you to look up car features that will be helpful for people with a variety of limitations. Available at https://seniordriving.aaa.com/maintain-mobility-independence/car-buying-maintenance-assistive-accessories/smartfeatures/.

DRIVING PREPAREDNESS CHECKLIST

* Be committed to recognizing when it is unsafe for you to drive and to stopping of your own accord at the appropriate time.
* Be attuned to signs that you or your loved one is having driving difficulties.
* Seek a comprehensive driving evaluation if there is uncertainty about driving abilities.
* Approach conversations with older drivers carefully. Be sensitive to their feelings and present them with evidence of specific driving problems.
* Keep transportation needs in mind when selecting a retirement community.
* Investigate transportation options before asking a loved one to stop driving.
* As you age, pay special attention to safety features and safety-oriented technology when purchasing automobiles.

CHAPTER 6

COORDINATED CARE: TREATING THE PERSON, NOT DISEASES

In April 2012, a little over a year before she died, something terrible happened to my mother. Eema, as we called her in Hebrew, had just returned from a trip to Israel with my sister, where they attended a young cousin's wedding. Seemingly overnight, Eema transformed from being a relatively active, alert 83-year-old to behaving as though she had advanced dementia. When she talked, she made no sense, and frequently, she was completely uncommunicative. She slept for much of the day and often sat in front of the television with a blank stare when she was awake. She showed little interest in eating and drinking and lost weight rapidly. The local hospital admitted Eema for a couple of days and then transferred her to a psychiatric ward elsewhere. My sister who lives in the same city soon demanded that Eema be released because her mental state deteriorated even further.

What had happened? Eema's treating physicians provided no answers. My three sisters and I decided to take matters into our own hands. We spent countless hours doing Internet searches, calling every acquaintance who was a medical professional, and e-mailing our findings to each other. We ultimately determined that the problem was severe drug interactions. Eema had been taking about a dozen medications, and then one more was added—an antidepressant that was prescribed after my father reported to their doctor that she seemed somewhat lethargic and glum. The internist vaguely told Eema that it was another pill to help her sleep, because he knew she would decline any psychiatric intervention and would resist being labeled as clinically depressed. The drastic change in her demeanor came days after she began taking the new drug.

The hospital and several doctors dismissed the possibility that the small dose of the antidepressant had led to instantaneous mental decline. Nevertheless, her doctor agreed that Eema should stop taking the medication. There was some improvement, but not a dramatic one. Upon learning about the phenomenon of drug-induced delirium, we urged my sister to take Eema to the emergency room again. Testing revealed that Eema's blood had dangerously high levels of digoxin, a heart medication. When this medication's level was stabilized, there was further improvement, but Eema was still far from her old self.

We continued our research, studying the side effects of all of her drugs and identifying several that were listed as potentially impacting cognitive functioning. Each of Eema's specialists argued against eliminating any drugs that he had prescribed, but we persisted, and one-by-one all medications that were not clearly medically necessary at her age were discontinued, until she was down to five instead of 12 prescriptions. I caution that you should not change medications for yourself or others on your own—you need professional medical oversight. In some cases, eliminating a medicine or stopping it too abruptly can have catastrophic consequences.

Miraculously, when all but five of the drugs were out of her system, Eema regained her full mental capacities. She had no memory of a two-month period spanning from mid-April to mid-June 2012.

Is this story unique? Apparently not. Richard Russo's book *Elsewhere: A Memoir* contains an account of a similar episode involving his mother. One day she was fine. Then the next morning he found her disheveled, confused, and incoherent, like "the madwoman in the attic, straight out of *Jane Eyre*." Once hospitalized, the author's mother was taken off all of her medications except for blood pressure pills. I was not surprised to read that she "returned to the old normal" after four days.[1]

Researchers have confirmed that over-prescription is a common medical error. According to the Lown Institute, "over the past few decades, medication use in the U.S., especially for older people, has gone far beyond necessary polypharmacy, to the point where millions are overloaded with too many prescriptions and are experiencing significant harm as a result."[2] Consequently, each day, 750 US seniors are hospitalized because of serious medication side effects. Experts estimate that in the next decade, adverse drug events among older adults will cause 4.6 million hospitalizations, 74 million outpatient visits, and almost 150,000 premature deaths.[3]

Approximately 40 percent of seniors take five or more prescription drugs, and almost 20 percent take ten or more.[4] In a book called *Overtreated: Why Too Much Medicine Is Making Us Sicker and Poorer*, Shannon Brownlee argues that the drug and

---

1. Richard Russo, *Elsewhere: A Memoir* (New York: Knopf, 2012), 167 and 181.

2. Shannon Brownlee and Judith Garber, "Medication Overload: America's Other Drug Problem," Lown Institute, April 1, 2019, https://lowninstitute.org/reports/medication-overload-americas-other-drug-problem/.

3. Shannon Brownlee and Judith Garber, "Overprescribed: High Cost Isn't America's Only Drug Problem," *STAT*, April 2, 2019, https://www.statnews.com/2019/04/02/overprescribed-americas-other-drug-problem/.

4. Christina J. Charlesworth, Ellen Smit, David S. H. Lee, Fatimah Alramadhan, Michelle C. Odden, "Polypharmacy among Adults Aged 65 Years and Older in the United States: 1988–2010," *Journals of Gerontology: Medical Sciences* 70, no. 8 (2015): 989–95; Brownlee and Garber, "Medication Overload."

device industries have persuaded "both patients and doctors that we're sicker than we really are, and that the path to wellness lies with medical intervention: with a pill, an operation, or a test." Thus these industries have transformed us "into a nation of the worried well."[5]

Some patients also undergo unnecessary surgeries. In elderly patients, surgery can sometimes exacerbate cognitive decline or other conditions. It can also cause complications and force people who were living independently to need aides or move to nursing homes. Thus, at times, elderly patients are better off tolerating some discomfort or health risks instead of having extensive operations.[6]

How can incidents such as the one that Eema endured be avoided? Medical oversight by a skilled internist or geriatric specialist who can coordinate the care of a patient with multiple medical problems may be the most promising answer. In addition, patients must learn to be active members of their own medical teams and to seek the support and counsel of advocates who can assist them with navigating the complexities of medical care.

THE PRACTICE OF GERIATRICS

Geriatricians are physicians with special training in evaluating and managing the care needs of older adults. Treating this population requires expertise not only in internal medicine but also in neurology, psychiatry, rehabilitative medicine, and other specialties. Elderly patients commonly suffer from multiple medical conditions, and geriatricians often must address some combination of dementia, depression, mobility impairments,

5. Shannon Brownlee, *Overtreated: Why Too Much Medicine Is Making Us Sicker and Poorer* (New York: Bloomsbury, 2007), 183.

6. Paula Span, "The Elderly Are Getting Complex Surgeries. Often It Doesn't End Well," *New York Times*, June 7, 2019, https://www.nytimes.com/2019/06/07/health/elderly-surgery-complications.html?smid=nytcore-ios-share.

incontinence, chronic pain, sensory limitations, and end-of-life decision-making.[7]

Geriatricians generally work with interdisciplinary teams to provide elderly patients with comprehensive care. They may partner with nurses, physician assistants, social workers, pharmacists, nutritionists, physical and occupational therapists, speech and hearing specialists, and geriatric psychiatrists.[8] Mental health services are often particularly important for elderly patients, who commonly suffer from depression because of health problems, loneliness, bereavement, or a sense of lacking purpose.[9]

One of the most important benefits geriatricians can provide to their patients is coordination of overall care. The elderly often see a number of different specialists, including cardiologists, oncologists, rheumatologists, endocrinologists, and others, and these specialists may not communicate with each other.[10] According to a Dartmouth Atlas report, 43 percent

7. Timothy Bates, Aubri Kottek, and Joanne Spetz, "Geriatrician Roles and the Value of Geriatrics in an Evolving Healthcare System," UCSF Health Workforce Research Center on Long-Term Care, July 8, 2019; New York Chapter, American College of Physicians, "A Better Understanding of Geriatric Medicine," New York Chapter, American College of Physicians, August 2018, https://www.nyacp.org/files/A%20Better%20Understanding%20of%20 Geriatric%20Medicine%20-%20A%20White%20Paper.pdf.

8. HealthinAging.gov, "Geriatrics Basic Facts," HealthinAging.org, updated August 2017, https://www.healthinaging.org/a-z-topic/geriatrics/basic-facts; Hallie Levine, "When It's Time to See a Geriatrician," AARP, February 11, 2019, https://www.aarp.org/health/conditions-treatments/info-2019/geriatrics-specialist.html.

9. Lawrence Robinson, Melinda Smith, and Jeanne Segal, "Depression in Older Adults: Signs, Symptoms, Treatment," *HelpGuide*, updated September 2020, https://www.helpguide.org/articles/depression/depression-in-older-adults.htm.

10. Monika Kastner et al., "Effectiveness of Interventions for Managing Multiple High-Burden Chronic Diseases in Older Adults: A Systematic Review and Meta-Analysis," *CMAJ* 190, no. 34 (2018): E1004–E1012.

of fee-for-service Medicare beneficiaries see specialists instead of primary care physicians (also called internists) for the majority of their doctor visits.[11] Another study estimated that seniors see an average of four different specialists.[12] The elderly's medical care can thus be fragmented. Sometimes each specialist focuses only on complaints that fall within his or her area of expertise and provides aggressive treatment for those problems without looking at the patient's full health profile.

Patients who suffer from chronic pain may be particularly persistent in pursuing the care of specialists and experimenting with new drugs and treatments. A considerable segment of the elderly population is included among chronic pain patients—30.8 percent of seniors report chronic pain, and 11.8 percent state they have "high-impact chronic pain."[13]

Although responsible doctors generally ask patients what other medications they are taking, patients may provide incomplete accounts (especially those with memory impairments). Note that even if your memory is good, you should carry a list of your drugs in your wallet and update it each time one of your doctors changes a medication or dosage. Another concern is that specialists will check only for well-established drug interactions

11. Julie P. W. Bynum, Ellen Meara, Chiang-Hua Chang, and Jared M. Rhoads, "Our Parents Ourselves: Health Care for an Aging Population," The Dartmouth Institute for Health Policy and Clinical Practice, February 17, 2016, 57, https://www.dartmouthatlas.org/downloads/reports/Our_Parents_Ourselves_021716.pdf.

12. Barbara Starfield, Hsien-Yen Chang, Klaus W. Lemke, and Jonathan P. Weiner, "Ambulatory Specialist Use by Nonhospitalized Patients in US Health Plans: Correlates and Consequences," *Journal of Ambulatory Care Management* 32, no. 3 (2009): 216–25.

13. Carla E. Zelaya, James M. Dahlhamer, Jacqueline W. Lucas, and Eric M. Connor, "Chronic Pain and High-Impact Chronic Pain among U.S. Adults, 2019," NCHS Data Brief, No. 390, November 2020, https://www.cdc.gov/nchs/data/databriefs/db390-H.pdf.

involving pairs of drugs rather than combinations of three or more medications. Without a geriatric expert, there may be nobody who will assess whether you are taking too many drugs, whether a combination of your drugs is causing you harm, or whether your most pressing problems are being addressed.

Both my mother and mother-in-law visited geriatricians for comprehensive work-ups. Our families were impressed with the attention both received at their initial visits. The appointment began with a social worker who asked questions about their living situations, social support, and ability to perform activities of daily living and then conducted cognitive testing. The geriatric physicians then spent a full hour taking a thorough medical history, reviewing all available documentation, and paying special attention to all the medications they were taking. After ordering blood tests, follow-up appointments were scheduled for the next month.

Dr. Atul Gawande, a surgeon and journalist, writes the following about geriatric care:

> Most of us in medicine [...] don't know how to think about decline. We're good at addressing specific, individual problems: colon cancer, high blood pressure, arthritic knees. Give us a disease, and we can do something about it. But give us an elderly woman with colon cancer, high blood pressure, arthritic knees, and various other ailments besides—an elderly woman at risk of losing the life she enjoys—and we are not sure what to do.[14]

Dr. Gawande published an article in the *New Yorker* in which he described sitting in on one patient's appointment at his hospital's geriatrics clinic. To his surprise, the geriatrician paid particular

---

14. Atul Gawande, "The Way We Age Now," *New Yorker*, April 30, 2007, http://www.newyorker.com/magazine/2007/04/30/the-way-we-age-now.

attention to the patient's feet. A primary concern, the doctor explained, is an elderly person's risk of falling,[15] and the condition of a patient's feet is highly relevant (poor balance, taking more than four prescription drugs, and muscle weakness also increase the probability of falling). At the end of the visit, the doctor formulated two key recommendations: the woman was to obtain regular care from a podiatrist and to increase her calorie intake.[16]

Gawande notes that geriatricians do not perform "high-tech medicine." Instead, they simplify medications and try to ensure that arthritis is controlled, feet are in acceptable shape, and nutritious meals are eaten. They also investigate whether the patient is socially isolated or living in a home that is unsafe. Gawande reports that research findings indicate that patients under the care of a geriatrics team are significantly less likely than other elderly people to become disabled or depressed or to require home health services.[17]

The shortage of geriatricians

Unfortunately, the United States faces a grave shortage of geriatricians, and thus you may not be able to find a geriatrician for your relatives or yourself when you need one.[18] There are currently only 6,952 board-certified geriatricians nationwide,

---

15. Approximately 30 percent of seniors fall each year, and, as a result, often suffer serious injuries, mobility impairments, diminished independence, and even death. Curtis S. Florence, Gwen Bergen, Adam Atherly, Elizabeth Burns, Judy Stevens, and Cynthia Drake, "Medical Costs of Fatal and Nonfatal Falls in Older Adults," *Journal of the American Geriatrics Society* 66, no. 4 (2018): 693–98; Elizabeth Burns and Ramakrishna Kakara, "Deaths from Falls among Persons Aged ≥65 Years—United States, 2007–2016," *Morbidity and Mortality Weekly Report* 67, no. 18 (2018): 509–14.

16. Gawande, "The Way We Age Now."

17. Gawande, "The Way We Age Now."

18. Paula Span, "Older People Need Geriatricians. Where Will They Come From?" *New York Times*, January 3, 2020, https://www.nytimes.com/2020/01/03/health/geriatricians-shortage.html.

of which only 3,590 practice geriatrics full time.[19] The supply is unlikely to increase any time soon because medical students rarely choose to specialize in the field. In 2019 only 213 of 415 available geriatric fellowship positions were filled, and over the prior five years, only 44–50 percent of geriatric fellowships were filled.[20] The shortage extends to geriatric medical specialties as well. For example, geriatric psychiatrists are difficult to locate because there are only 1,523 board-certified geriatric psychiatrists practising in the United States (2.6 for every 100,000 seniors).[21] Likewise, experts estimate that in the entire country there are only 250–300 dentists with special training in geriatric dentistry.[22] The shortage of geriatricians is particularly acute in rural areas.[23]

19. Geriatrics Healthcare Professionals, "Geriatrics Workforce by the Numbers," Geriatrics Healthcare Professionals, accessed December 24, 2020, https://www.americangeriatrics.org/geriatrics-profession/about-geriatrics/geriatrics-workforce-numbers.

20. Bates, Kottek, and Spetz, "Geriatrician Roles," 7.

21. American Board of Medical Specialties, "ABMS Board Certification Report 2019–2020," American Board of Medical Specialties, accessed December 24, 2020, 54, https://www.abms.org/wp-content/uploads/2020/11/ABMS-Board-Certification-Report-2019-2020.pdf; Angela J. Beck, Cory Page, Jessica Buche, Danielle Rittman, and Maria Gaiser, "Estimating the Distribution of the US Psychiatric Subspecialist Workforce," University of Michigan Behavioral Health Workforce Research Center, December 2018, www.behavioralhealthworkforce.org/wp-content/uploads/2019/02/Y3-FA2-P2-Psych-Sub_Full-Report-FINAL2.19.2019.pdf ("The AMA Masterfile showed 1,265 geriatric psychiatrists active in the United States, with New York having the most GPs (218) and two states having none—Mississippi and North Dakota.").

22. Ronald L. Ettinger, Zachary S. Goettsche, and Fang Qian, "Postdoctoral Teaching of Geriatric Dentistry in US Dental Schools," *Journal of Dental Education* 81, no. 10 (2017): 1220–26; Leonardo Marchini et al, "Geriatric Dentistry Education and Context in a Selection of Countries in 5 Continents," *Special Care in Dentistry* 38, no. 3 (May/June 2018): 123–32 ("In this new study, 57.1% [of U.S. dental schools] had some form of compulsory clinical education in geriatric dentistry.").

23. Lars E. Peterson, Andrew Bazemore, Elizabeth J. Bragg, Imam Xierali, and Gregg A. Warshaw, "Rural-Urban Distribution of the U.S.

When my parents, in their mid-80s, finally sought the care of a geriatrician in East Lansing, Michigan, they learned that there was only one geriatric medicine practice in the area. Those clinicians were so overwhelmed that they declined to accept new patients. Instead, my mother turned to a geriatrics practice in Ann Arbor, which was more than an hour away.

And matters are likely to get worse as baby boomers age. Some commentators predict that by 2025 the nation will have 27,000 fewer geriatricians than it needs.[24]

What explains the alarming shortage of geriatricians? A significant barrier to entry into the field of geriatrics is a comparatively low earning potential, which likely concerns medical students who are encumbered by significant educational debt. Geriatricians are reimbursed largely by Medicare. In mid-2019, the average salary of geriatricians was $202,050 (with a range of $185,840–$220,750), while specialists earned $346,000 on average.[25] In addition, medical students may consider geriatrics to be a more challenging and less satisfying field than others. Elderly patients generally have multiple, complex, chronic conditions. Their geriatricians

Geriatrics Physician Workforce," *Journal of the American Geriatrics Society* 59, no. 4 (2011): 699–703; Annette Hintenach, Oren Raphael, and William W. Hung, "Training Programs on Geriatrics in Rural Areas: A Review," *Current Geriatrics Reports* 8, no. 2 (2019): 117–22.

24. Ellen Flaherty and Stephen J. Bartels. "Addressing the CommunityBased Geriatric Healthcare Workforce Shortage by Leveraging the Potential of Interprofessional Teams," *Journal of the American Geriatrics Society* 67, no. S2 (2019): S400–S408; Geriatrics Healthcare Professionals, "Geriatrics Workforce by the Numbers."

25. Salary.com, "Geriatric Medicine Specialist Salary in the United States," Salary.com, accessed December 24, 2020, https://www.salary.com/research/salary/alternate/geriatric-medicine-specialist-salary; Leslie Kane, "Medscape Physician Compensation Report 2020," *Medscape*, May 14, 2020, https://www.medscape.com/slideshow/2019-compensation-overview-6011286#2.

work long hours managing health problems and trying to alleviate symptoms but often cannot cure their patients' chronic illnesses.[26]

PLANNING FOR MEDICAL CARE IN OLD AGE

As noted above, geriatricians treat only elderly individuals, and thus, even the most dedicated planners for old age cannot obtain care from a geriatric specialist earlier in life. Nevertheless, forming good habits regarding medical care in middle age is essential to good health later in life.

Finding a doctor

Those of us who have experienced significant health problems at a relatively young age are often particularly careful about checkups and preventive care. Nevertheless, by age 50, everyone should be diligent about following medical guidelines regarding checkups and preventive care. To this end, if you are middle-aged, you should have a primary care physician who is familiar with your medical history and can coordinate your care if you develop multiple medical ailments. If you have a good primary care physician who knows you well, you likely will not need to switch to a geriatrician in older age. As noted by several experts "the importance of a primary care physician in the care of all conditions, except those that are highly complex or rare, is increasingly recognized."[27]

---

26. Maria Castellucci, "Geriatrics Still Failing to Attract New Doctors," *Modern Healthcare*, February 27, 2018, https://www.modernhealthcare.com/article/20180227/NEWS/180229926/geriatrics-still-failing-to-attract-new-doctors.

27. Barbara Starfield, Klaus W. Lemke, Robert Herbert, Wendy D. Pavlovich, and Gerard Anderson, "Comorbidity and the Use of Primary Care and Specialist Care in the Elderly," *Annals of Family Medicine* 3, no. 3 (2005): 220; David M. Levine, Bruce E. Landon, and Jeffrey A. Linder, "Quality and

Unfortunately, even finding a primary care physician who accepts new patients and who is available and attentive may be easier said than done. Our country is experiencing not only a shortage of geriatricians but also a significant dearth of internists. Experts predict a shortfall of between 21,100 and 55,200 primary care physicians by 2032.[28] This deficit is expected in part because of the large discrepancy[29] between the salaries of internists and those of other specialists.[30] Furthermore, the rate of primary care physician retirements is outpacing the rate of entry into the profession. In the coming years, approximately 8,500 primary care physicians will likely retire each year, while only 8,000 new primary care physicians will join the profession annually.[31]

Thus, identifying and selecting a good internist can be difficult work in and of itself. Friends and acquaintances are

---

Experience of Outpatient Care in the United States for Adults with or without Primary Care," *JAMA Internal Medicine* 179, no. 3 (2019): 363–72.

28. IHS Markit Ltd., "The Complexities of Physician Supply and Demand Projections from 2017 to 2032," Association of American Medical Colleges, April 2019, 6, https://aamc-black.global.ssl.fastly.net/production/media/filer_public/31/13/3113ee5c-a038-4c16-89af-294a69826650/2019_update_-_the_complexities_of_physician_supply_and_demand_-_projections_from_2017-2032.pdf.

29. According to Medscape, in 2020, the average salary of primary care physicians was $243,000 compared to an average salary of $346,000 for specialists. Leslie Kane, "Medscape Physician Compensation Report 2020," *Medscape*, May 14, 2020, https://www.medscape.com/slideshow/2020-compensation-overview-6012684#4.

30. Victoria Knight, "America to Face a Shortage of Primary Care Physicians within a Decade or So," *Washington Post*, July 15, 2019, https://www.washingtonpost.com/health/america-to-face-a-shortage-of-primary-care-physicians-within-a-decade-or-so/2019/07/12/0cf144d0-a27d-11e9-bd56-eac6bb02d01d_story.html.

31. Flaherty and Bartels, "Addressing Community-Based Geriatric Healthcare."

often a trustworthy source of information, so you should not hesitate to ask for recommendations. Patient reviews on the Internet are a more dubious source. Frequently there are only a handful of comments, so they are not necessarily representative of most patients' experiences. Moreover, there is no way to verify that those who post comments anonymously are actually the doctors' patients rather than family members, friends, competitors, or others with a personal agenda.

You may want to find a practice that employs nurse practitioners or physician assistants because such practices may provide more accessibility and responsiveness to patients. Although the number of primary care physicians is declining, the number of nurse practitioners and physician assistants is growing significantly.[32] Nurse practitioners and physician assistants are highly trained professionals and sometimes receive special instruction in geriatric matters.[33] Because they are paid lower salaries and bill at lower rates than doctors, they are often the ones who spend extensive time interacting with patients while the doctor moves quickly from one exam room to another. Patients may find that nurse practitioners and physician assistants take time to answer questions thoroughly either in person or by phone and to provide reassuring explanations. Thus, access to these health-care professionals may significantly enhance patients' medical experiences.

Many seniors will never see a geriatrician either because they cannot find one or because they are satisfied with the treatment they receive from their primary care physicians. Those suffering discomfort from multiple and complex conditions, however, should make a special effort to obtain regular care from a

---

32. Flaherty and Bartels, "Addressing Community-Based Geriatric Healthcare."

33. Gawande, "The Way We Age Now"; Erin Sarzynski, and Henry Barry, "Current Evidence and Controversies: Advanced Practice Providers in Healthcare," *American Journal of Managed Care* 25, no. 8 (2019): 367.

geriatric expert, or, at the very least, to visit a geriatrician for a one-time thorough exam and evaluation. Such a consultation can enable elderly people (or relatives who accompany them) to determine whether they are receiving appropriate care from their primary care physicians or whether they need to switch doctors or see specialists.

Concierge medicine and direct primary care

Concierge medicine (also known as "boutique medicine" or "retainer-based medicine") is an option for individuals who are financially comfortable. Under this model, primary care physicians charge annual out-of-pocket fees and can thus afford to see fewer patients so that they can dedicate more time to them. The fees reportedly average $183 per month.[34] In return, concierge doctors promise patients same-day or next-day care, thorough preventive medical services, and 24-hour-a-day access through cell phones and e-mail so that they can be contacted anytime from anywhere in the country or the world.[35]

---

34. Laura Daily, Before You Pay Extra to Join a Concierge Medical Practice, Consider These Questions," *Washington Post*, October 22, 2019, https://www.washingtonpost.com/lifestyle/home/before-you-pay-extra-to-join-a-concierge-medical-practice-consider-these-questions/2019/10/21/90d8206a-ef8b-11e9-b648-76bcf86eb67e_story.html (stating that the average annual fee is between $1,500 and $2,400); Jeff Lagasse, "Concierge Medicine Being Embraced by a Growing Number of Primary Care Physicians," *Healthcare Finance News*, June 12, 2018, https://www.healthcarefinancenews.com/news/concierge-medicine-being-embraced-growing-number-primary-care-physicians ("The average annual fee is $2,000—equivalent to most people's cable bill.").

35. Hallie Levine, "What to Know about Concierge Medicine," AARP, April 25, 2019, https://www.aarp.org/health/conditions-treatments/info-2019/what-to-know-about-concierge-medicine.html.

Concierge doctors have adopted a variety of charge structures. Some physicians charge only a monthly fee, while others require both a monthly fee and payment for individual office visits. Some bill insurance companies; some prefer to avoid the administrative burdens of billing insurers; and still others continue to run regular primary care practices, setting aside a few hours a day for their concierge patients.[36]

It is difficult to know how many concierge doctors there are in the United States because there is no formal registry. Estimates range from 5,000 to over 20,000.[37]

A less common but more affordable option is a direct primary care (DPC) physician. DPC doctors charge lower monthly fees, often under $100 (sometimes with discounts for additional family members). They do not bill insurers and thereby save considerable administrative and staffing costs.[38] However, currently there are only about 1,200 DPC offices located in 48 states.[39]

---

36. Nissa Simon, "Is a 'Boutique' Doctor for You? Here's What You Need to Know Before Signing Up With A 'Concierge' Practice," AARP, January 7, 2013, http://www.aarp.org/health/healthy-living/info-01-2013/boutique-doctors.html; Levine, "What to Know about Concierge Medicine."

37. Concierge Medicine Today, "25+ Concierge Medicine Industry Statistics, Graphics and Trends, 2021," *Concierge Medicine Today*, accessed December 24, 2020, https://conciergemedicinetoday.org/25-concierge-medicine-industry-statistics-graphics-and-trends-2021/; Neil Freedman, "Is It Time for Pulmonary Concierge Practices? Yes," *Chest* 151, no. 2 (2017): 255–57 (estimating that there were 12,000 concierge practices in 2014).

38. Seka Palikuca, "5 Things to Know about Direct Primary Care," *The DO*, March 13, 2019, https://thedo.osteopathic.org/2019/03/5-things-to-know-about-direct-primary-care/.

39. Christine Lehmann, "More Patients Turning to 'Direct Primary Care'," *WebMD Health News*, February 6, 2020, https://www.webmd.com/health-insurance/news/20200206/more-patients-turning-to-direct-primary-care.

Both Concierge and DPC practices have far fewer patients than their primary care physician counterparts. They accept 600–800 patients rather than the 2,000–2,500 that family physicians typically treat.[40] Consequently, they can devote 30–60 minutes to each patient appointment and see 8 patients a day rather than 24 or more.[41] Concierge and DPC doctors can provide patients with far more accessibility, attentiveness, and time than ordinary primary care physicians with much busier practices. Many patients find this to be well worth the cost. It is important to understand, however, that if you have a DPC or concierge doctor, you still need health insurance to cover other medical costs, such as visiting specialists and hospitalizations.

Being a member of your own medical team

On October 15, 2013, we learned that my husband, then aged 55, has Parkinson's disease. He had had a tremor for many months, and when it grew more persistent and was accompanied by stiffness and other discomforts, Andy decided it was time to see a neurologist. We had been anxious for days before the appointment. Hours of Internet searches encouraged us to cling to the hope that the tremor was benign, as many are. But we also knew that we could get life-changing news from the doctor.

The neurologist did a very thorough examination. Then, without indicating that he was ready to deliver his decree,

---

40. American Academy of Family Physicians, "Direct Primary Care: An Alternative Practice Model to the Fee-For-Service Framework," American Academy of Family Physicians, accessed December 24, 2020, https://www.aafp.org/dam/AAFP/documents/practice_management/payment/DirectPrimaryCare.pdf; Freedman, "Is It Time for Pulmonary Concierge Practices?"

41. James E. Dalen, "Concierge Medicine Is Here and Growing!!," *American Journal of Medicine* 130, no. 8 (2017): 880–81; Levine, "What to Know about Concierge Medicine."

he blurted out, "Well, this is clearly Parkinson's disease." He explained that it was an incurable, degenerative, neurologic disease caused by loss of dopamine cells in the brain and that it usually progresses over decades. The doctor discussed a variety of drugs and recommended one for Andy to try first, assuring us that "most patients tolerate this one well." He instructed us to make another appointment in three months and left the exam room to see his next patient.

What followed were some of the most difficult days of our marriage. Life had changed in an instant. We were consumed by fear that our future was bleak and uncertain, that our place in the world had permanently shifted, that our sense of ourselves would never be the same. And our next medical appointment was not for three months.

Although our friends were incredibly patient, affectionate, and encouraging, we were left on our own to construct professional support systems. In the turmoil of the days and weeks after the diagnosis, what Andy needed was someone to call frequently to discuss his symptoms, his reaction to the new medication, his mood. He very much would have appreciated having access to a nurse practitioner or a physician assistant who could spend time providing reassurance that this disease could be managed and that life could go on. Waiting for several months for our next contact with a medical professional was not a viable option.

I don't think Andy's doctor was atypical or that he deviated from standard protocol. But patients receiving life-changing diagnoses need much more intensive attention, and they need to benefit from a team approach. In 1994, when my mother became a breast cancer patient at MD Anderson Cancer Center in Houston, a social worker literally ran after us as we left one of the first doctors' appointments to make sure that we learned about a variety of resources that the cancer center offered to promote patients' mental and emotional well-being. How I wish that all medical centers adopted similar practices!

According to experts, up to 60 percent of Parkinson's disease patients experience depression. Overlooking these symptoms can have devastating consequences for them. We took initiative, sought a second opinion regarding the diagnosis, and consulted several mental health professionals. But we had to figure out on our own that all this should be done.

Perhaps the most important part of planning for proper medical care in old age is to learn to become an active participant in your own medical care. Doctors have approximately 15 minutes to spend with each patient during a typical office visit.[42] The patient, therefore, needs to feel empowered to guide the physician and to be a key member of his or her medical team.

This principle applies not only to what happens after a serious diagnosis but also to the doctor's visit itself. When a doctor prescribes a medication or recommends a treatment course, the patient should ask questions. For example:

- How will this drug interact with others that I'm taking?
- I'm already on several other daily medications, is it really necessary to add another?
- You are recommending aggressive intervention (e.g., surgery), but are there other options that I should consider first?
- What should I expect during my recovery period?

When accompanying relatives to medical appointments, I have found the following cliché but pointed question to be

---

42. Andy Lazris, Alan Roth, and Shannon Brownlee, "No More Lip Service; It's Time We Fixed Primary Care (Part One)," *Health Affairs Blog*, November 20, 2018, https://www.healthaffairs.org/do/10.1377/hblog20181115.750150/full/; Colorado Health Institute, "Direct Primary Care: A New Way to Deliver Health Care," Colorado Health Institute, updated June 30, 2018, https://www.coloradohealthinstitute.org/research/direct-primary-care-new-way-deliver-health-care.

particularly effective: If this were your mother or sister, which alternative would you select for her?

In the book *When Doctors Don't Listen*, Leana Wen and Joshua Kosowsky develop a set of recommendations to help patients avoid misdiagnosis and unnecessary tests. Their "8 Pillars to Better Diagnosis" are the following:

1. Tell your whole story.
2. Assert yourself in the doctor's thought process.
3. Participate in your physical exam.
4. Make the differential diagnosis together.
5. Partner for the decision-making process.
6. Apply tests rationally.
7. Use common sense to confirm the working diagnosis.
8. Integrate diagnosis into the healing process.[43]

Central to their book is the assertion that the patient must transform "from being a passive participant who answers yes or no, and submits to tests to being an active storyteller and equal partner in the diagnostic process."[44]

Other commentators refer to an approach of "shared decision making." They urge clinicians to employ decision aids in written, audiovisual, or web-based form to educate patients and families about treatment options, outcomes, risks, and costs.[45] Such educational efforts may improve care, better align treatment with patient preferences, and even reduce

---

43. Leana Wen and Joshua Kosowsky, *When Doctors Don't Listen: How to Avoid Misdiagnoses and Unnecessary Tests* (New York: St. Martin's Press, 2012): 196–98.

44. Wen and Kosowsky, *When Doctors Don't Listen*, 275.

45. Emily Oshima Lee and Ezekiel J. Emanuel, "Shared Decision Making to Improve Care and Reduce Costs," *New England Journal of Medicine* 368, no. 1 (2013): 6–8; Advanced Care Planning Decisions, "4 Best Practices for Effective Shared Decision Making," Acpdecisions.org, May 26, 2018, https://acpdecisions.org/4-best-practices-for-effective-shared-decision-making/.

costs. Studies have shown that patients participating in shared decision-making more frequently select less aggressive, more conservative care options, though it is not clear that these choices consistently lead to better outcomes.[46]

Patients' reluctance to ask their doctors questions has been labeled "white coat silence," and experts have blamed both patients and physicians for this phenomenon. However, you should fight the inclination to be silent, and don't be intimidated. Write down your questions for your doctor, and do not hesitate to come to your appointment with a list of multiple queries. Do not rely on your memory. Do not feel embarrassed or hesitant to ask all of your questions and press the doctor for thorough answers.

Early in Andy's Parkinson's disease treatment, a doctor suggested that he add a new drug and spoke enthusiastically about it. I noticed, however, that he did not mention any side effects. I asked the doctor about potential side effects, and he responded, "Don't worry, most people tolerate this drug very well." As a trained lawyer, however, I listened carefully and focused on the word "most." I persisted and asked, "How many people have problems with this drug, and what happens to them?" Finally, the doctor disclosed that about 20 percent of patients find that the drug clouds their minds and causes some confusion. In light of our experience with Eema and because Andy was still working as a computer science professor, we declined to try the drug. But we would not have known to do so if I hadn't insisted that the doctor answer my questions.

The Internet is also an invaluable resource for medical information. Baby boomers are largely comfortable with navigating the Internet, and there is nothing wrong with conducting background research before going to the doctor.

---

46. Lee and Emanuel, "Shared Decision Making," 6–8; Wolters Kluwer, "Shared Decision Making: Informed Patients Make Safer, More Cost-Effective Choices," *Wolters Kluwer*, July 9, 2018, https://www.wolterskluwercdi.com/blog/shared-decision-making/.

Although not all websites are reliable, many are operated by very reputable entities, such as the National Institutes of Health, the Centers for Disease Control and Prevention, the American Medical Association, and various prestigious professional organizations. When my mother suffered from her mysterious and precipitous cognitive deterioration, we learned a great deal about possible causes and remedies through simple Google searches. Years earlier, I was able to self-diagnose a thyroid problem based on several common symptoms. I made an appointment with my internist and asked him to test for a thyroid disorder before trying to explore other possibilities.

Of course, Internet searches should not replace consultation with medical experts, and you should recognize their pitfalls. You should not panic based on what you have learned from the Internet and torment yourself with thoughts of disability and death before you have even been examined by a physician. You should not go to the doctor with a closed mind, convinced that you know exactly what your malady is and what treatment you require. However, research can equip you to discuss your symptoms more intelligently, ask the right questions, and have more productive and satisfying visits with your health-care providers.

If you receive a serious diagnosis, reading relevant literature and communicating with similar patients through social media, support groups, or other means can be very helpful. Ask your doctor to recommend reliable websites, books, support groups, and additional resources. The best advice often comes from fellow patients who have coped with the illness and navigated through treatment longer than you have, and thus, finding ways to connect with them is well worth the effort.

Involving trusted advocates and obtaining adequate support

Patients who are too ill or mentally impaired to participate fully in their own medical decision-making will need to have an advocate. As indicated in Chapter 4, this arrangement should be formalized through a power of attorney document that will authorize a proxy to make medical decisions if you become incompetent.

However, regardless of mental status, at least one close friend or relative should be involved whenever a patient of any age is having surgery or suffering from a serious illness. If no friend or relative is available, you can turn to a geriatric care manager whose job it is to be a patient advocate and care coordinator (see Chapter 3).[47] No matter how strong your mind is, you might be nervous, anxious, or feeling unwell during your doctor's appointments. Therefore, having a companion and a second pair of ears is important.

My rules of thumb for my own medical care and that of family members are the following:

1. Don't be shy about sharing health problems with loved ones and asking for reasonable assistance.
2. Don't go to any important medical appointment or to the hospital alone.

It is vital to have another individual in the room to hear the doctor's explanations, take notes, formulate appropriate questions, and help you review what happened during the medical encounter. In the hospital, it is also important to have someone who can find the nurses when they do not respond to the call button quickly, urge nurses to page the doctor in order to ask for further measures to relieve discomfort, and pose appropriate questions about treatment and prognosis whenever a doctor pops in briefly.

---

47. Carol Bradley Bursack, "Geriatric Care Managers Can Help Busy Caregivers," AgingCare, updated April 22, 2020, https://www.agingcare.com/articles/geriatric-care-managers-help-for-elders-needs-138976.htm.

Be aware that the HIPAA Privacy Rule prohibits health-care providers from discussing any details about you with third parties without your authorization. Therefore, even in the hospital, health-care providers should not speak with your family members and friends about your condition unless you explicitly permit them to do so. If you are not able to make your own decisions, clinicians should speak only to your legally named health-care agent (as discussed in Chapter 4), unless you have provided "HIPAA authorization" for others to receive health information about you.[48] To that end, you should ask your doctors for a HIPAA authorization form that names the individuals with whom they can discuss your medical condition. You should make sure that all of your physicians have a copy of your completed form and that you provide a copy to any hospital to which you are admitted.

You may feel uncomfortable asking others for favors and feel that you are a burden to them. However, people are most often glad to help, especially in the face of medical challenges. And they will know that they can turn to you when they are the ones that need support. As I learned from my experience of caring for my mother through breast cancer just five months after she rushed to my side for my surgery,[49] there are plenty of opportunities in life to reciprocate.

---

48. US Department of Health & Human Services, "Under HIPAA, When Can a Family Member of an Individual Access the Individual's PHI from a Health Care Provider or Health Plan?" HHS.gov, last reviewed January 31, 2020, https://www.hhs.gov/hipaa/for-professionals/faq/2069/under-hipaa-when-can-a-family-member/index.html; Office for Civil Rights, "Sharing Health Information with Family Members and Friends," Office for Civil Rights, accessed December 24, 2020, https://www.hhs.gov/sites/default/files/ocr/privacy/hipaa/understanding/consumers/sharing-family-friends.pdf.

49. See introduction to this book.

Undergoing major medical procedures can be particularly challenging for individuals without relatives or friends who can meet their care needs. Short-term paid help from home care agencies is often the answer in such circumstances. Although the cost of $23.50 per hour[50] may be unaffordable in the long run, having an attentive aide when you are incapacitated for a few days may well be worth the investment. On average, home care agencies require that their aides be hired for a minimum of four hours, though some have no hourly minimum.[51] You can usually request service on short notice. Aides can accompany clients to outpatient procedures, stay with recuperating patients at home for a few days after surgery, or even sit with you in a hospital room if your discomfort, anxiety, or other needs are not fully addressed by overtaxed nurses on a busy hospital floor. The option of acquiring temporary paid help through an agency is one that I keep on my radar for myself and that I find particularly reassuring.

Those who learn to be active members of their own care team earlier in life will be well served as they age. Forming the habits of doing background research, asking educated questions, involving trusted advocates, obtaining adequate support through paid help, and being assertive when you have clear and reasonable care preferences is vital to old-age preparedness.

---

50. Genworth, "Cost of Care Survey 2020," Genworth, December 2, 2020, https://www.genworth.com/aging-and-you/finances/cost-of-care.html; Richard W. Johnson and Claire Xiaozhi Wang, "The Financial Burden of Paid Home Care on Older Adults: Oldest and Sickest Are Least Likely to Have Enough Income," *Health Affairs* 38, no. 6 (2019): 994–1002.

51. Paula Span, "Help by the Hour, or Less," *New York Times*, November 23, 2012, http://newoldage.blogs.nytimes.com/2012/11/23/1123-help-by-the-hour/?_r=0; AARP, "How to Hire a Caregiver," AARP, updated November 7, 2019, https://www.aarp.org/caregiving/home-care/info-2018/hiring-caregiver.html.

COORDINATED CARE PREPAREDNESS CHECKLIST

* Find a primary care physician whom you trust and with whom you are comfortable, and get regular checkups starting in middle age.
* Carry a list of your drugs in your wallet and update it each time there is a change in your medications or dosages
* If you are a senior with complex medical problems or a caregiver for such an individual, consult a geriatrician if one is available in your area.
* If you are not satisfied with the care you or a loved one is receiving, consider a concierge or direct primary care doctor if these options are available and affordable for you.
* Learn to be an active member of your own medical team.
  o Before visiting the doctor, do your research (but don't panic about anything you read on the Internet);
  o Prepare questions before your appointment, and during your visit with the doctor, don't be afraid to ask questions regarding your symptoms, diagnosis, and the prescribed treatment;
  o If you receive a serious diagnosis, seek a second opinion and consult mental health professionals even if your doctor does not suggest doing so.
* When you have acute medical problems, obtain adequate support. Have someone accompany you to medical appointments and to the hospital. Hire help during your recovery period if family members or friends are unavailable and you can afford it.

CHAPTER 7

LONG-TERM CARE

As much as we all wish to avoid it, many of us will need professional long-term care at some point in our lives. Those of us with aging parents are likely to face a decision about obtaining long-term care for them in the last years of their lives, and we may well need the same for ourselves in the future.

Experts expect that almost half of the people who are currently 65 or older will require paid long-term care.[1] Spending on such care in the United States exceeds $400 billion annually, including over $61 billion that is paid out of pocket.[2] Among those needing paid assistance, approximately half will require it for less than a year, but slightly over 10 percent will use it for five years or more. The average lifetime cost of long-term care is estimated to be $172,000 per person (in 2016 dollars).[3] In some instances, certain long-term care costs are tax deductible,

---

1. Christine Benz, "100 Must-Know Statistics about Long-Term Care: Pandemic Edition," *Morningstar*, December 8, 2020, https://www.morningstar.com/articles/1013929/100-must-know-statistics-about-long-term-care-pandemic-edition.

2. FEDweek, "Report Details How Long-Term Care Expenses Are Paid," FEDweek, May 27, 2020, https://www.fedweek.com/retirement-financial-planning/report-details-how-long-term-care-expenses-are-paid/.

3. William E. Gibson, "Long-Term Care Costs May Double to $5.6 Trillion by 2047," AARP, March 19, 2018, https://www.aarp.org/health/health-insurance/info-2018/costs-long-term-care-fd.html.

so it is worth consulting an accountant if you have significant care expenses.[4]

Many older adults receive at least some of the care they need from informal caregivers, most often, family members. A 2019 US Bureau of Labor Statistics report indicated that, on average, 40.4 million Americans provided unpaid eldercare during 2017 and 2018.[5] The economic value of the care provided to adults with functional limitations (not just seniors) was estimated to be $470 billion in 2017.[6]

Even those with strong support systems and dedicated and knowledgeable informal caregivers can face significant challenges as their frailties and needs become more acute. Beth Ann Swan, a nursing school dean, described the obstacles she and her husband faced after his stroke in an article published in *Health Affairs*.[7] "How can we expect not-yet-well people to suddenly begin managing all of the complex medical and personal issues that just the day before were being handled by an entire team of trained professionals?" she asks as she describes her husband's transition from a rehabilitation hospital to home. For those with no family members to help, the situation can be all the more difficult.

4. SeniorLiving.org, "Health Care Tax Deductions," SeniorLiving.org, updated February 27, 2019, https://www.seniorliving.org/finance/tax-deductions/.

5. US Bureau of Labor, "Unpaid Eldercare in the United States—2017–2018 Summary," US Bureau of Labor Statistics, November 22, 2019, https://www.bls.gov/news.release/elcare.nr0.htm.

6. Susan Reinhard, Lynn Friss Feinberg, Ari Houser, Rita Choula, and Molly Evans, "Valuing the Invaluable 2019 Update: Charting a Path Forward," AARP Public Policy Institute, November 14, 2019, https://www.aarp.org/ppi/info-2015/valuing-the-invaluable-2015-update.html?cmp=RDRCT-VALUN_JUN23_015.

7. Beth Ann Swan, "A Nurse Learns Firsthand That You May Fend for Yourself after a Hospital Stay," *Health Affairs* 31, no. 11 (2012): 2579–82.

What options are available to older adults who can no longer manage to live independently with or without help from unpaid caregivers such as spouses and children? The choices come down to nursing homes, assisted living, and paid home care obtained through agencies or by independently hiring caregivers.

NURSING HOMES

Nursing homes can provide two types of care. Many nursing homes provide skilled nursing care by licensed health professionals to patients needing rehabilitation after an injury, illness, or surgery. Such residents often stay at the facility for a limited period of time and then return to their homes, though severely disabled patients may need long-term skilled nursing care.[8] Skilled nursing facilities provide treatments such as wound care, physical and occupational therapy, or tube feeding if you cannot eat.

Others move to a nursing home late in life because it is the only safe option for them. Nursing homes can serve as permanent homes for individuals who need nonmedical assistance with activities of daily living (e.g., bathing and dressing).[9] Permanent nursing home residents are among the most frail seniors. Most commonly, they are there because they have severe dementia, incontinence, behavioral problems, no family, or a combination of these problems.[10]

---

8. Marlo Sollitto, "What's the Difference between Skilled Nursing Care and a Nursing Home?" AgingCare, accessed December 26, 2020, https://www.agingcare.com/articles/difference-skilled-nursing-and-nursing-home-153035.htm.

9. Scott Witt and Jeff Hoyt, "Nursing Home vs Skilled Nursing," SeniorLiving.org, updated June 24, 2020, https://www.seniorliving.org/compare/nursing-home-vs-skilled-nursing/.

10. Paula Span, *When the Time Comes: Families with Aging Parents Share Their Struggles and Solutions* (New York: Springboard Press, 2009), 161.

Sadly, many of my visits with elderly relatives who were receiving either skilled medical or nonmedical care in nursing homes have been discouraging. A number of the facilities I have seen over the years seemed understaffed, and the residents complained that they did not receive prompt attention when they needed to use the bathroom, to obtain medication for pain relief, or to be transported to another area of the nursing home. In one case, staff members placed residents with dementia in wheelchairs around the nursing station for hours at a time so that they did not have to walk to different rooms to check on them. My relatives and acquaintances complained that they were bathed only twice a week and that it happens in the middle of the night because night shift staff members are less busy than day shift personnel. To the extent that activities were offered, many were not intellectually stimulating and seemed more appropriate for small children than for adults. Residents who had their full mental faculties had few opportunities for social interaction because so many of the other residents had dementia or were otherwise unable or unwilling to form new friendships.

My mother-in-law, Helen, complained bitterly about the lack of social opportunities during a two-month stay in a nursing home in which she received physical therapy after a fall. One day, after learning how to maneuver on her own in a wheelchair, Helen wheeled herself into a common room and was glad to see a fellow resident sitting on a sofa. The woman motioned to Helen to come close and then grabbed Helen's hand and put it to her own face, clearly craving another human being's touch. When Helen asked for the woman's name, she was able to say "Mary" but was not able to converse any further. Helen saw Mary the next day and said hello, but the woman stared at her blankly without any recognition.

Yet, nursing home stays are sometimes a necessary and welcome step to recovery from a medical crisis. A large percentage of us will have at least a short sojourn in a nursing home. Experts estimated in 2017 that people aged 57–61 at the time had a 56 percent chance of spending at least one night in a nursing home during their lifetimes.[11]

According to the American Association for long-term care insurance, among nursing home residents, the average lengths of stay are as follows:

- five years or more—12 percent
- three to five years—12 percent
- one to three years—30.3 percent
- six months to 1 year—14.2 percent
- three to six months—10 percent
- less than three months—20 percent.[12]

However, a large government study concluded that among *all* seniors, only 15 percent received 90 days or more of nursing home care by age 85.[13] The report provides additional details:

Women are more likely to receive at least 90 days of nursing home care than men, and people who were single before they developed [long-term care] […] needs are more likely to receive

11. Michael D. Hurd, Pierre-Carl Michaud, and Susan Rohwedder, "Distribution of Lifetime Nursing Home Use and Out-of-Pocket Spending," *Proceedings of the National Academy of Sciences of the United States of America*, August 28, 2017, https://www.rand.org/news/press/2017/08/28/index1.html.

12. American Association for Long-Term Care Insurance, "What Is the Probability You'll Need Long-Term Care? Is Long-Term Care Insurance A Smart Financial Move?" American Association for Long-Term Care Insurance, accessed December 26, 2020, http://www.aaltci.org/long-term-care-insurance/learning-center/probability-long-term-care.php.

13. Richard W. Johnson, "What Is the Lifetime Risk of Needing and Receiving Long-Term Services and Support?" Department of Health and Human Services, Assistant Secretary for Planning and Evaluation, Research Brief, April 2019, 7, https://aspe.hhs.gov/system/files/pdf/261036/LifetimeRisk.pdf.

nursing home care than people who were married. People with less income and wealth before they became disabled are more likely to spend more than two years in a nursing home than people with more income and wealth, and they tend to enter nursing homes earlier.

Quality of care

Unfortunately, research confirms that the quality of many nursing homes leaves much to be desired. A 2019 study found that staffing levels in nursing homes were highly variable and were "often below the expectations of the Centers for Medicare and Medicaid Services."[14]

According to the Kaiser Family Foundation, on average, US nursing homes had 10 deficiencies in 2020.[15] Deficiencies are problems that "can result in a negative impact on the health and safety of residents." The five most common deficiencies in 2016 were categorized as follows:

1. poor infection control (found in 45.4 percent of certified nursing facilities);
2. inadequate food sanitation (in 42.6 percent);
3. accident hazards (found in 39.8 percent);
4. poor quality of care (in 34.3 percent); and
5. pharmacy consultation problems (26.8 percent).[16]

---

14. Fangli Geng, David G. Stevenson, and David C. Grabowski, "Daily Nursing Home Staffing Levels Highly Variable, Often Below CMS Expectations," *Health Affairs* 38, no. 7 (2019): 1095–100.

15. Kaiser Family Foundation, "Average Number of Deficiencies per Certified Nursing Facility," Kaiser Family Foundation, accessed August 17, 2021, https://www.kff.org/other/state-indicator/avg-of-nursing-facility-deficiencies/?currentTimeframe=0&sortModel=%7B%22colId%22:%22Location%22,%22sort%22:%22asc%22%7D.

16. Charlene Harrington, Helen Carrillo, Rachel Garfield, and Ellen Squires, "Nursing Facilities, Staffing, Residents and Facility Deficiencies,

In a statement to Congress in 2019, in conjunction with a hearing on nursing homes, advocates asserted:

> Abuse and neglect of nursing home residents occurs far too often. They are at increased risk due to the prevalence of dementia and dependency on caregivers for personal care. The systems designed to protect residents and hold facilities and perpetrators accountable have not been as effective as they should be.[17]

The COVID-19 pandemic highlighted the importance of finding a high-quality nursing home. Shockingly, 39 percent of people who died of COVID-19 as of December 2020 (over ten thousand individuals) were residents and staff members of long-term care facilities.[18] According to the AARP, poor government oversight and lack of accountability in nursing homes are substantially to blame.[19] A study of nursing homes in West Virginia revealed that the odds of a COVID-19 outbreak were far lower in facilities that were highly rated. Nursing homes with 4- to 5-star ratings were 94% less likely to have

2009 through 2016," Kaiser Family Foundation, April 2018, 17, http://files.kff.org/attachment/REPORT-Nursing-Facilities-Staffing-Residents-and-Facility-Deficiencies-2009-2016.

17. Tony Chicotel et al., "Statement on 2019 Nursing Home Hearing, Not Forgotten: Protecting Americans from Abuse and Neglect in Nursing Homes," Center for Medicare Advocacy, hearing held March 6, 2019, https://www.medicareadvocacy.org/statement-not-forgotten/.

18. Halley Bondy, "39% of Covid-19 Deaths Have Occurred in Nursing Homes—Many Could Have Been Prevented: Report," NBC News, December 8, 2020, https://www.nbcnews.com/know-your-value/feature/39-covid-19-deaths-have-occurred-nursing-homes-many-could-ncna1250374.

19. Joe Eaton, "Who's to Blame for the 100,000 COVID Dead in Long-Term Care?," AARP, December 3, 2020, https://www.aarp.org/caregiving/health/info-2020/covid-19-nursing-homes-who-is-to-blame.html.

an outbreak than 1-star-rated facilities, and 2- to 3-star-rated facilities were 87% less likely to suffer outbreaks than nursing homes with only 1-star ratings.[20]

Those without families may be the worst off in nursing homes. Family members provide both emotional support and crucial medical and other information to nursing home staff, especially when the patient is cognitively impaired. They also serve an oversight role, ensuring that the patient's needs are met to the extent possible. By some accounts, staff members sometimes prioritize care for those who receive frequent visits in order to ensure that these residents appear clean, dressed, and in good spirits to whomever stops by.[21] Therefore, it is important to visit loved ones in nursing homes as frequently as possible and to ask people to visit you if you become a nursing home resident.

The most recently compiled data shows that in 2016, there were 1.7 million beds available in 15,600 certified nursing facilities throughout the United States with an average occupancy rate of 80.8 percent. Among nursing homes, 69 percent were for-profit, 23.5 percent were nonprofit, and 6.9 percent were government-owned facilities.[22]

If you or a loved one needs nursing home care, you do not have to leave the quality of the facility up to chance. Rather, you should research nursing homes as thoroughly as possible. A useful resource is "Nursing Home Compare" on the

---

20. David P. Bui et al., "Association between CMS Quality Ratings and COVID-19 Outbreaks in Nursing Homes—West Virginia, March 17– June 11, 2020," Morbidity and Mortality Weekly Report 69, no. 37 (2020): 1300–1304.

21. Span, *When the Time Comes*, 184.

22. Elaine K. Howley, "Nursing Home Facts and Statistics," *U.S. News & World Report*, November 2, 2020, https://health.usnews.com/health-news/ best-nursing-homes/articles/nursing-home-facts-and-statistics; Harrington, Carrillo, Garfield, and Squires, "Nursing Facilities, Staffing," 7 and 9.

Medicare.gov website, which features nursing home ratings.[23] Further information can be obtained from the website of your state's health department or by calling the department and requesting any reports it has produced concerning nursing homes that interest you.[24]

You should be mindful, however, that federal and state ratings and reports may not be based on comprehensive information. For example, government authorities may rely excessively on self-reporting by nursing homes, fail to take into account significant information such as lawsuits filed by aggrieved residents' family members, and be duped by manipulative practices such as hiring additional staff members right before scheduled inspections and then laying them off.[25] Thus, recommendations from friends who have personal knowledge about nursing homes are particularly valuable, and, if time permits, you should visit potential nursing homes in order to form a firsthand impression of their atmosphere and quality of care. One factor to consider is that there is some

---

23. "Find a Nursing Home," Medicare.gov, accessed December 26, 2020, http://www.medicare.gov/nursinghomecompare/search.html.

24. See Aging and Long-Term Support Administration, "Long-term Care Residential Options," Washington State Department of Social and Health Services, accessed December 26, 2020, http://www.altsa.dshs.wa.gov/pubinfo/housing/other/.

25. Editorial Board, "When Five-Star Care Is Substandard: Medicare's Flawed Ratings for Nursing Homes," *New York Times*, August 25, 2014, http://www.nytimes.com/2014/08/26/opinion/medicares-flawed-ratings-for-nursing-homes.html?_r=0; Kira L. Ryskina, Tamara Konetzka, and Rachel M. Werner, "Association between 5-Star Nursing Home Report Card Ratings and Potentially Preventable Hospitalizations," *Inquiry* 55 (2018): 6; Jessica Silver-Greenberg and Robert Gebeloff, "Maggots, Rape and Yet Five Stars: How U.S. Ratings of Nursing Homes Mislead the Public", *New York Times*, March 13, 2021, updated August 4, 2021, https://www.nytimes.com/2021/03/13/business/nursing-homes-ratings-medicare-covid.html?referringSource=articleShare.

evidence that nonprofit facilities often provide better care than
for-profit entities, which may be tempted to cut corners in order
to increase their profits.[26]

Costs

One reason for a move to a nursing home is that it may be the
only affordable alternative for the very frail because Medicare
and Medicaid can cover costs. In 2020, on average, a private
room in a US nursing home cost $106,000 per year, while the
price tag for a semi-private nursing home room was $93,000.[27]
Medicare covers some of the costs for rehabilitation in a nursing
home in limited circumstances.[28] Residents who meet Medicare
requirements can receive 20 days of free care per benefit period
and then pay a daily copay for days 21 to 100 (up to $185.50 per
day in 2021), after which no Medicare funds are available until
the next benefit period.[29]

---

26. Span, *When the Time Comes*, 135; Michael O. Schroeder, "Nonprofit versus For-Profit Senior Care—Is There a Difference?" *U.S. News & World Report*, October 30, 2018, https://health.usnews.com/wellness/aging-well/articles/2018-10-30/is-there-a-difference-between-nonprofit-and-for-profit-senior-care.

27. Genworth, "Cost of Care Survey 2020," Genworth, last updated December 2, 2020, https://www.genworth.com/aging-and-you/finances/cost-of-care.html.

28. Medicare.gov, "Skilled Nursing Facility (SNF) Care," Medicare.gov, accessed December 26, 2020, https://www.medicare.gov/coverage/skilled-nursing-facility-snf-care.

29. Medicare explains the term "benefit period" as follows:

A benefit period begins the day you're admitted as an inpatient in a
hospital or [a skilled nursing facility (SNF)]. The benefit period ends
when you haven't received any inpatient hospital care (or skilled care
in a SNF) for 60 days in a row. If you go into a hospital or a SNF
after one benefit period has ended, a new benefit period begins. […]
There's no limit to the number of benefit periods.

"Glossary-B," Medicare.gov, https://www.medicare.gov/glossary/b.

To be eligible for Medicare coverage, residents must enter a nursing home within 30 days of having spent at least three consecutive days as admitted patients in a hospital and must need skilled nursing care. Medicare will discontinue coverage as soon as you stop needing skilled services or stop making progress. Some patients remain in the hospital "under observation," and this status does not qualify them for nursing home payment.[30] Days spent on observational status do not count toward Medicare's required three days. I learned the meaning of this distinction through my mother-in-law's difficult experience.

Observational status

At the age of 93, my mother-in-law, who lived alone, fell and broke her ankle in three places. We knew that after her hospitalization, she would need to be in a rehabilitation facility until, hopefully, she regained mobility. But on her first full day in the hospital, we received upsetting news: Helen, who was too frail for surgery, was under observation rather than admitted, and thus was considered to be an outpatient. Consequently, she would be ineligible for Medicare coverage of her rehabilitation care and, even during her hospitalization, would incur copayments for doctors' fees and hospital services. She would also have to pay for the many drugs she ordinarily takes at home that the hospital was now providing.

After persistent begging and pleading, the hospital admitted her, much to our relief. Our take-away lesson was that you should always ask right away whether you are an admitted patient or under observation. Hospitals are required to give you a Medicare Outpatient Observation Notice (MOON) but only

30. Center for Medicare Advocacy, "Outpatient Observation Status," Center for Medicare Advocacy, accessed December 26, 2020, https://www.medicareadvocacy.org/medicare-info/observation-status/.

within 36 hours of the initiation of observational status or upon hospital discharge, whichever is earlier.[31] If you want to change your status to admitted and begin accumulating time toward Medicare's three-day hospitalization requirement, you should pursue the matter with hospital officials as soon as possible.

You should also be aware of Medicare's "two-midnight rule."[32] The rule establishes that inpatient admission (as opposed to observational status) is appropriate if the admitting physician expects the patient's stay to last through two midnights. Medicare may also pay for shorter inpatient admissions that physicians deem medically necessary.[33] However, you should understand that hospitals have a financial incentive to err on the side of placing patients under observation rather than admitting them. Medicare pays hospitals only two-thirds as much for observational care as it does for inpatient care. However, if Medicare auditors determine that a hospital inappropriately admitted a patient, the hospital must return the entirety of its payment to Medicare and earn nothing.[34] This potential penalty has led to a dramatic increase in observational stays.[35]

---

31. Centers for Medicare and Medicaid Services, "Medicare Outpatient Observation Notice (MOON)," CMS.gov, December 8, 2016, https://www.cms.gov/newsroom/fact-sheets/medicare-outpatient-observation-notice-moon.

32. 42 CFR §412.3 (2018); Charles Locke and Edward Hu, "Medicare's Two-Midnight Rule: What Hospitalists Must Know," *The Hospitalist*, February 22, 2019, https://www.the-hospitalist.org/hospitalist/article/194971/medicares-two-midnight-rule.

33. Centers for Medicare and Medicaid Services, "Fact Sheet: Two-Midnight Rule," CMS.gov, October 30, 2015, https://www.cms.gov/newsroom/fact-sheets/fact-sheet-two-midnight-rule-0.

34. Howard Gleckman, "Understanding Medicare Observation Status," *Forbes*, January 2, 2019, https://www.forbes.com/sites/howardgleckman/2019/01/02/understanding-medicare-observation-status/#5a257ba27876.

35. In 2011 they accounted for $690 million in Medicare spending, but by 2016 Medicare paid $3.1 billion for observational stays. Howard

Medicaid eligibility

Although short stays in a nursing home can be covered by Medicare, another public form of insurance, Medicaid, pays for many permanent residencies. Medicare is available to anyone who is 65 and older and to some people with disabilities. Medicaid, on the other hand, is a program for only low-income individuals. To be eligible for nursing home coverage by Medicaid, you must "spend down" your assets, and "spending down" is a fairly literal term.[36] It requires you to drain most assets other than your home, personal effects, and vehicle. Detailed guidelines determine Medicaid eligibility, but typically, single people who are seniors can have no more than $2,000 in "countable resources" (cash, financial accounts, stocks, bonds, available assets in trust). In addition, in 2021, single Medicaid recipients' monthly income had to be under $2,382.[37]

Moreover, individuals cannot simply transfer their assets in order to become Medicaid eligible. The law restricts transfers made during the five years before you apply for Medicaid, a window of time commonly known as the "look-back" period (note that California's look-back period is only 30 months). The law does not prohibit all transfers, but rather, it addresses those made for less than fair market value. For example, if you own jewelry appraised at $30,000, you cannot give it away or sell it for anything less than that amount during the look-back period.

Gleckman, "Understanding Medicare Observation Status," *Forbes*, January 2, 2019, https://www.forbes.com/sites/howardgleckman/2019/01/02/under standing-medicare-observation-status/#5a257ba27876.

36. Geoff Williams, "How a Medicaid Spend Down Works," *U.S. News & World Report*, May 17, 2019, https://money.usnews.com/money/ retirement/baby-boomers/articles/how-a-medicaid-spend-down-works.

37. American Council on Aging, "Medicaid Eligibility: 2019 Income, Asset & Care Requirements for Nursing Homes & Long-Term Care," American Council on Aging, updated January 3, 2020, https://www.medicaid planningassistance.org/medicaid-eligibility.

Thus, sale of the jewelry should yield $30,000 that you count as assets for Medicaid eligibility purposes.

Transferring assets for less than fair market value during the look-back period does not disqualify you from Medicaid eligibility forever, but it will result in a penalty period. To calculate the length of this period, divide the overall value of the assets you transferred or undersold by the average monthly cost of a nursing home in your state. For example, if you gave away $30,000 in assets, and the average cost of a nursing home in your state is $6,000 per month, you would be ineligible for Medicaid for five months ($30,000 divided by $6,000). The penalty period usually begins on the date of application for Medicaid, assuming you meet all other requirements.[38]

Be aware that spouses who have considerable separate assets will not be able to retain all of those assets if their sick spouse wishes to enroll in Medicaid for purposes of nursing home care. When a married couple applies for Medicaid, a snapshot is taken of the couple's total assets, whether they are held jointly or separately. Medicaid disregards prenuptial agreements. State law will allow the "community spouse" (the healthy person who continues to live in the community) to keep a "community spouse resource allowance." In 2021, this amount ranged from a maximum of $130,380 to a minimum of $26,076, depending on the state. State law also addresses the amount of income working community spouses may keep from their ongoing earnings or, if they have little to no monthly income, the amount they may obtain from the income of the spouse in a nursing home to meet their living expenses. These amounts may vary significantly from state to state.[39]

---

38. 42 U.S.C. §1396p(c); American Council on Aging, "Understand Medicaid's Look-Back Period; Penalties, Exceptions & State Variances," American Council on Aging, updated June 15, 2020, https://www.medicaidplanningassistance.org/medicaid-look-back-period/.

39. Medicaid.gov, "2021 SSI and Spousal Impoverishment Standards," Medicaid.gov, accessed December 26, 2020, https://www.medicaid.gov/medicaid/eligibility/downloads/ssi-and-spousal-impoverishment-standards.pdf.

Note that if you hope to become eligible for Medicaid coverage, you would be wise to consult an elder law or estate planning attorney. A lawyer can answer your questions about Medicaid eligibility and may be able to help you protect some of your assets from the Medicaid spend-down requirement through tools such as an irrevocable trust.[40]

In 2020, 62 percent of nursing home residents were covered by Medicaid, 12 percent were covered by Medicare, and 26 percent paid from private sources.[41] Sadly, according to one study, individuals who have lived in a nursing home for six months or more have a median total household wealth of only $5,518.[42] This is most likely because wealthier people often choose options other than nursing homes, and nursing home residents must spend down their assets before Medicaid will pay for their care. Thus, some people who have worked hard for their earnings and take pride in having money to leave as an inheritance for their loved ones must instead hand over their life savings to nursing home operators.

ASSISTED LIVING

Seniors whose health is declining but who can still live with some degree of independence may opt for assisted living settings.

---

40. David A. Cutner, "Top 5 Strategies for Protecting Your Money from Medicaid," AgingCare, accessed December 26, 2020, https://www.agingcare.com/articles/strategies-to-protect-money-from-medicaid-175434.htm.

41. Kaiser Family Foundation, "Distribution of Certified Nursing Facility Residents by Primary Payer Source: Timeframe 2020," Kaiser Family Foundation, accessed August 17, 2021, https://www.kff.org/other/state-indicator/distribution-of-certified-nursing-facilities-by-primary-payer-sourc e/?currentTimeframe=0&sortModel=%7B%22colId%22:%22Lo cation%22,%22sort%22:%22asc%22%7D.

42. Sudipto Banerjee, "Effects of Nursing Home Stays on Household Portfolios," Employee Benefits Research Institute, Issue Brief 372, June 12, 2012, 4–18, https://www.ebri.org/content/effects-of-nursing-home-stays-on-household-portfolios-5078.

These facilities allow residents to have their own apartments or rooms along with assistance that is available around the clock, including prepared meals, cleaning services, activities, transportation, and some health care.[43] They do not, however, provide skilled nursing services.

Assisted living offers seniors a more active, autonomous life than nursing homes. Residents typically have apartments and can cook for themselves if they wish. Nevertheless, seniors are rarely enthusiastic about leaving their homes for an assisted living facility and most often do not enter assisted living settings until they are simply unable to live on their own. More than half (52.1 percent) of the 811,500 people in assisted living in 2016 were 85 and older.[44] Residents take an average of 12–14 drugs per day, including both prescription and over-the-counter medications.[45] A large percentage of residents require assistance with activities of daily living such as bathing, dressing, toileting, transferring in and out of bed, eating, and mobility.[46] Approximately 70 percent have experienced cognitive decline.[47]

---

43. American Health Care Association and National Center for Assisted Living, "Resources for Consumers," American Health Care Association and National Center for Assisted Living, accessed December 26, 2020, https://www.ahcancal.org/ncal/about/assistedliving/Pages/What-is-Assisted-Living.aspx.

44. US Department of Health and Human Services, "Long-Term Care Providers and Services Users in the United States, 2015–2016," National Center for Health Statistics, *Vital and Health Statistics*, series 3, no. 43 (February 2019): 1 and 19, https://www.cdc.gov/nchs/data/series/sr_03/sr03_43-508.pdf.

45. PharMerica,"Medication Management Issues in Assisted Living" PharMerica, November 10, 2020, https://pharmerica.com/medication-management-issues-in-assisted-living/.

46. US Department of Health and Human Services, "Long-Term Care Providers and Services," 24.

47. Paula Span, "Where There's Rarely a Doctor in the House: Assisted Living," *New York Times*, March 29, 2019, https://www.nytimes.com/2019/03/29/health/assisted-living-doctors-house-calls.html.

In the words of writer Paula Span, assisted living is sometimes "sardonically called a nursing home with a chandelier."[48]

The cost of assisted living is a significant barrier for many consumers, though it is less expensive than nursing home care. In 2020, the average total monthly charge per resident for assisted living care in the United States was approximately $4,300.[49] Prices can vary greatly by region. For example, in 2020, you could expect a monthly price tag of $3,638 in South Dakota and $5,000 in California.[50] Facilities may also charge additional fees for extra services. Residents generally pay for assisted living out-of-pocket.[51] Consequently, assisted living residents who exhaust their financial resources may be transferred to nursing homes for which Medicaid will pay.

On average, residents live in assisted living facilities for 22 months (as of 2020).[52] About 60 percent of residents transfer to nursing homes as their health fails (or finances dwindle). Assisted living facilities may in fact involuntarily discharge residents as their

---

48. Span, *When the Time Comes*, 118.

49. Genworth, "Cost of Care Survey 2020."

50. Genworth, "Cost of Care Survey 2020."

51. A small percentage of assisted living residents (16.5 percent in 2020) obtain some degree of assistance from Medicaid. Medicaid reimbursement for assisted living varies by state. Payment rates, however, are generally low, and not every assisted living facility accepts Medicaid. Also, there are typically enrollment caps and waiting lists for Medicaid assisted living support. For a state-by-state explanation of benefits, see Paying for Senior Care, "Medicaid's Assisted Living Benefits: Availability and Eligibility," *Paying for Senior Care*, updated August 14, 2020, https://www.payingforseniorcare.com/medicaid-waivers/assisted-living.html.

52. American Health Care Association and National Center for Assisted Living, "Facts and Figures," accessed December 26, 2020, https://www.ahcancal.org/Assisted-Living/Facts-and-Figures/Pages/default.aspx.

needs intensify.[53] Because seniors often do not move to assisted living until their 80s, when they are physically or mentally frail (or both), these facilities may not provide a robust social setting and frequently constitute a temporary rather than a permanent, final home.

Although residents may enter nursing homes directly from the hospital, leaving very little time for extensive investigation of choices, the same is not true for assisted living facilities. The decision to move to assisted living is generally made without the pressure of an emergency or acute medical needs so that you should have adequate time to explore alternatives. Websites such as Angie's List and Caring.com provide reviews and ratings. States regulate assisted living facilities and often survey them as part of their regulatory enforcement process. Some states post their surveys on government websites. In addition, you may call your state's department of health and request any assessments it has concerning facilities that interest you.[54] You should also seek recommendations from friends and acquaintances and visit assisted living residences that you are considering.

Though many assisted living providers are large facilities, more intimate settings are available as well. For example, residential care homes offer lodging, meals, and assistance with activities of daily living to small groups of adults in a private

53. Brad Breeding, "So I'll Probably Need Long-Term Care, but for How Long?" myLifeSite.net, July 6, 2016, https://www.mylifesite.net/blog/post/so-ill-probably-need-long-term-care-but-for-how-long/; Timothy J. Ford, "How to Prepare for and Facilitate an Involuntary Discharge," *McKnight's Senior Living*, April 1, 2019, https://www.mcknightsseniorliving.com/home/columns/guest-columns/how-to-prepare-for-and-facilitate-an-involuntary-discharge/.

54. See Minnesota Attorney General, "Nursing Homes and Assisted Living," Office of the Minnesota Attorney General, accessed December 26, 2020, https://www.ag.state.mn.us/Consumer/Publications/NursingHomes AssistedLiving.asp.

home setting.[55] They may be less expensive than larger facilities, costing on average between \$3,500 and \$4,500 a month. In California, these arrangements are often known as "six-bed board and care facilities," and their cost typically ranges between \$3,000 and \$7,000 per month.[56]

HOME CARE AGENCIES

The vast majority of American seniors wish to live out their lives in their own homes. Even among those 85 and older, only 7 percent live in nursing homes.[57] For elderly people who want to avoid institutional settings, home care can be a godsend.

Home care is supportive care that elderly people receive in their homes. The terminology for this type of care, however, can be confusing and is inconsistently used. Some states differentiate between "home health care," which includes visits by licensed medical personnel such as those providing skilled nursing or rehabilitation services, and "in-home care," which covers a lower level of services. In-home care may

---

55. "Residential Care Home: Senior Care in a Home-Like Setting," aPlaceforMom.com, accessed December 26, 2020, https://www.aplaceformom.com/care-homes; Merritt Whitley, "Everything You Need to Know about Residential Care Homes," aPlaceforMom.com, June 8, 2020, https://www.aplaceformom.com/planning-and-advice/articles/residential-care-homes.

56. "Residential Care Homes for Seniors (AKA Board and Care Homes)," California Registry, accessed December 26, 2020, https://www.calregistry.com/residential-care-homes-for-seniors/.

57. Administration for Community Living and Administration on Aging, "2019 Profile of Older Americans," May 2020, 8, https://acl.gov/sites/default/files/Aging%20and%20Disability%20in%20America/2017OlderAmericansProfile.pdf; Karan Kaul, "American Seniors Prefer to 'Age in Place'—But What's the Right Place?" *Urban Wire*, June 3, 2019, https://www.urban.org/urban-wire/american-seniors-prefer-age-place-whats-right-place.

include companionship, assistance with daily living activities (e.g., cooking, dressing, and bathing), driving, and medication reminders.[58]

In 2019, Americans spent \$113.5 billion on home care.[59] The median cost of an aide from a home care agency was \$23.50 per hour.[60]

Medicare pays for limited home care for homebound elderly people. Services may include skilled nursing, physical therapy, social services, and assistance with activities of daily living typically for up to 28 hours a week for a limited period of time, typically after discharge from a hospital or rehabilitation facility.[61] In some states, Medicaid also provides some degree of home care coverage for Medicaid-eligible, low-income seniors[62] and support may also be available through local programs, charities, or the Veterans Administration.

An aide hired through a home care agency can be a very good solution for frail elderly people who live alone and wish

---

58. See PA STAT. ANN. Tit. 28 § 611.5.

59. Robert Holly, "National Home Health Spending Reaches All-Time High of \$113.5 Billion," *Home Health Care News*, December 16, 2020, https://homehealthcarenews.com/2020/12/national-home-health-spending-reaches-all-time-high-of-113-5-billion/.

60. Genworth, "Cost of Care Survey 2020"; Richard W. Johnson and Claire Xiaozhi Wang, "The Financial Burden of Paid Home Care on Older Adults: Oldest and Sickest Are Least Likely to Have Enough Income," *Health Affairs* 38, no. 6 (2019): 994–1002.

61. Medicare Interactive, "Home Health Hours," Medicare Interactive, accessed December 26, 2020, https://www.medicareinteractive.org/get-answers/medicare-covered-services/home-health-services/home-health-hours#:~:text=Medicare's%20home%20health%20benefit%20covers,case%2Dby%2Dcase%20basis.

62. PayingforSeniorCare.com, "Medicaid's Home Care Benefits: Eligibility, Waivers & Application Information," PayingforSeniorCare.com, updated August 14, 2020, https://www.payingforseniorcare.com/medicaid-waivers/home-care.html.

to avoid moving to an institutional setting. Agencies ideally screen employees, supervise workers, dispatch substitutes if assigned aides become unavailable, and allow clients to request personnel changes when they are dissatisfied with particular aides. Agencies also handle the paperwork, which can be an invaluable service to elderly individuals who are trying to navigate the system on their own.

Nevertheless, although agency-provided home care allows the elderly to remain in their homes, this approach too has its drawbacks. The cost is an obvious barrier, but it is not the only concern. Home care aides are largely female, minority, and immigrant, and they are often underpaid and overworked.[63] In 2020, the average hourly wage of home health aides, who provide basic medical services such as wound care, was $13.49, and the average annual salary was $28,060, though many work only part-time.[64] The salary of home care aides who do not provide medical care ranged from $23,621 to $28,551.[65] Consequently, aides' annual turnover rate is alarming, reaching over 22 percent in 2020.[66] Having to get used to new caregivers on a frequent basis can be distressing, especially for people with

---

63. Andy Newman, "On the Job, 24 Hours a Day, 27 Days a Month," *New York Times*, September 6, 2019, https://www.nytimes.com/2019/09/02/nyregion/home-health-aide.html?smid=nytcore-ios-share.

64. United States Department of Labor, Bureau of Labor Statistics, "Occupational Employment and Wages, May 2020, 31-1120 Home Health and Personal Care Aides," US Bureau of Labor Statistics, accessed August 17, 2021, http://www.bls.gov/oes/current/oes311011.htm.

65. "Home Care Aide Salary in the United States," Salary.com, accessed December 26, 2020, https://www.salary.com/research/salary/benchmark/home-care-aide-i-salary.

66. Robert Holly, "Home Health Turnover Rate Hits 22.18%," *Home Health Care News*, October 27, 2020, https://homehealthcarenews.com/2020/10/home-health-turnover-rate-hits-22-18/#:~:text=Released%20Monday%2C%20this%20year's%20Home,home%20health%20positions%20in%202020.

dementia. In addition, agencies might have somewhat rigid policies, such as refusing to allow workers to drive clients for fear of liability or requiring that you use aides for a minimum number of hours per day.

Another concern is that current immigration policies will significantly reduce the home care aide workforce. At least a quarter of these employees are from other countries, and they may not be able to gain legal status to work in this country. A shrinking supply will likely drive up costs and reduce access to quality caregivers.[67]

Regulatory oversight and compliance are yet another concern. Medicare oversees home health care agencies that provide skilled nursing care, physical therapy, occupational therapy, speech therapy, medical social services, and home health aide services. The Medicare website provides useful quality surveys on certified home health agencies.[68] However, agencies that provide nonmedical services are not governed by Medicare rules. Some states post similar information about in-home care agencies on their websites, but others do not regulate in-home care agencies at all. Furthermore, even states with robust regulations often have inadequate enforcement resources, and, therefore, they cannot effectively prevent or punish most violations of the law.

Before employing aides from a home care agency, you should do as much research as possible. This includes not only looking for rankings and quality surveys on the Internet but also asking acquaintances for recommendations based on

---

67. Howard Gleckman, "Where Will Our Home Care Aides Come From?" *Forbes*, February 28, 2018, https://www.forbes.com/sites/howardgleckman/2018/02/28/where-will-our-home-care-aides-come-from/#7a667659383f.

68. They are available at "Find & Compare Nursing Homes, Hospitals & Other Providers Near You," Medicare.gov, http://www.medicare.gov/HomeHealthCompare/search.aspx.

personal experience. Ascertaining the quality of the agency is especially important if your loved one is mentally impaired and will not be able to explain her needs to the caregiver, advocate for herself, or report that she is dissatisfied with her care. In-home care aides spend many hours alone with their clients and have their clients' welfare, and, frequently, even lives, in their hands. Thus, you cannot underestimate the importance of your decision about which agency to employ.

HIRING AIDES INDEPENDENTLY

A less expensive and more flexible alternative to using an agency is to hire an aide independently. You can initiate the process of hiring an aide independently by posting an ad through Internet services such as Craigslist or Care.com. Some states, such as Oregon, also have state-run registries that enable workers and employers to specify their criteria and conduct searches in order to be matched.[69]

However, this may be an overwhelming undertaking for many seniors and impossible for those with cognitive impairment and no family support. A sound hiring process entails advertising, interviewing, performing background and reference checks, and formulating a detailed contract. Because individuals who respond to ads on Craigslist or Care.com are not licensed or prescreened, conducting reference calls and a background check through a reliable service is essential. Once you select a caregiver, be sure that the contract specifies tasks, hours, payment, conditions for termination, and the terms of a short probationary or trial period during which you can determine

---

69. "Registry," Oregon.gov, accessed December 26, 2020, https://www.oregon.gov/DHS/SENIORS-DISABILITIES/HCC/Pages/Registry.aspx. See also, AARP, "How to Hire a Caregiver," AARP, updated November 7, 2019, https://www.aarp.org/caregiving/home-care/info-2018/hiring-caregiver.html.

whether you are satisfied with the caregiver's performance.[70] In addition, if you employ an aide independently, you will need to arrange to pay social security and state unemployment compensation taxes.

After my mother died, my 86-year-old father, who suffered from congestive heart failure, decided that he wanted to stay in his home but was not prepared to live alone. He wanted to hire a male caregiver who would sleep at the house, provide transportation, help with household chores, and serve as a companion.

We initially met with a home health care agency and learned that round-the-clock service would cost up to $480 per day or approximately $175,000 per year (in Michigan in 2013). In order to find a less expensive alternative, we posted an ad on Craigslist. A young man in his mid-20s responded with an articulate and compelling e-mail explaining why he was interested in the job. We interviewed him in person twice, conducted a criminal background check through the Internet, called his references, and hired him for $20,000 a year plus room and board.

Although calling references is helpful, other research, including a Google search and a thorough background check is critical. Remember, the applicant is providing the names of references, and therefore, you can assume that the individuals you call think highly of him or her. Nevertheless, you should make the phone calls because you may be able to evaluate the references' level of enthusiasm about the candidate from their tone or wording. To further judge their credibility, you may want to ask surprising questions, such as "Please tell me two negative things about the applicant."

A simple Google search of the candidate's name may reveal very useful information, such as whether the individual has

---

70. Span, *When the Time Comes*, 38–61.

been involved in litigation and what prior jobs he or she has had. Searching Facebook and other social media can be equally productive. For the background check, we used a service called "Intelius," which produces a report based on the person's last name and social security number for $49.95.

At the time, my father did not have severe cognitive impairment, and one of my sisters lived 10 minutes away and could visit him almost daily, so the risk of elder abuse or neglect seemed small. Happily, my father was pleased with his live-in caregiver for over a year. This came as a shock to many acquaintances who had warned me that it was nearly impossible to find a good aide on the first try and that their relatives had fired one individual after another, usually after trial periods that lasted just days. When my father's health deteriorated and he began to require constant attention, we switched to round-the-clock care supplied by a home care agency for the last four months of his life.

A potential concern stemming from all forms of home care is that it will cause the elderly person to become socially isolated. If the individual does not receive regular visits from friends and family members, the aide may be the only one with whom the client interacts in person for weeks at a time. Experts who have studied the benefits of social contact have found that interaction with hired personnel is not as beneficial as naturally occurring social relationships.[71] Caregivers should thus be asked to help clients remain active in religious or other communities or become newly involved in appropriate activities, such as those offered by senior centers (discussed in Chapter 2).

As in every other setting, quality of care is of serious concern. Both agencies and independently employed aides can provide subpar services. Seniors with cognitive impairment and

---

71. Julianne Holt-Lunstad, Timothy B. Smith, and J. Bradley Layton, "Social Relationships and Mortality Risk: A Meta-Analytic Review," *PLoS Medicine* 7, no. 7 (2010): 14, https://doi.org/10.1371/journal.pmed.1000316.

those without frequent visitors may be particularly vulnerable to receiving less-than-optimal services from a caregiver. Unannounced visits by friends and family members are an invaluable form of oversight and quality control.

We cannot ignore the all-too-common phenomenon of elder abuse. Experts believe that approximately 10 percent of people 60 and older are victims of some form of abuse.[72] However, according to the National Center on Elder Abuse, there are no accurate figures as to how many elderly people are abused or neglected because only a small fraction of cases are reported. Research suggests that authorities receive reports of only 7–20 percent of elder abuse cases and as few as 4 percent of instances of financial exploitation. In as many as 60 percent of cases, the abuser is a relative.[73] Therefore, you should not take for granted that your loved ones are well cared for even if you have hired help for them.

PART-TIME CARE: ADULT DAY SERVICES

Those seeking part-time care for seniors should consider one additional option—adult day services. In 2020 there were 4,600 adult day service centers, in which 286,300 people participated each day.[74] There are three types of adult day care:

72. National Council on Aging, "Elder Abuse Facts," National Council on Aging, accessed December 26, 2020, https://www.ncoa.org/public-policy-action/elder-justice/elder-abuse-facts/.

73. National Council on Aging, "Elder Abuse Facts"; National Center on Elder Abuse, "Statistics and Data," National Center on Elder Abuse, accessed December 26, 2020, https://ncea.acl.gov/What-We-Do/Research/Statistics-and-Data.aspx; Nursing Home Abuse Center, "Elder Abuse Statistics: Statistics over Time," Nursing Home Abuse Center, updated January 16, 2020, https://www.nursinghomeabusecenter.com/elder-abuse/statistics/.

74. National Center for Health Statistics, "Adult Day Services Centers," Centers for Disease Control and Prevention, reviewed May 20, 2020, https://www.cdc.gov/nchs/fastats/adsc.htm.

1. Adult social day care, which emphasizes social activities, meals, and recreation;
2. Adult day health care, which offers more intensive therapeutic and social services for individuals who suffer from serious problems such as diabetes, hypertension, stroke, and dementia; and
3. Specialized day care, which serves individuals with particular diagnoses, such as dementia or developmental disabilities.[75]

Adult day health care may be used for short-term, post-hospitalization care and rehabilitation or as a longer-term solution for frail elderly people. For the latter group, it can supplement or replace in-home care and also delay or prevent placement in assisted living or nursing homes.

Adult day service centers offer health monitoring, social opportunities, activities, and assistance with daily functions. Approximately 80 percent have a nurse on staff; about half have a social worker; half also offer physical, occupational, or speech therapy; and 60 percent provide case management services. The majority have special programs for people living with dementia. They also offer caregiver support in the form of education, support groups, and counseling. On average, adult day service centers have one care worker for every six participants.[76]

In 2020, adult day services charged an average of $74 per day, though prices ranged from $30 to $150 per day.[77] Many clients must pay out of pocket, but in some cases, public

---

75. National Adult Day Services Association, "Overview and Facts," National Adult Day Services Association, accessed January 3, 2020, https://www.nadsa.org/consumers/overview-and-facts/.

76. AginginPlace.com, "Adult Day Care," AginginPlace.com, updated December 2020, https://www.aginginplace.org/adult-day-care/.

77. Genworth, "Cost of Care Survey 2020" AgingInPlace.com, "Adult Day Care."

programs such as Medicaid, the Veterans Administration, or state social services will pay part or all of the expense, depending on the client's income and eligibility. Private medical insurance policies might also cover a portion of adult day care center costs if licensed medical professionals provide care, and long-term care insurance policies often provide coverage as well.

The National Adult Day Services Association urges seniors and their caregivers to visit facilities (perhaps more than once) and speak to participants before choosing a program. The association also recommends that you ask the following questions:

- How many years has the center been in operation?
- Does the center have a license, certification, or accreditation?
- What are the hours of operation?
- Are transportation services offered?
- What is the cost?
- Is it an hourly or daily charge? Are there other charges?
- What types of payment are accepted?
- Is financial assistance available?
- Is specialized care provided for conditions such as memory loss?
- What is the staff-to-client ratio?
- What kinds of training do staff receive?
- Do participants have access to services such as physical or occupational therapy?
- What types of activities are provided?
- Are meals and/or snacks provided? Are special diets accommodated?[78]

Although some states regulate adult day service centers and require licenses and certification, others do not. You can find

---

78. National Adult Day Services Association, "Site Visit Checklist," National Adult Day Services Association, accessed December 27, 2020, https://www.nadsa.org/wp-content/uploads/2015/08/Site-Visit-Checklist-for-the-web.pdf.

local adult day service centers through online resources such as Caring.com.[79] You may also contact the Eldercare Locator, a service of the US Administration on Aging.[80]

LONG-TERM CARE PREPAREDNESS CHECKLIST

* If you (or a loved one) will need rehabilitation care after a hospitalization, inquire as to whether you are admitted or under observation as soon as possible. Be aware that Medicare will not pay for inpatient rehabilitation unless you were admitted and stayed in the hospital for at least three days.

* Do your research before selecting a nursing home, assisted living facility, home care agency, or adult day services center. Search the Internet, seek word-of-mouth recommendations, and visit the facilities in person.

* If you want to avoid living in a long-term care facility, consider obtaining home care either through an agency or by hiring a caregiver independently.

* Consider supplementing care by family members or paid aides with care at an adult day service center.

* If you hire a caregiver on your own, be sure to call references, Google the applicant, and conduct a comprehensive background check using a reputable Internet service.

* Visit loved ones who are receiving care in nursing homes, assisted living, or at home as frequently as possible. Ask friends and family members to visit you if you are the one needing care.

* Consult an accountant to determine whether any of your long-term care costs are tax deductible.

---

79. See Caring.com "Find Adult Day Care Options Near Me," https://www.caring.com/senior-living/adult-day-care/.

80. The phone number is 800-677-1116.

CHAPTER 8

EXIT STRATEGIES: MAINTAINING CONTROL AT THE END OF LIFE

Most of this book has focused on planning for living a fulfilling and comfortable life as you age. Life, however, inevitably ends in death. What, if any, planning can or should you do for the end of life's journey?

Few individuals die suddenly without some period of physical and/or cognitive decline. End-of-life studies reveal that only 7–15 percent of people studied experienced sudden deaths.[1] Sudden death can be defined as occurring "when a person progresses quickly from normal functioning to death." Causes of sudden death included "sudden cardiac failure, aneurysms, toxins, and accidents."[2]

Although longevity is generally perceived as a blessing, many who have watched the decline of elderly loved ones are more dubious about its benefits. A prolonged existence devoid of the ability to enjoy even simple pleasures can hardly be described as good fortune.

---

1. Jiska Cohen-Mansfield, Michal Skornick-Bouchbinder, and Shai Brill, "Trajectories of End of Life: A Systematic Review," *Journals of Gerontology: Psychological Sciences* 73, no. 4 (2017): 564–72.

2. Cohen-Mansfield, Skornick-Bouchbinder, and Brill, "Trajectories of End of Life," 567.

The hero of Jonathan Swift's *Gulliver's Travels* describes the "Stulbrugs" or "Immortals" about which he learned during one of his voyages:

> At Ninety they lose their Teeth and Hair; they have at that Age no Distinction of Taste, but eat and drink whatever they can get, without Relish or Appetite. The Diseases they were subject to, still continue without increasing or diminishing. In talking they forget the common Appellation of Things, and the Names of Persons, even of those who are their nearest Friends and Relations. For the same Reason they never can amuse themselves with reading, because their Memory will not serve to carry them from the Beginning of a Sentence to the End; and by this Defect they are deprived of the only Entertainment whereof they might otherwise be capable.[3]

This description is fictional, but for one of my relatives, Mae, who lived to be 104, it was quite apt during the last 18 months of her life. Mae and her sister Nettie, who was five years younger, lived in different apartments in the same building in Cleveland, each with round-the-clock aides hired through a home care agency. They visited each other daily, enjoyed occasional outings, and sometimes talked about how Nettie would move to Boston after Mae's death so she could be closer to her son and grandchildren. Nettie, however, died in 2011 at age 96 from breast cancer that was not diagnosed until she had a tumor the size of a large apricot breaking through her skin. Although she visited her internist every few months, she said he spent only a couple of minutes with her, taking her

---

3. Jonathan Swift, *Gulliver's Travels* in *The Cambridge Edition of the Works of Jonathan Swift*, ed. Claude Rawson, Ian Gadd, Ian Higgins, James McLaverty, Valerie Rumbold, Abigail Williams, and Linda Bree (Cambridge: Cambridge University Press, 2012), 318–19.

blood pressure and listening to her heart. Because the doctor never asked if anything else was wrong, Nettie thought it was inappropriate to trouble him with a question about the growing lump in her breast.

At 102, Mae, who had never married, was inconsolable. She spent large portions of the day sleeping, lost her appetite, and exhibited rapid mental deterioration. During her last few months, it was unclear whether she recognized her visitors, and she did not remember even the simple details of her life, such as where she lived and what relatives she had. On good days, she could ask a question such as "How are your parents?" But she asked it repeatedly throughout the visit. She also expressed her profound distress about her circumstances, uttering phrases such as, "I never thought this would happen to me," "I wouldn't wish this on my worst enemy," and "My whole family is gone." Mae died on her 104th birthday because of fluid in her lungs.

Mae was never combative or uncooperative with caregivers. However, I have seen firsthand that other dementia patients can become hostile, verbally abusive, and even violent with paid caregivers and loved ones alike. For family members, it can be agonizing to watch relatives who were gentle souls and highly respected professionals undergo a radical change in personality at the end of life.

Some acquaintances have told me that they or their relatives have a concrete plan to commit suicide at a particular age (e.g., 85) or at the first sign of dementia. This approach has even been discussed in academic literature. For example, Professor Dena Davis, a bioethics scholar who teaches at Lehigh University, has argued that "suicide is one rational response to the knowledge that one will have Huntington's disease or Alzheimer's disease."[4] It is noteworthy that according to the National Institute of

---

4. Dena S. Davis, "Rational Suicide and Predictive Genetic Testing," *Journal of Clinical Ethics* 10, no. 4 (1999): 316–23.

Mental Health, the suicide rate for men is highest in the age group of 75 and older (39.9 per 100,000 in 2018).[5]

In contrast, other individuals are certain that every moment of life is precious and emphasize the sanctity of human life. They would not consider any acts to shorten their lives because they view such acts as morally impermissible.[6] Perhaps they are in an enviable position because they are free of moral uncertainty and the need to make difficult end-of-life decisions.

Still others, myself included, occupy a middle ground. Formulating a plan to commit suicide before suffering significant age-related deterioration is out of the question for any number of reasons: religion, culture, social norms, or lack of courage. Yet, we contemplate with horror the prospect of having no control over our fate at the end of life no matter what suffering befalls us. As a 29-year-old, I developed a very large, borderline malignant ovarian tumor, as described in the introduction to this book. Before surgery, I endured nearly unbearable pain and, decades later, still experience occasional episodes of similar pain because of internal scar tissue. If such agony were long lasting and could not be stopped through medical interventions, I could well imagine wanting my life to end and contemplating doing something about it.

So now back to the original question: Can you do any planning in order to reduce your risk of prolonged suffering before death? What are your existing options and for what further choices might you lobby?

---

5. National Institute of Mental Health, "Suicide," National Institute of Mental Health, updated September 2020, https://www.nimh.nih.gov/health/statistics/suicide.shtml.

6. Heike Baranzke, " 'Sanctity-of-Life'—A Bioethical Principle for a Right to Life?," *Ethical Theory and Moral Practice* 15, no. 3 (2012): 296–302.

HOSPICE AND PALLIATIVE CARE

Hospice is a common approach to avoiding unwanted life-prolonging treatment at the end of life. Hospice care is available to terminally ill patients and provides treatments that promote comfort but are not intended to cure their illnesses. Thus, hospice patients do not undergo aggressive curative therapies such as chemotherapy and radiation and do not go to the hospital for medical care. They do receive plenty of medications to address pain, nausea, shortness of breath, and other sources of discomfort. To be eligible, a patient must obtain certification from her doctor and the hospice director that she has a terminal illness and is expected to die within six months.[7]

According to the National Hospice and Palliative Care Organization, approximately 4,639 Medicare-certified hospices existed in 2018, serving 1.55 million Medicare beneficiaries.[8] About 50 percent of deaths involve hospice care, if only for a few days.[9]

Hospice services are provided primarily in patients' homes, though they can also be provided in nursing homes, assisted living facilities, freestanding hospices, and hospitals.[10] Medicare will pay for hospice-related medical expenses, including five

---

7. Centers for Medicare & Medicaid Services, "Medicare Hospice Benefits," Center for Medicare & Medicaid Services, revised November 2020, https://www.medicare.gov/pubs/pdf/02154-medicare-hospice-benefits.pdf.

8. National Hospice and Palliative Care Organization, "NHPCO's Facts and Figures, 2020 Edition," 6, 20, National Hospice and Palliative Care Organization, August 20, 2020, https://www.nhpco.org/wp-content/uploads/NHPCO-Facts-Figures-2020-edition.pdf.

9. Sarah H. Cross and Haider J. Warraich, "More Americans Are Dying at Home. Is That a Good Thing?" *STAT*, December 11, 2019, https://www.statnews.com/2019/12/11/more-americans-die-at-home/.

10. AginginPlace.com, "Hospice Care," AginginPlace.com, updated December 2020, https://aginginplace.org/hospice-care/.

days of respite care at a Medicare-approved inpatient facility in order to give the patient's usual caregiver (e.g., a family member) a break. However, Medicare will not reimburse for curative treatments, room and board, or emergency room and inpatient care unless the visit to the hospital is arranged by the hospice team or is unrelated to the patient's terminal illness.[11] Medicare recipients who spend time in residence at a hospice facility must be prepared to pay a daily rate to cover room and board. Patients also retain the right to leave hospice and resume treatment at any time.

My first exposure to hospice came when my mother (Eema in Hebrew) spent the last two days of her life at an inpatient hospice facility. After we learned that she had advanced pancreatic cancer, we were told that if we wanted to pursue treatment, the doctors would need to intubate her and use a ventilator because she was experiencing respiratory failure. The attending physician advised us to consider giving her only comfort care. We had no difficulty deciding to follow this advice and spare Eema further torments.

The next day, we met with the palliative care team, which consisted of a nurse and social worker. They told us that Eema could not stay in the intensive care unit (ICU) now that she would receive no curative treatment. We were distressed to leave the familiar environment of the hospital, but we dutifully followed the ambulance that moved her to the nearby hospice facility.

Eema's private hospice room was small, though in addition to the bed, it had enough chairs to seat her five family members. Other rooms appeared to be larger and well decorated and presumably belonged to longer-term patients. We especially appreciated the spaces with sofas that could be reserved by family members who wanted to sleep at the hospice. Two of my sisters slept there on both nights of Eema's stay.

---

11. Centers for Medicare & Medicaid Services, "Medicare Hospice Benefits."

The nursing staff was attentive, appearing almost instantly when we pressed the call button and frequently checked on Eema on their own. Eema received oxygen to ease her breathing and was given pain and anti-anxiety medications. She had no monitors and no food or water because she could not eat or drink on her own. Although she was semiconscious and at times agitated during the first evening and night, she fell into a deep sleep the next morning and seemed at peace for her last 24 hours. When she died mid-morning the following day, the staff members treated us with respect and sensitivity. Several days later, they sent a condolence card in which each wrote a personal note. They also offered my father grief counseling for several months.

A year later, my husband and I were equally impressed by the devoted care my mother-in-law received during the last six weeks of her life at a hospice unit in a Veterans Administration hospital (she had been a woman marine during World War II). My father too spent his last three months in hospice care, though he remained at home. A highly competent and compassionate hospice nurse visited him twice a week, and hospice provided medical equipment, such as a hospital bed, wheelchair, and oxygen tanks. Hospice providers also came to his home to bathe him and cut his hair and nails, and on-call nurses were available 24 hours every day of the week. At the end, when he required far more attention, he was transferred to the same inpatient facility that had served my mother and received the same high-quality care in his final three days.

Nevertheless, hospices, like all service providers, can vary in quality. For-profit hospices in particular have been criticized at times for providing inadequate care.[12] If time permits, you

---

12. Reed Abelson, "When a Health Insurer Also Wants to Be a Hospice Company," *New York Times*, June 22, 2018, https://www.nytimes.com/2018/06/22/health/hospice-humana-private-equity.html; Blake Dodge, "Dozens of For-Profit Hospices Fail to Visit Dying People in Their Final

should research potential hospices and select one that is highly reputable.

If you are not a hospice patient, you nevertheless have the option of receiving palliative care. It is available to anyone with significant discomfort, including those who wish to receive curative therapies (such as surgery or chemotherapy) at the same time. Palliative care focuses on relieving suffering caused by pain, shortness of breath, fatigue, insomnia, digestive problems, nausea, loss of appetite, and stress. The palliative care team can include nurses, social workers, pharmacists, chaplains, physical therapists, dieticians, and volunteers.[13] In 2019, 72 percent of hospitals with 50 or more beds and 94 percent of hospitals with at least 300 beds had palliative care programs.[14]

Palliative care specialists may refer patients to psychologists or even to attorneys if psychiatric or legal problems are causing distress and thus exacerbating the patient's suffering. To that end, some hospitals and health centers have formal medical-legal partnerships through which lawyers work directly with their patients to resolve problems related to housing, child custody, public assistance programs, and other matters.[15]

Days," *Newsweek*, November 15, 2019, https://www.newsweek.com/dozens-profit-hospices-fail-visit-dying-people-final-days-gao-1472098; United States Government Accountability Office, "Medicare Hospice Care," Government Accountability Office, October 2019, https://www.gao.gov/assets/710/702149.pdf.

13. MedlinePlus, "What Is Palliative Care?" U.S. National Library of Medicine, updated December 22, 2020, https://medlineplus.gov/ency/patientinstructions/000536.htm.

14. R. Sean Morrison and Diane E. Meier, "America's Care of Serious Illness: 2019," Center to Advance Palliative Care and National Palliative Care Research Center, updated May 2020, 6, 12, https://reportcard.capc.org/wp-content/uploads/2020/05/CAPC_State-by-State-Report-Card_051120.pdf.

15. National Center for Medical-Legal Partnership, "The Response," National Center for Medical-Legal Partnership, accessed December 27, 2020, https://medical-legalpartnership.org/response/.

Patients who receive early palliative care for serious diseases often have better outcomes even with less aggressive treatment. When you have less pain, you are able to heal and thrive to a greater extent. In one study involving 151 patients with advanced lung cancer, those receiving early palliative care scored 6.5 points higher on assessments of mood and quality of life. In addition, their median survival was 11.6 months, compared to 8.9 months for those receiving standard care, even though fewer of the palliative care patients received aggressive end-of-life treatment.[16]

BEING AN ACTIVE MEMBER OF YOUR HEALTH CARE TEAM

There are many ways for patients to exert control over their end-of-life treatment beyond entering hospice or receiving palliative care. All patients are empowered to make choices about their medical treatment. If you are uncertain about the advice that a particular doctor gave you, you can seek a second opinion from a different doctor. As long as you have decision-making capacity, you have an *absolute right* to refuse unwanted treatment even if doing so will expedite your death. This prerogative rises to the level of a constitutional right that was confirmed by the US Supreme Court in the 1990 case *Cruzan v. Director, Missouri Dept. of Health.*[17]

---

16. Jennifer S. Temel et al., "Early Palliative Care for Patients with Metastatic Non–Small-Cell Lung Cancer," *New England Journal of Medicine* 363, no. 8 (2010): 733–42. See also Ravi B. Parikh, Rebecca A. Kirch, Thomas J. Smith, and Jennifer S. Temel, "Early Specialty Palliative Care—Translating Data in Oncology into Practice," *New England Journal of Medicine* 369, no. 24 (2013): 2347–51; David Oliver, "Improving Patient Outcomes through Palliative Care Integration in Other Specialised Health Services: What We Have Learned So Far and How Can We Improve?" *Annals of Palliative Medicine* 7, sup. 3 (2018): S219–S230, http://apm.amegroups.com/article/view/19628/19608.

17. *Cruzan v. Director, Missouri Dept. of Health*, 497 U.S. 261 (1990).

The problem of overtreatment

The contemporary norm is to battle disease forcefully until the patient's last breath. This trend, however, can sometimes cause patients to endure great misery and generates high end-of-life care costs. According to one study, in 2015, Medicare spending for treatment during the last year of life represented 21 percent of total Medicare expenditures.[18] Other researchers found that spending in the last 12 months of life accounts for 8.5 percent of *all* health expenditures in the United States.[19]

Today, there are mounting objections to the traditional approach of treating medical problems aggressively even at the end of life.[20] In the book *Overtreated: Why Too Much Medicine Is Making Us Sicker and Poorer*, Shannon Brownlee decries the "medicalization of aging" and deems it to be "elder abuse."[21] She observes that patients and doctors tend to see "the inevitable breakdown of the body as a series of treatable diseases," which at times leads literally to torturing the dying. The author tells

---

18. Ian Duncan, Tamim Ahmed, Henry Dove, and Terri L. Maxwell, "Medicare Cost at End of Life," *American Journal of Hospice & Palliative Medicine* 36, no. 8 (2019): 705–10.

19. Eric B. French et al., "End-of-Life Medical Spending in Last Twelve Months of Life Is Lower Than Previously Reported," *Health Affairs* 36, no. 7 (2017): 1211–17; Eric French, John Jones, Elaine Kelly, and Jeremy McCauley, "End-of-Life Medical Expenses," *Vox*, September 22, 2019, https://voxeu.org/article/end-life-medical-expenses. On average, Medicare pays $40,000–$50,000 for beneficiaries' medical care during the final year of life. Matthew Allen Davis, "Identification of Four Unique Spending Patterns among Older Adults in the Last Year of Life Challenges Standard Assumptions," *Health Affairs* 35, no. 7 (2016): 1316–23.

20. Geoffrey Hosta, "Doctors Are Torturing Dementia Patients at the End of Their Life. And It's Totally Unnecessary," *Washington Post*, November 28, 2019, https://www.washingtonpost.com/opinions/2019/11/28/doctors-are-torturing-dementia-patients-end-their-life-its-totally-unnecessary/.

21. Shannon Brownlee, *Overtreated: Why Too Much Medicine Is Making Us Sicker and Poorer* (New York: Bloomsbury, 2008), 205.

of one hospitalized lung cancer patient who clearly had only days to live. Yet he was subjected to the placement of a painful nasogastric feeding tube in his nose because he refused food and was tied to the bed with restraints at his wrists and ankles because he was thrashing and likely to pull out the nasogastric tube. The staff had prioritized the futile continuation of nutrition over allowing the man to spend his last days in dignity and comfort.[22]

Dr. Jessica Nutik Zitter provides similar accounts in her book, *Extreme Measures: Finding a Better Path to the End of Life.* She relates that one day, as she was about to insert a catheter in a dying patient's neck, a nurse "lifted an imaginary phone to her ear" and said "Nine-one-one, get me the police. [...] They're torturing a patient in the ICU at University Hospital."[23] You can watch a short documentary called *Extremis* about Dr. Zitter's work in the ICU. It was nominated for a 2017 Academy Award and is available on YouTube. It is a bit difficult to watch but will give you a good idea of what aggressive care in the ICU looks like and what decisions need to be made about it.

In a moving article titled "A Life Worth Ending," Michael Wolff describes his mother's travails.[24] When his mother suffered a worsening of her aortic stenosis (narrowing of the aortic valve), doctors recommended surgery. The author reports that it never occurred to him and his siblings to ask: "You want to do major heart surgery on an 84-year-old woman showing progressive signs of dementia? What are you, nuts?" According to at least some experts, general anesthesia and major surgery

---

22. Brownlee, *Overtreated*, 205–8.

23. Jessica Nutik Zitter, *Extreme Measures: Finding a Better Path to the End of Life* (New York: Avery, 2017), 23.

24. Michael Wolff, "A Life Worth Ending," *New York Magazine*, May 20, 2012, http://nymag.com/news/features/parent-health-care-2012-5/.

(especially cardiac operations) are frequently associated with the deterioration of cognitive abilities.[25]

The operation successfully repaired Mrs. Wolff's heart and added years to her life. But here is the real outcome:

> Where before she had been gently sinking [mentally], now we were in free fall. She was reduced to a terrified creature— losing language skills by the minute. [...] Unmoored in time, she began to wander the halls and was returned on regular occasions to the emergency room: Each return, each ambulance, each set of restraints, each catheter, dealt her another psychic blow.[26]

Jonathan Rauch adds his clear and strong voice of protest in the article "How Not to Die," published in the *Atlantic*. The author decries "the war on death," which he attributes to the American medical system's often unreasonable "determination to save lives" and its astonishing ability to do so through "technological virtuosity." He writes:

> Unwanted treatment is American medicine's dark continent. No one knows its extent, and few people want to talk about it. The U.S. medical system was built to treat anything that might be treatable, at any stage of life—even near the end, when there is no hope of a cure, and when the patient, if fully

25. Michael S. Avidan and Alex S. Evers, "Review of Clinical Evidence for Persistent Cognitive Decline or Incident Dementia Attributable to Surgery or General Anesthesia," *Journal of Alzheimer's Disease* 24, no. 2 (2011): 201–16; BMJ, "Major Surgery Associated with Small, Long Term Decline in Brain Functioning," *Science Daily*, August 7, 2019, https://www.sciencedaily.com/releases/2019/08/190807190827.htm; Mitch Leslie, "Will Surgery Sap Your Brain Power?" *Science*, May 31, 2017, https://www.sciencemag.org/news/2017/05/will-surgery-sap-your-brain-power.
26. Wolff, "A Life Worth Ending."

informed, might prefer quality time and relative normalcy to all-out intervention.[27]

Happily, not all doctors are overly aggressive in treating the ailments of the elderly. Five months before she died of other causes, Eema learned that she had a small and slow-growing kidney cancer. We consulted top-notch experts in Ann Arbor, Michigan, and at the Cleveland Clinic, and they advised against surgery because of her advanced age and several risk factors (low kidney function, high blood pressure, heart problems). It was difficult for Eema, a long-time breast cancer survivor, to adjust to the idea that this time she would not be battling her cancer but rather, coexisting with it. Yet our family was comfortable with the decision, and we believed Eema was fortunate to have seen skilled doctors who focused on her overall well-being, sparing her needless suffering.

It is also true that some doctors may embrace the approach of providing solely palliative care too quickly or be unjustifiably reluctant to provide wanted interventions to the elderly. One friend told me that her mother, who had been diagnosed with cancer over a year earlier, was hospitalized in the ICU. When the doctors observed that she was refusing food, they interpreted this as a sign that she no longer wanted to live and urged my friend "to let her go." Jennifer pointed out that her mother was saying that it hurt too much to eat, which was entirely possible because she had severe chemotherapy-related mouth sores. After appropriate treatment to alleviate the symptoms, the patient began eating again.

Along the same lines, in a short article published in the *Journal of the American Medical Association,* a medical student told the story of her grandmother's hip replacement at the age of

---

27. Jonathan Rauch, "How Not to Die," *The Atlantic,* April 24, 2013, http://www.theatlantic.com/magazine/archive/2013/05/how-not-to-die/309277/.

90. Although physicians were hesitant to operate and urged her to accept her pain and mobility limitations, the elderly woman insisted on having the arduous operation. The author proudly relates that just 12 weeks after surgery, her grandmother "strolled, though at a slow pace, into her surgeon's office [...] with the use of no walking aids."[28]

The power to choose

Given alternatives and a doctor who is willing to provide care, the choice of what treatment route to follow is ultimately up to the patient or her health-care proxy. Elderly patients can opt for aggressive interventions in an effort to prolong life or to enhance its quality. They also have a right to decline standard therapies if they wish to hasten death. The key is for you or your decision maker to understand the risks and implications of each procedure and your long-term prognosis with and without treatment.

Chapter 6, which addressed geriatric care, emphasized the importance of doing your research before, during, and after medical encounters. This point needs to be reiterated here. There is junk on the Internet, but there are also many excellent resources, such as government websites or the websites of highly respected professional organizations, many of which I cite in the book's footnotes. Do not be reluctant to read information from reliable authorities about your medical conditions and potential treatments. You may find useful answers to some of your questions and think of new questions that you should ask your doctors. Moreover, do not forget that you have a right to question your doctors about their recommendations and what is best for you (or your loved one) overall in the long term.

---

28. Kelly Lauren Sloane, "If Only Grown-Ups Would Pay Attention," *Journal of American Medical Association* 309, no. 8 (2013): 779–80.

Likewise, in discussing the topic of the durable power of attorney for health care in Chapter 4, I elaborated on the need to have extensive discussions with your agent concerning end-of-life care. Do you want aggressive treatment even in the face of irreversible mental deterioration? Would you want to be put on a ventilator at the end of life? Do you want measures that will prolong life if they come at the expense of quality of life? If you are terminally ill or have advanced dementia, do you want family members to call an ambulance in the event of a medical crisis or do you wish to avoid hospitalization at all costs?

Even the most well-intentioned substitute decision makers can make mistakes. Michael Wolff notes painfully that his mother's "wishes ha[d] always been properly expressed, volubly and in writing: She urgently did not want to end up where she ultimately ha[d] ended up."[29] And he acknowledges that the family did not question the doctor who suggested cardiac surgery about its implications for his mother's deteriorating mental capacities. Thus, you must make sure that your health-care agent is prepared to do both of the following: (1) think carefully about what your wishes would be under the circumstances and (2) research suggested interventions and question clinicians to determine which option will best fit your wishes.

DNRs, out-of-hospital DNRs, and POLST

Advance directives are created and signed by patients (see Chapter 4), but do not resuscitate (DNR) orders, out-of-hospital DNRs and portable medical order sets (POLST)[30] are

---

29. Wolff, "A Life Worth Ending."

30. POLST orders may also be called POST (physician orders for scope of treatment), MOLST (medical orders for life-sustaining treatment), and MOST (medical orders for scope of treatment). POLST previously was an abbreviation for "physician orders for life-sustaining treatment," but this terminology is no longer used.

prepared by physicians after speaking with patients or their agents. DNR orders apply in hospitals and nursing homes in limited circumstances. They instruct that the patient should not be resuscitated if her heart stops. Out-of-hospital DNRs are recognized in most states and are portable orders that follow patients wherever they go. Patients with these orders wear identification tags indicating that they do not wish to be resuscitated by emergency personnel. POLST are medical orders that are more comprehensive than DNRs, covering not only cardiopulmonary resuscitation (CPR) but also decisions such as hospitalization, feeding tubes, antibiotics, and ventilation.[31]

Although DNRs provide clear instructions to caregivers, they have not escaped controversy. DNRs are designed to impact care only if the patient's heart actually stops. However, evidence suggests that patients with DNR orders may be denied other therapeutic interventions because physicians tend to interpret the orders broadly as indicating that the patient generally wishes to reject aggressive treatment. For example, one study found that patients who arrive at an ICU unit with a DNR order are more likely to die within 28 days than are ICU patients without a DNR order (33.9 percent vs. 18.4 percent).[32] Consequently, some experts advise against premature placement of a DNR order. Instead, according to these experts, patients should ensure that their health-care proxies have a detailed understanding of their wishes for decision-making purposes, and put a DNR order in place only close to the time of anticipated death.[33]

31. Compassion & Choices, "Do Not Resuscitate (DNR) and POLST," Compassion & Choices, accessed December 27, 2020, https://compassion andchoices.org/end-of-life-planning/plan/dnr/; National POLST Paradigm, "Programs in Your State," POLST.org, accessed December 27, 2020, http:// www. polst.org/programs-in-your-state/.

32. Lior Fuchs et al., "Quantifying the Mortality Impact of Do-Not-Resuscitate Orders in the ICU," *Critical Care Medicine* 45, no. 6 (2017): 1019–27.

33. Derek K. Richardson, Dana Zive, Mohamud Daya, and Craig D Newgard, "The Impact of Early Do Not Resuscitate (DNR) Orders on

POLST were introduced by clinicians at the Center for Ethics and Health Care at the Oregon State Health and Science University in the early 1990s. POLST forms are appropriate for seriously ill or frail individuals. According to the National POLST Paradigm, these are

- People whose health-care provider would not be surprised if they died within 1–2 years; or
- People at an increased risk of experiencing a medical emergency because of serious medical problems who wish to clarify their preferences regarding CPR, mechanical ventilation, ICU, and other aggressive treatment; or
- People who have had multiple unexpected hospital admissions in the last 12 months along with more frailty and worse functioning.[34]

Advocates are enthusiastic about POLST because these orders cover a broader range of end-of-life treatments than DNRs and transform advance directives into actual physician orders. Because they are medical orders, they are more likely to be seen by treating physicians than are advance directives, which are not always incorporated into the patient's chart or are not prominently placed in it, and thus POLST can promote greater adherence to patients' wishes.[35] In addition, you can wear a bracelet indicating that you have a POLST. The forms also travel with the patient, so that orders concerning end-of-life

---

Patient Care and Outcomes Following Resuscitation from Out of Hospital Cardiac Arrest," *Resuscitation* 84, no. 4 (2013): 483–87.

34. National POLST Paradigm, "National POLST Paradigm: Intended Population & Guidance for Health Care Professionals," POLST.org, revised January 14, 2019, https://polst.org/wp-content/uploads/2020/03/2019.01.14-POLST-Intended-Population.pdf.

35. Sharona Hoffman, "Portable Medical Order Sets (POLST®): Ethical and Legal Landscape," *NAELA Journal* 15 (Fall 2019): 1–11.

care can be followed in all care settings, not just hospitals.[36] However, like DNRs, POLST forms generate concern that clinicians will take a low-intensity approach to caring for patients who have them and withhold interventions that the patient would want and did not mean to prohibit.[37]

Religious beliefs

If religion is important to you, you should investigate its teachings about end-of-life care. In my own religion, Judaism, the transition to comfort care is governed by the concept of *goses*. A *goses* is a moribund person, that is, a person who is dying. All rabbinical authorities agree that no further medical efforts need to be undertaken to prolong the life of one who has become a *goses*, though comfort measures must be continued. The problem is that there is considerable disagreement as to when the *goses* stage is reached. Some hold that you become a *goses* when your doctors believe that you will die within 72 hours. More liberal authorities offer a broader definition and teach that you can be deemed a *goses* as soon as you receive a diagnosis of an incurable, terminal illness, even if the dying process could take a year or longer.[38] According to this view, it would be acceptable to stop aggressive treatments earlier on.

---

36. Information about the POLST program in your sate can be found at "State Programs," POLST.org, https://polst.org/programs-in-your-state/.

37. Stanley A. Terman, "It Isn't Easy Being Pink: Potential Problems with POLST Paradigm Forms," *Hamline Law Review* 36, no. 2 (2013): 177–211; Judith Graham, "You May Have Signed a Living Will, but Scary Mistakes Can Happen at the ER," *Washington Post*, August 5, 2018, https://www.washingtonpost.com/national/health-science/you-may-have-signed-a-living-will-but-scary-mistakes-can-happen-at-the-er/2018/08/03/418ec3e8-6fed-11e8-bf86-a2351b5ece99_story.html.

38. Elliot N. Dorff, *Matters of Life and Death: A Jewish Approach to Modern Medical Ethics* (Philadelphia, PA: Jewish Publication Society, 1998), 199–200.

When we made the decision to discontinue Eema's treatment in the ICU, we were all in agreement and did not struggle with its moral implications. Eema was clearly already dying—she was gasping for breath even with oxygen and had had no food or water by mouth for 10 days. In fact, she was gone within fewer than 72 hours after entering hospice care. However, I know that in many cases, circumstances are more ambiguous, and disagreements can tear families apart and traumatize the patient.

For those who value religious doctrine, clarity about what your faith teaches concerning end-of-life care can be very helpful. Moreover, postponing the study of religious medical ethics until you are in the midst of a medical crisis, urgently needing to make decisions, is unwise. As a member of a hospital ethics committee, I know that at times, patients or their families insist that their religion dictates certain decisions, but clergy from their denomination tell us that the individuals' understanding does not reflect formal religious doctrine. People who study religious teachings at leisure, without the pressures of a medical emergency, are more likely to obtain a deep understanding of the subject and to determine for themselves what they believe their faith requires of them.

MEDICAL AID IN DYING

In 10 jurisdictions, it is legal for doctors to help patients end their lives if they no longer wish to endure suffering. This was previously known as physician-assisted suicide, but the preferred term is now medical aid in dying.

Doctors who follow detailed protocols can prescribe barbiturates to qualifying patients, and the patients then take the drugs themselves when they wish to die.[39] Oregon,

---

39. Timothy E. Quill and Bernard Sussman, "Physician-Assisted Death," The Hastings Center, September 23, 2015, https://www.thehastingscenter.org/briefingbook/physician-assisted-death/.

Washington, Vermont, California, Colorado, the District of Columbia, Hawaii, Maine, and New Jersey legalized the practice by statute. Oregon's law was famously the first in the United States, having been enacted in 1994, and as of this writing, Maine and New Jersey are the most recent to accept medical aid in dying with 2019 statutes.[40] In addition, in 2009, Montana's Supreme Court held that physicians who provide aid in dying pursuant to patients' wishes are immune from criminal liability, though the state has not established a legal protocol for the practice.[41]

In truth, very few people seek a physician's assistance in ending their lives even when they have a legal option to do so. Let us consider statistics from the two states that have had the longest experience with medical aid in dying: Oregon and Washington.

Oregon's Death with Dignity Act (DWDA) 2020 report provides the following data:

- A total of 370 people received prescriptions under the DWDA in 2020 (compared with 297 in 2019).
- A total of 245 people died in 2020 from ingesting the prescribed medications, an increase from 191 during 2019.
- This figure includes 22 individuals who had received the prescriptions in previous years.
- Among patients who died using DWDA prescriptions, 81 percent were 65 and older.
- During 2020, the estimated rate of DWDA deaths was 65.5 per 10,000 total deaths (0.65 percent).

---

40. Death with Dignity, "Death with Dignity Acts," DeathwithDignity.org, accessed December 28, 2020, https://www.deathwithdignity.org/learn/death-with-dignity-acts/.

41. *Baxter v. State*, 224 P.3d 1211 (Mont. 2009).

- A total of 2,895 prescriptions were written under the DWDA since 1997, and 1,905 people (66 percent) died from ingesting the prescribed medications.[42]

Washington State's most recently published report (for 2018) provides the following details:

- In 2018, 267 patients received medication pursuant to its Death with Dignity Act.
- Of these, 251 died, but only 203 are known to have ingested the medication. The others died of natural or unknown causes.
- The 251 deceased individuals ranged in age from 28 to 98.
- Among the 251 decedents, 75 percent had cancer; 10 percent had neurodegenerative disease (such as Lou Gehrig's disease); and 15 percent had heart and respiratory disease or other illnesses.[43]

Those who are concerned that the legalization of medical aid in dying will frequently lead to the deaths of frail individuals who are pressured to end their lives should be encouraged by these statistics. Although a 2018 Gallup poll[44] showed that

42. Oregon Health Authority, Public Health Division, "Oregon Death with Dignity Act: 2020 Data Summary," Oregon Health Authority, February 26, 2021, 5–6, https://www.oregon.gov/oha/PH/ PROVIDERPARTNERRESOURCES/EVALUATIONRESEARCH/ DEATHWITHDIGNITYACT/Documents/year23.pdf.

43. Katherine Hutchinson and Zachary Smithingell, "2018 Death with Dignity Act Report," Washington State Department of Health, July 2019, 5, https://www.doh.wa.gov/Portals/1/Documents/Pubs/422-109-DeathWithDignityAct2018.pdf.

44. Megan Brenan, "America's Strong Support for Euthanasia Persists," *Gallup*, May 31, 2018, https://news.gallup.com/poll/235145/americans-strong-support-euthanasia-persists.aspx.

72 percent of Americans believe physicians should be able to help people with terminal illnesses die,[45] very few take advantage of this option when it is available to them.

This may be attributable to the statutory safeguards that exist in the United States.[46] The state statutes establish strict eligibility criteria for patients seeking medical aid in dying.

- The patient must be at least 18 years old and a resident of the state in which medical aid in dying is sought.
- The patient must be able to make and communicate health-care decisions him- or herself.
- Two physicians must diagnose the patient as having a terminal illness that will lead to death within six months. (Note that it is often very difficult to predict with any degree of confidence when death will occur).[47]
- If either physician determines that the patient's judgment is impaired by depression or another condition, the individual must undergo a psychological examination.[48]
- Patients with dementia are ineligible for medical aid in dying because the statutes do not permit anyone other than the patient (e.g., a health-care agent) to make the decision and prohibit physicians from honoring requests

---

45. Note that the question's wording influences the response rate. When asked if doctors should be permitted to help terminally ill patients "commit suicide," only 65 percent answered yes. Only 54 percent said yes when they were asked specifically if physician-assisted suicide was *morally* acceptable.

46. See Or. Rev. Stat. Ann. Tit. 13, §§ 127.800–897; Wash. Rev. Code Ann. §§70.245.010 – 70.245.904; Vt. Stat. Ann. Tit. 18, §§5281–5292.

47. Katrina Hedberg and Susan Tolle, "Putting Oregon's Death with Dignity Act in Perspective: Characteristics of Decedents Who Did Not Participate," *Journal of Clinical Ethics* 20, no. 2 (2009): 133–35.

48. In Hawaii, a mental health evaluation is mandatory for all patients requesting medications under the Death with Dignity law. "How Death with Dignity Laws Work," DeathwithDignity.org, accessed January 6, 2020, https://www.deathwithdignity.org/learn/access/.

for medical aid in dying that were made in advance directives.

- Attending physician must be licensed in the state.
- Attending physicians must inform patients of alternatives such as palliative care and, in Oregon and Washington, must ask patients to notify their next of kin of their prescription requests.

The request procedures are also somewhat elaborate. There is a mandatory 15-day[49] waiting period between a first and second oral request to a physician followed by submission of a written request to the doctor. Thereafter, in most states, the physician must wait 48 hours before writing the prescription. In Oregon and Washington, physicians must report to the state all prescriptions that they write for medical aid in dying purposes.

Finally, the statistics reported by Oregon and Washington suggest that in about one-quarter to one-third of cases, individuals find comfort in having the option of taking the drugs but die naturally before deciding to do so.[50] Some people never reach the point of deciding that life is no longer worth living, and for some, taking the irreversible step of initiating death may turn out to be more complicated or frightening than they thought it would be.

---

49. The waiting period is 20 days in Hawaii.

50. Vermont issued its first report in 2018, and its statistics confirm this trend. Because Vermont is a small state, there were far fewer participants in its program. Between May 31, 2013, and June 30, 2017, 52 prescriptions were filled under Vermont's statute, and 48 of these patients died. However, only 29 died by ingesting the prescribed drugs. The others died because of their disease or other causes. See Vermont Department of Health, "Report to the Vermont Legislature: Report Concerning Patient Choice at the End of Life," Vermont Department of Health, January 15, 2018, http://legislature.vermont.gov/assets/Legislative-Reports/2018-Patient-Choice-Legislative-Report-12-14-17.pdf.

Americans may also have an option for medical aid in dying outside of the United States. Dignitas is a Swiss organization founded in 1998 that accepts clients from all over the world for purposes of assistance in dying at a facility in Zurich. According to its website, it uses a fast-acting and painless barbiturate dissolved in drinking water. To qualify for "accompanied suicide" an individual must be a member of Dignitas, of sound judgment, able to self-administer the drug, and have one of the following: (1) a terminal illness, (2) "unendurable incapacitating disability," or (3) "unbearable and uncontrollable pain."[51] A film called *The Suicide Tourist* (available on YouTube) portrays Dignitas in a very positive light. However, not surprisingly, the organization has been controversial and occasionally faces misconduct accusations. According to Dignitas' data sheet, it helped 3,027 people die between 1998 and 2019.[52]

ENDING YOUR LIFE WITHOUT MEDICAL ASSISTANCE

Residents of states in which medical aid in dying is not legal are left to their own devices if they wish to end their lives before they die naturally. A variety of websites and publications offer chemical and drug recipes and equipment that aim to help patients end their lives as painlessly as possible. An organization called Final Exit Network (originally the Hemlock Society) offers "education, support, and a compassionate presence" to those who meet its medical evaluation committee criteria.[53]

51. Dignitas, "Accompanied Suicide," Dignitas, updated December 18, 2020, http://www.dignitas.ch/index.php?option=com_content&view=article& id=20&Itemid=60&lang=en.

52. Statista, "Annual Number of Accompanied Suicides to Dignitas in Switzerland from 1998 to 2019," Statista, February 11, 2020, https:// www.statista.com/statistics/675701/dignitas-number-of-accompanied- suicides-europe/.

53. Homepage, FinalExitNetwork.org, accessed December 28, 2020, https://finalexitnetwork.org/.

Experts, however, warn that those following suicide manuals on their own are at risk of making mistakes that can render them seriously disabled but still alive. This is because "underlying disease states and chronic drug therapy may affect the absorption, distribution, metabolism and excretion of substances ingested."[54]

In most states in the United States, physicians whose patients seek their aid in dying can do little more than advise them to stop accepting food and fluids. This is known in medical parlance as VSED—voluntary stopping eating and drinking. Death from starvation and dehydration can take 7–10 days or longer. This seems like a terrible way to die, but patients at the end of life often do not feel hunger or thirst. There are a number of published accounts of patients who have made this choice. A particularly poignant one is Zoe FitzGerald Carter's *Imperfect Endings*. In this book, she recounts the story of her mother, a long-time Parkinson's disease sufferer, who died after 12 days of fasting, supplemented by a morphine overdose.[55]

What about patients with dementia who do not have the capacity to decide to stop eating and drinking? One controversial approach is to address the matter in your advance directive.[56] In fact, a new form of advance directive is called an "advance directive for dementia."[57] Two scholars, Paul. T. Menzel and

---

54. Barbara Insley Crouch, "Toxicological Issues with Drugs Used to End Life," in *Drug Use in Assisted Suicide and Euthanasia*, ed. Margaret P. Battin and Arthur G. Lipman (Binghamton, NY: Haworth Press, 1996), 219.

55. Zoe FitzGerald Carter, *Imperfect Endings: A Daughter's Story of Love, Loss, and Letting Go* (New York: Simon & Schuster, 2010); David Muller, "Physician-Assisted Death Is Illegal in Most States, So My Patient Made Another Choice," *Health Affairs* 31, no. 10 (2012): 2343–46.

56. Jonel Aleccia, "'Aggressive' Advance Directive Permits Halting Food and Water in Severe Dementia," *NPR*, March 29, 2018, https://www.npr.org/sections/health-shots/2018/03/27/597499464/-aggressive-advance-directive-authorizes-stopping-food-in-cases-of-dementia.

57. "Advance Directive for Dementia," https://dementia-directive.org/, accessed December 28, 2020; JoNel Aleccia, "Diagnosed with Dementia,

M. Colette Chandler-Cramer, have argued that individuals should be able to direct that they not be given food and water if they have severe dementia and resist being fed or show no signs of enjoying the activity of eating. The authors write that "with an appropriate directive, full withholding is [ethically] justified when the current experiential value of survival to the patient has diminished enough that it is outweighed by the critical interests and autonomy represented in the directive."[58] Other ethicists would find this approach morally unacceptable and posit that patients with dementia should be fed as long as eating and drinking does not cause them real distress.[59] If you feel that you would want to have food and water withheld if you develop severe dementia, you should certainly address the matter in your advance directive.[60] However, many caregivers will undoubtedly feel too uncomfortable to honor this instruction.[61]

She Documented Her Wishes for the End. Then Her Retirement Home Said No," *Washington Post*, January 18, 2020, https://www.washingtonpost.com/health/diagnosed-with-dementia-she-documented-her-wishes-for-the-end-then-her-retirement-home-said-no/2020/01/17/cf63eeaa-3189-11ea-9313-6cba89b1b9fb_story.html.

58. Paul T. Menzel and M. Colette Chandler-Cramer, "Advance Directives, Dementia, and Withholding Food and Water by Mouth," *Hastings Center Report* 44, no. 3 (2014): 33.

59. Rebecca Dresser, "Toward a Humane Death with Dementia," *Hastings Center Report* 44, no. 3 (2014): 38–40.

60. In 2019, Nevada passed a law that recognizes the legitimacy of advance directive instructions that ask caregivers to stop providing food and fluids by mouth to a person with advanced dementia. It is the first state to have enacted such a statute. Thaddeus Mason Pope, "Avoiding Late-Stage Dementia with Advance Directives for Stopping Eating and Drinking," *KevinMD.com*, October 6, 2019, https://www.kevinmd.com/blog/2019/10/avoiding-late-stage-dementia-with-advance-directives-for-stopping-eating-and-drinking.html.

61. Aleccia, "Diagnosed with Dementia, She Documented Her Wishes for the End. Then Her Retirement Home Said No."

CODA

Admittedly, it is difficult to anticipate our thoughts and wishes in times of crisis. Even those who adamantly assert that they would reject life-prolonging treatment if they were grievously ill may find that, at the moment of decision, they are far more ambivalent than they ever imagined they would be. The *New York Times Magazine* piece "A Life or Death Situation" crystallizes this point in a poignant story about bioethicist Peggy Battin and her husband, Brooke Hopkins, who became a quadriplegic after an accident in 2008 and consequently suffered many life-threatening health problems.[62] Both were strong advocates of patient autonomy and the right to choose to end life rather than endure terrible suffering. Yet, they came back from the brink of declining further treatment several times. Despite her copious writing on the subject, Battin found her theories very difficult to apply to her own personal situation.

Nevertheless, familiarity with options such as the possibility of rejecting unwanted care, requesting a DNR or POLST order, or medical aid in dying can promote better decision-making. Likewise, engaging in soul-searching about your preferences and, if relevant, understanding your own religious beliefs should facilitate your decision-making when the time comes.

These ideas are embraced by a movement called The Conversation Project that promotes discussion of death and dying matters among loved ones in small social gatherings. The project provides conversation starter kits and a wealth of information on its website.[63] A significant number of Americans do not think about end-of-life issues at all. According to a 2017 Kaiser Family Foundation report, only

---

62. Robin Marantz Henig, "A Life or Death Situation," *New York Times Magazine,* July 17, 2013, 27.

63. Available at "Homepage," TheConversationProject.org, https://theconversationproject.org/.

56 percent of American adults say they have had a serious conversation with a loved one about their end-of-life care wishes.[64] The Conversation Project aims to increase that number dramatically.

Planning for aging should include preparation not only for living as an elderly person but also for the dying process. Doing so can be of great benefit when we face our loved ones' final illnesses and ultimately, when we face our own.

END-OF-LIFE PREPAREDNESS CHECKLIST

* Understand that you have a right to refuse unwanted treatment.
* Ask for a palliative care consult if you or your loved one is experiencing significant discomfort.
* If you are ill and have significant legal problems, ask your doctor or hospital if your health-care facility has a medical-legal partnership.
* Consider hospice if you (or a loved one) do not want life-prolonging treatment and are in the last six months of life according to your doctors.
* Consider requesting a DNR or out-of-hospital DNR order or POLST if you wish to limit care and are near the end of life.

---

64. Laz Hamel, Bryan Wu, and Mollyan Brodie, "Views and Experiences with End-of-Life Medical Care in the U.S.," The Henry J. Kaiser Family Foundation, April 2017, http://files.kff.org/attachment/Report-Views-and-Experiences-with-End-of-Life-Medical-Care-in-the-US. See also Amy Goyer and Andy Markowitz, "How to Start a Conversation about of End-of-Life Care," AARP, September 17, 2020, https://www.aarp.org/caregiving/basics/info-2020/end-of-life-talk-care-talk.html (stating that only 32 percent of people have talked with their loved ones about their end-of-life wishes).

* If you or a loved one may one day be interested in medical aid in dying and live in a state in which it is permissible, learn about the conditions under which it is potentially appropriate.
* Examine your religious or moral beliefs about end-of-life care.

CHAPTER 9

CONCLUSION

I began writing the first edition of this book as a way to address my own anxieties about growing old without children, and I hoped that my work would also help others. I ask myself now: Has what I have learned provided me with reassurance about planning for old age and my ability to take steps that will enhance my quality of life in later years? The answer is yes.

As I write this concluding chapter of the second edition, it is May of 2021, and we have grappled with the COVID-19 pandemic for well over a year. I am working remotely and spending almost all my time at home. I know more about life's unpredictability and social isolation than ever before.

Indeed, there are aspects of life in general and aging in particular that are largely outside our control. Pandemics are one example. Another is dementia, though some research indicates that even this ailment can be delayed or diminished through exercise, good diet, control of blood pressure and cholesterol, social engagement, and continued employment.[1]

---

1. National Institute on Aging, "Preventing Alzheimer's Disease: What Do We Know?" National Institute on Aging, last reviewed September 24, 2018, https://www.nia.nih.gov/health/preventing-alzheimers-disease-what-do-we-know; Muriel R. Gillick, *The Denial of Aging: Perpetual Youth, Eternal Life, and Other Dangerous Fantasies* (Cambridge, MA: Harvard University Press, 2006), 257–58; Fiona E. Matthews et al., on behalf of the Medical Research Council Cognitive Function and Ageing Collaboration, "A Two-Decade Comparison of Prevalence of Dementia in Individuals Aged 65 Years and

245

In my own life, my husband's Parkinson's disease has added a great deal of uncertainty because the condition's progression varies from person to person. We do not know how long he will be able to work, how severe his disabilities will become and when, what his care needs will be, and how much financial strain his care will place on us. I must accept that as much as I love planning, some of my plans may not come to fruition because of the hurdles that life will throw my way. I am also striving not to be excessively focused on the future and to shift to a greater extent to enjoying every day in the present because I don't know what tomorrow will bring.

Yet, there are many potential misfortunes, such as acute loneliness or inappropriate medical care, that you might be able to avoid or whose impact you could lessen through forethought, preparedness, and a variety of interventions. The prospect of aging should not be bleak even for those without strong family support systems. In the words of physician, Harvard professor, and author Muriel Gillick, "We need to see old age as neither all bad nor [...] all good, but rather not unlike adolescence or other challenging stages of life, as both."[2]

Have I begun to practise what I preach? Yes, in the process of writing this book, I did several things to initiate my own aging preparedness, and I have recommitted myself to a few good habits that I had already formed.

1. **Retirement communities:** I learned a lot about retirement communities in general and continuing care retirement communities (CCRCs) in particular and developed an interest in moving to a community setting after retirement. As I grow older, I will continue

---

Older from Three Geographical Areas of England: Results of the Cognitive Function and Ageing Study 1 and II," *Lancet* 382, no. 9902 (2013): 1405–12.

2. Gillick, *The Denial of Aging*, 267.

to investigate CCRCs and other less expensive options. I know several people who, prior to retirement, spent a week of vacation every year traveling to retirement communities in different locations. I now understand why and know that I too will need to spend considerable time at any facility that is of real interest to me.

2. **Legal documents:** I revisited and updated my will, advance directive, durable power of attorney for finances and property, and durable power of attorney for health care. I made sure that my agent (my husband) and substitute agent (my sister) have copies of my documents, and I talked with them about my wishes should I become unable to make decisions for myself. I will make sure to initiate similar conversations periodically in the future.

3. **Savings and financial management:** I have always been committed to saving as much as possible. I will now continue to do so with renewed purpose, having learned much more about the cost of a comfortable retirement. I will continue to consult our excellent financial adviser and be sure to meet with him at least twice a year for a thorough assessment of our investments.

4. **Diet and exercise:** I have exercised regularly for years and don't feel that I need to change my routine in this area. Diet is a different story. I love sweets and do not love vegetables. Am I likely to change my eating habits? Sure, but maybe not until next year!

5. **Social interaction:** My research emphasized to me the importance of having a large network of friends and relatives. Social engagement has numerous psychological and other health benefits.[3] Unfortunately, I tend to prioritize work over socializing, and I need to improve in this regard. I have tried harder to stay in touch with friends and to get

---

3. See Chapter 2.

together regularly (before the pandemic) with those who live nearby. I also have made more of an effort to contact people I know when I travel to other cities and to make sure I see them and renew or maintain old friendships. During COVID-19, I had many Zoom get-togethers with friends, including those whom I had not seen in several years. It turned out that with a little effort, even stay-at-home practices could yield some social opportunities.

A friend of mine, who had been a high achiever in her career, told me that the year after she retired was her "year of yes." She tried multiple activities for which she had never had time and accepted invitations whenever friends asked her to join them even if she was not sure she would enjoy the gathering or outing. "A year of yes" sounds like an excellent idea to me.

6. **Intellectual pursuits:** My work occupies my mind too much of the time, and I am trying to devote more effort to developing other intellectual interests, hobbies, and volunteer work that will sustain me after retirement. I enjoy taking nonwork-related continuing education classes and attending public lectures, reading, going to movies and the theater, being active in my synagogue, and serving as a member of a hospital ethics committee. For a couple of years before the pandemic, I took ballroom dancing classes twice a month and enjoyed learning this new skill. I know that reading and writing can prevent cognitive decline in older adults, and I will never abandon these activities so long as I am capable of doing them.[4] To add a social element to reading, I have joined a book club. Still, my leisure life needs improvement, and I will work on cultivating it in the future.

---

4. Roger J. Kreuz, "One Skill That Doesn't Deteriorate with Age," *Salon*, September 7, 2019, https://www.salon.com/2019/09/07/one-skill-that-doesnt-deteriorate-with-age_partner/.

7. **Medical care:** As someone who had major surgery at a young age, I tend to become quite concerned about any unusual symptoms and to seek the care of specialists. As I age and my health problems become more numerous, I need to worry more about coordinated care and to take greater initiative to become a member of my own medical team. I now try routinely to ask about drug–drug interactions, side effects, and whether treatment is actually necessary. In addition, I often prepare for medical appointments by looking at reliable Internet sources. Finally, as much as I am inclined to trust the expertise of doctors, I keep in mind that I am empowered to decline unwanted treatments, seek second opinions, and not return to doctors with whom I am dissatisfied.

All in all, writing this book has provided me with reassurance. There are already many resources available to the elderly, although finding and using them may require effort. As the large population of baby boomers ages, the number and types of resources will hopefully increase considerably.

HELP FROM THE GOVERNMENT

To what extent can American seniors count on the government to provide them with needed support in old age? We are fortunate in this country to have several public safety net programs for the elderly, although I would argue that they do not go far enough. Most retirees qualify for social security payments, which depend on their earnings and how much they paid into the system.[5] Medicare covers some but not all

---

5. Social Security Administration, "Retirement Benefits," *Social Security Administration Publication No. 05-10035*, July 2020, 1–3, http://www.ssa.gov/pubs/EN-05-10035.pdf.

medical expenses for those who are 65 and older, and Medicaid provides additional coverage for low-income seniors, including for nursing home care.

In addition, the Older Americans Act of 1965 (OAA),[6] helps fund the delivery of certain social services to the aging population.[7] The law established the Administration on Aging within the Department of Health and Human Services and provides for grants that support state, local, and private agencies furnishing services such as meals, transportation, home care, aid for family caregivers, and disease prevention and health promotion programs. In fiscal year 2021, OAA funding totaled 2.129 billion, which is far from adequate.[8] Approximately 11 million older adults benefit from OAA programming each year (out of a population of 54 million seniors).[9]

By contrast, the governments of some countries play a more proactive role in ensuring the welfare of their elderly.

---

6. 42 U.S.C. §§ 3001–3057.

7. Tamara Lytle, "Older Americans Act Needs Money, Support: Lawmakers Can Strengthen This Vital Program," AARP, April 5, 2019, https://www.aarp.org/politics-society/advocacy/info-2019/older-americans-act-funding.html.

8. Kirsten J. Colello and Agnela Napili, "Older Americans Act: Overview and Funding," 9, Congressional Research Service, updated April 22, 2021, https://crsreports.congress.gov/product/pdf/R/R43414#:~:text=116%2D94)%20provided%20discretionary%20appropriations,more%20than%20the%20FY2019%20level. The Coronavirus Aid, Relief and Economic Security (CARES) Act added over $800 million for OAA programs. Administration for Community Living, "Older Americans Act," Administration for Community Living, updated December 2, 2020, https://acl.gov/about-acl/older-americans-act-oaa.

9. Dena Bunis, "Older Americans Act Reauthorized for 5 Years," AARP, March 26, 2020, https://feeds.aarp.org/politics-society/government-elections/info-2020/oaa-reauthorization.html?_amp=true.

Not surprisingly, these countries often have higher tax rates than we do in the United States. For example, Sweden's Social Services Act establishes that people of all ages have a right to receive services if their needs cannot otherwise be met. Swedish municipalities offer meals that are home delivered or available at adult day care centers whose cost varies with income. The government provides public and special transportation services that are accessible to individuals with disabilities. Home care assistance is also widely available with fees that are calculated based on household income and living expenses. Informal caregivers, such as family members, can also obtain payment in the form of a "carer's allowance" and four hours of cost-free respite coverage per week. Services are offered through either a public provider or a private company subsidized by the government.[10]

Given our aversion to high taxes, it is unlikely that the US government will significantly increase funding for programs or services in the foreseeable future. Nevertheless, many charitable organizations, religious institutions, and private enterprises offer a wealth of services and programs for seniors, as discussed throughout this book.

WHAT THE FUTURE HOLDS

The resources that I have described in these chapters are already available to seniors. The future, however, promises

---

10. Susan M. Collins, Robbyn R. Wacker, and Karen A. Roberto, "Considering Quality of Life for Older Adults: A View from Two Countries," *Generations* 37, no. 1 (2013): 82–84; "Elderly Care in Sweden," The Official Site of Sweden, updated July 3, 2020, https://sweden.se/society/elderly-care-in-sweden/.

to bring support mechanisms that are only in early stages of development today.

Technology may significantly extend seniors' ability to remain independent and mobile. For example, as noted in Chapter 5, autonomous cars may enable elderly individuals to drive even in the face of impairments that would otherwise affect their reaction time and driving ability. Similarly, robots may help elderly individuals with various tasks and allow them to continue living at home.[11]

Entrepreneurs are also creating technology for "smart homes." These include a large number of safety and comfort-enhancing features such as the following:

- Smart door locks and security systems that can be operated remotely;
- Smart doorbells with video surveillance, speakers, and microphones;
- Smart refrigerators that keep track of people's grocery lists and deliver them to participating nearby grocery stores;
- Automatic stove turn-off devices;
- Automatic medication dispensers;
- Smart thermostats that learn their owners' preferences and provide remote access;
- Key finders that can be attached to keys;
- Smart light switches that can be controlled using timers or voice commands and a smartphone app;
- Smart toilets that can analyze urine to detect urinary tract infections, kidney disease, diabetes, how you are metabolizing your medications, and details about your diet, exercise, and even sleep;

---

11. Luke Dormehl, "The Promise and Pitfalls of Using Robots to Care for the Elderly," *Digital Trends*, June 1, 2019, https://www.digitaltrends.com/cool-tech/robots-caregiving-for-the-elderly/.

- Wearable health monitoring sensors that communicate information relating to heart health, and chronic conditions directly to health-care providers.[12]

It is not clear how expensive such items will be if they are widely marketed and whether they would be affordable for people of modest means. Nevertheless, in planning for old age, we should familiarize ourselves with existing and emerging resources.

I have developed several other essential planning themes in this book. They are worth highlighting again in this concluding chapter.

THE IMPORTANCE OF SOCIAL LIFE

A robust social life is critical to happiness at any time in life and especially after retirement, when people no longer interact with others through work on a daily basis. The elderly are vulnerable to becoming socially isolated for a variety of reasons. You may no longer be able to travel to visit loved ones. Some people withdraw from social, civic, or intellectual activities because of disability or transportation challenges. Some have difficulty communicating with others and participating in conversations because of hearing loss. You may become housebound because of severe mobility or cognitive impairments. If you are very elderly, you may not have visitors because your contemporaries are frail or predecease you. At the same time, many seniors cherish their autonomy and prioritize "aging in place" and

---

12. Taylor Gadsden "Smart Home Adjustments Every Senior Can Make for Better Living," AllConnect.com, June 18, 2020, https://www.all connect.com/blog/smart-home-technology-seniors/;KevinWheeler,"Urine Luck: Your Toilet Could Spot Signs of Disease," *USA Today*, December 20, 2019, https://www.pressreader.com/usa/usa-today-us-edition/2019 1220/281676846811864.

continuing to live independently in their longtime homes, no matter how lonely or disabled they are.

This approach, however, is misguided. In the words of Dr. Muriel Gillick, "baby boomers will need to give up our single-minded devotion to individual autonomy and to accept the fact that community is tremendously important as we age."[13]

Baby boomers should seriously consider moving to retirement communities while they are robust enough to enjoy their offerings. Such facilities foster social integration and furnish safe and accessible homes for the elderly. Aging within a close and vibrant community is of far greater value than aging in a home that is spacious and holds memories of decades past.

All of us should emphasize nurturing friendships and expanding our social circles throughout life. Involvement in a church, synagogue, mosque, or other religious entity often provides a natural mechanism for social contact, as does membership in other organizations. If you grew comfortable with Zoom or similar technology during the pandemic, do not lose this skill and continue to stay in touch with people whom you cannot often see. Do not give up opportunities to meet new people, see friends, and build a network of people who care about each other.

RETAINING A SENSE OF PURPOSE AND USEFULNESS

To be happy, you need not only friends but also meaning and purpose in life. After retirement, you need to replace your career with other meaningful and rewarding activities, such as volunteer work, a creative outlet, or advocacy for a good cause.

Several months after he was widowed, my father wrote a short memoir and reported that this undertaking gave him a

---

13. Gillick, *The Denial of Aging*, 259.

"renewed appetite for life." Other acquaintances volunteer for charitable organizations, take classes, become politically active, pursue hobbies such as fishing, and develop their artistic talents in areas such as painting or photography, to which they could devote only minimal time in the past. Younger retirees could also contribute to the well-being of older seniors by assisting them with driving, errands, and household chores either as volunteers or for a modest fee.

If you need income or simply enjoy working, you can seek a part-time job. Like volunteering and leisure activities, so-called bridge work can enhance life satisfaction after retirement.[14]

You should not postpone involvement in nonwork-related activities until old age, when it might be difficult to take on completely new endeavors. To prepare for retirement, middle-aged individuals should cultivate hobbies, interests, and volunteer work that they can continue to pursue later in life.

WRITE YOUR LEGISLATOR

Baby boomers have a strong political voice and are a vital economic force in the United States. We should use these advantages to advocate for ourselves and persuade policymakers to address the needs of elderly members of society.[15]

In 2016, there were 74 million baby boomers living in the United States, accounting for approximately 23 percent of the population. Baby boomers and older generations represented 43 percent of eligible voters and cast 49 percent of ballots in

---

14. Isabelle Hansson, Sandra Buratti, Valgeir Thorvaldsson, Boo Johansson, and Anne Ingeborg Berg, "Changes in Life Satisfaction in the Retirement Transition: Interaction Effects of Transition Type and Individual Resources," *Work, Aging, and Retirement* 4, no. 4 (2018): 352–66.

15. Sharona Hoffman, "The Perplexities of Age and Power," *Elder Law Journal* 25, no. 2 (2018): 327–75.

2016.[16] Baby boomers spend \$3.2 trillion annually and have as much as 70 percent of the nation's disposable income.[17]

Seniors are active voters, and political candidates invest considerable effort in courting them. In the 2020 presidential election, 78 percent of individuals who were 65 and older voted, compared with 66.8 percent of the general eligible electorate.[18] Seniors cast 22 percent of the votes in 2020, although they comprised only 16.5 percent of the population.[19]

The elderly in this country experience many challenges, and many of these are not likely to be alleviated in the near future. We face the threat of significant cuts to Medicare and Social Security benefits, insufficient savings, very costly long-term care insurance, a dearth of accessible transportation options, and a scarcity of geriatric and palliative care specialists, to name just a few. We must frequently remind government officials that baby boomers and seniors care deeply about these issues and press them to take action in the form of public programs and legislative solutions. In the words of author Susan Jacoby, "Like climate change, the aging of America demands serious reconsideration of the way we live."[20]

16. Anthony Cilluffo and Richard Fry, "An Early Look at the 2020 Electorate," *Pew Research Center*, January 30, 2019, https://www.pewsocialtrends.org/essay/an-early-look-at-the-2020-electorate/. The authors note that people who will be 56 and older "are expected to account for fewer than four-in-ten eligible voters in 2020."

17. Glenn Geller, "Baby Boomers Spend More Than Millennials—Yet Are Ignored by Advertisers," *The Marketing Insider*, May 22, 2019, https://www.mediapost.com/publications/article/336177/baby-boomers-spend-more-than-millennials-yet-ar.html.

18. Scott Clement and Daniela Santamariña, "What We Know about the High, Broad Turnout in the 2020 Election," *Washington Post*, May 13, 2021.

19. Timothy Noah, "America Is Run by Geezers," *New Republic*, November 25, 2020, https://newrepublic.com/article/160380/2020-election-exit-polls-elderly-turnout-senior-vote.

20. Susan Jacoby, "We're Getting Old, but We're Not Doing Anything about It," *New York Times*, December 23, 2019, https://www.nytimes.com/2019/12/23/opinion/america-aging.html?smid=nytcore-ios-share.

As just one example, Congress and state legislatures could implement a variety of measures to address the shortage of primary care and geriatric physicians. More generous Medicare reimbursement for geriatric services would be an obvious way to increase the attractiveness of the field. The same is true of loan forgiveness programs, scholarships, and other financial incentives for medical students.[21] More extensive requirements for education about elder care in medical school and for licensure and certification purposes would also be of benefit. President Obama tried to make progress with his signature legislation, the Patient Protection and Affordable Care Act ("Obamacare"). The law established a program that enabled primary care physicians to receive a 10 percent bonus for seeing Medicare patients, but the program expired in 2015. The law also dedicated money to programs designed to help train thousands of new primary care physicians.[22]

The issues that affect seniors can become a priority if we make them so. As Dr. Muriel Gillick asserts, "our voices matter, although we may need to speak in unison to be heard."[23]

REMAIN ADEPT AT USING TECHNOLOGY

Technology is evolving at a dizzying pace, and it is at times frustrating and difficult to keep up with its many changes. Although I use computers every day, whenever I buy a new laptop, I need to seek help from my university's information technology specialists in order to set it up. Getting it to work

21. Bruce Steinwald, Paul B. Ginsburg, Caitlin Brandt, Sobin Lee, and Kavita Patel, "We Need More Primary Care Physicians: Here's Why and How," Brookings, July 8, 2019, https://www.brookings.edu/blog/usc-brookings-schaeffer-on-health-policy/2019/07/08/we-need-more-primary-care-physicians-heres-why-and-how/.

22. Kathleen Klink, "Incentives for Physicians to Pursue Primary Care in the ACA Era," *AMA Journal of Ethics* 17, no. 7 (2015): 637–46.

23. Gillick, *The Denial of Aging*, 257.

just as I want it to often takes multiple visits and many hours of frustrating work.

Technology is just as important for the old as it is for the young. Elderly people who are sophisticated about e-mail and the Internet are less likely to become the victims of scams and fraudulent schemes that target the naive and gullible.

In addition, patients increasingly rely on computers and electronic devices for their health needs. Electronic personal health records allow patients to view test results, appointment schedules, and other information in their medical records. Using the Internet, you can research your symptoms, treatments, and medical conditions prior to seeing your physicians or obtain additional information after a doctor's visit. Telehealth enables clinicians to monitor physiological health data and to conduct patient visits remotely so that patients need not come to the clinic as frequently. Electronic medication dispensers can provide timed reminders, monitoring, and alerts to caregivers when medications are forgotten or taken improperly. During the COVID-19 pandemic, many patients and physicians opted for telemedicine appointments rather than in-person visits, and the use of telemedicine is likely to remain popular thereafter.[24]

Technology can also promote the social, intellectual, and physical fitness of the elderly. E-mail, Facebook, and Zoom enable you to remain in close contact with friends and relatives who live far away. Hobby forums, online courses, and many other offerings create opportunities for intellectual engagement. Wii games enable seniors to exercise their bodies and minds in their own living rooms.[25]

---

24. Cara Murez, "Health Care after COVID: The Rise of Telemedicine," *U.S. News & World Report*, January 5, 2021, https://www.usnews.com/news/health-news/articles/2021-01-05/health-care-after-covid-the-rise-of-telemedicine.

25. Anne-Marie Botek, "4 Reasons Why Your Elderly Parent Needs a Wii," AgingCare, accessed December 28, 2020, https://www.agingcare.com/articles/wii-for-elderly-155746.htm.

As we age, we should continue to embrace technology and remain updated about its uses and changes. You should feel comfortable navigating a computer and using sophisticated technological devices throughout life. The first-generation iPhone was released only in 2007, and now a billion people worldwide cannot conceive of life without it.[26] We cannot even begin to imagine what the future will bring us. To enjoy the benefits of communication, entertainment, and information, we must not allow our technology skills to atrophy no matter how old we are.

A FINAL PREPAREDNESS CHECKLIST

I have provided checklists at the end of each chapter. Now, I will further streamline the primary points of *Aging with a Plan* into a single preparedness checklist. Here is what you can do to prepare for your later years:

- Save as much money as possible for retirement. Do not underestimate your expenses or how much money you will need after you stop working.
- If possible, obtain financial advice from professional experts.
- Prepare legal documents: a will and possibly a trust, a living will, a durable power of attorney for finances and property, a durable power of attorney for health care, an anatomical gift form if desired, and, if relevant, an advance directive for mental health treatment.
- Have periodic conversations with your agents for health care and financial matters concerning your wishes

---

26. Stuti Mishra, "There Are Now 1 Billion iPhones Being Used in the World, Analyst Says," *Independent*, October 29, 2020, https://www.independent.co.uk/life-style/gadgets-and-tech/apple-iphone-1-billion-sales-neil-cybart-b1415796.html.

regarding finances, medical treatment, and end-of-life care should you become incapacitated.

- Designate property as "transfer on death" if you want to keep it out of probate.
- Supplement your will with a list of valuables, such as jewelry and cars, indicating who should get them after you die. This list should be updated periodically and accessible to the executor of your estate or trustee.
- Create a list that explains where important financial documents and items can be found (e.g., drawers at home, a safe, a safe deposit box in a bank) and give it to your agent for financial matters and the alternate.
- Provide instructions as to your preferred funeral and burial or cremation arrangements.
- Exercise regularly and maintain a healthy diet in order to prevent, delay, and diminish the impact of health problems in old age.
- Become a sophisticated user of technology.
- Learn about resources such as senior centers and transportation options that are available to the elderly and about professionals, such as daily money managers and geriatric care managers, who can provide assistance.
- Begin to explore retirement communities. Recognize that "aging in place" can have significant disadvantages in terms of social isolation and boredom.
- Accept the fact that you may not be able to drive forever and commit to stopping on your own before you become an unsafe driver.
- As you age, pay special attention to safety features and safety-oriented technology when purchasing automobiles.
- Find a good primary care physician and pursue appropriate preventive care. Plan to see a geriatric specialist if you develop multiple, complicated health problems when you are elderly.

- Develop good habits as a patient. Become an active member of your own medical team. Do research, ask questions, and seek second opinions when you are uncertain about which option is best.
- Do not make important medical decisions or undergo serious treatments alone. Have a close friend or relative accompany you, and hire aides when you require extra support at home or in the hospital.
- Determine what your moral beliefs are concerning end-of-life care. Read ethics literature and study religious doctrine, if it is meaningful for you.
- Keep the option of hospice in mind. It is a legal and widely available way to transition from aggressive treatment of a terminal illness to comfort care that can alleviate suffering at the end of life.
- Nurture strong friendships and relationships with family members, pursue hobbies, and become involved in volunteer work.
- Dream about retirement and plan for it to be life-enriching and fulfilling.

Despite being a workaholic, I look forward to retirement and imagine a variety of activities that will make me happy. I think about studying to be a docent at an art museum and then using my teaching skills to serve as a tour guide for museum visitors. I look forward to attending courses, lectures, and the theater. I will continue to exercise regularly and volunteer in the community. I will frequently get together with friends, and I dream of traveling extensively.

Baby boomers are reluctant to think about our own old age, much less plan for it.[27] We often watch our elderly relatives

---

27. Gillick, *The Denial of Aging*, 266.

suffer, we shudder, and we fervently hope that we will be able to avoid a similar fate. Nevertheless, we can reduce our loved ones' angst by having conversations with them about difficult topics such as moving to an appropriate residential setting, driving, and end-of-life care long before they need to make immediate decisions in a crisis. Moreover, we can surely help ourselves by planning ahead.

Having a high quality of life as we grow older requires effort and forethought, especially for those of us who will not have a strong family support network. The good news is that however unpredictable the aging process may be, it need not be left entirely to chance. We can take the initiative to remain active physically, mentally, and socially and implement antidotes to isolation and depression.

Having done my research and written this book, I'm reassured about our prospects as seniors. Armed with information and a plan, we can do much to direct our future and achieve a high quality of life no matter how old we are.

INDEX

AAA 147, 150
  educational courses for older
    drivers 147
  Roadwise rx 150. *See also* Internet
    resources
  See also AARP; driving
AARP 32, 37, 107, 147, 150, 191
  conversations about driving 151–
    53, 157
  educational courses for older
    drivers 147
  What to Ask and Observe when
    Visiting Continuing Care Retirement
    Communities 81
  See also AAA; elderly driving
Administration on Aging 213, 250. *See also*
  Older Americans Act of 1965 (OAA)
adult day services 210–13
  adult day health care 211
  adult social day care 68, 211
advance directives 89, 102–21, 137–40
  for dementia 102, 111, 121–23, 229,
    236–37, 239–40
  for health care 102–16, 118,
    123, 138–40
  instructions for 103–17, 120–21
  for mental health treatment 116–
    17, 138
  portability 118–20
  precedent autonomy 121–23
  quality 120–21
  registries of 115–16, 118–20

See also durable power of attorney for
  health care; elder law attorneys
Aging with Dignity's Five Wishes 106. *See
  also* Internet resources
Alzheimer's disease 10–11, 69, 121–
  23, 217
American Association of Daily Money
  Managers (AADMM) 84–85
  website 84
American Bar Association 90
American Bar Association Commission
  on Law and Aging 136–37
  Consumer's Tool Kit for Health Care
    Advance Planning 138. *See also*
    Internet resources
  guidance on choosing a health care
    proxy 109, 112–13
  What To Do After Signing Your Health
    Care Advance Directive 136–37
American Medical Association 179
anatomical gift form 114–16, 138, 259
assisted living 21, 31, 61–66, 72, 77–79,
  199–202, 213
  cost of 20–21, 31, 62–63, 201–03
  facilities 62–66, 72, 199–202

baby boomers 8, 17, 19, 24, 57, 74, 99,
  156, 168, 249, 254, 255, 256, 261
Battin, Peggy 241
Benjamin Rose Institute on Aging 60
Brookdale Senior Living 80–81
Brownlee, Shannon 161, 224

car safety features 156, 157, 260
Care.com 154, 207. *See also* Internet
    resources
caregivers 23, 31, 32, 55, 86–88, 99, 127,
    185–86, 191, 206, 207–10, 213, 217,
    230, 240, 250
Caring Connections 108, 109, 110, 111,
    115. *See also* Internet resources
Carter, Zoe FitzGerald 239
CCRC. *See* continuing care retirement
    communities
CDC. *See* Centers for Disease Control and
    Prevention
Census Bureau 9
Centers for Disease Control and
    Prevention 7, 179
Chandler-Cramer, M. Colette 240
childlessness 11–12
Commission on Accreditation of
    Rehabilitation Facilities (CARF) 77
Community Living Assistance Services
    and Supports (CLASS) Act 42
Compassion & Choices 230. *See also* end
    of life
concierge doctors/medicine 172–74, 183.
    See also coordinated medical care
continuing care retirement communities
    (CCRC) 61–81, 246
  benefits of 66–70
  CCRC without Walls 78
  contract options 72–73
  costs 70–75
  features 62–66
  financial and organizational structure
    63–64, 73–74
  state regulation 75–78
  risks 75–78
  See also retirement communities
coordinated medical care 159–83. *See*
    also concierge medicine; drug
    interactions; end of life; geriatricians;
    primary care physicians
COVID-19, 7, 48, 102, 155, 191, 245,
    248, 258
Craigslist 154, 207, 208. *See also* Internet
    resources

daily money managers 83–86, 97–100. *See*
    also American Association of Daily
    Money Managers
Davis, Dena 217
default surrogates 103, 113, 123
dementia 7, 10–11, 65, 69, 102–03, 109,
    111, 121–22, 130, 159, 162, 187–88,
    191, 205–06, 211, 217, 229, 236,
    239–40, 245
Didion, Joan 12
diet 212, 245, 247, 252, 260
direct primary care 172–74, 183
Dignitas 238. *See also* medical aid in dying
DMM. *See* daily money managers
do not resuscitate (DNR) orders 229–30,
    241, 242. *See also* end of life
Dresser, Rebecca 122
driving 69, 141–57, 204, 252, 255, 260
  conversations about 151–53
  danger signs 150–51
  driving evaluations 150–51
  risks 141–43
  state regulation 144–50
  statistics 143–44
  technology aids 155–56
  transportation resources 153–55
  See also AAA; AARP
drug interactions 159–62, 164, 176, 249.
    See also coordinated medical care;
    geriatricians
durable power of attorney 99, 104, 109–
    13, 125–28, 137, 138, 229, 247, 259
  for health care 109–11, 136–37, 179–
    80. *See also* advance directives
  for property and finances 125–28,
    137, 138
Dworkin, Ronald 122

elder abuse 209–10, 224
  statistics 210
elder law attorneys 89–91, 97–100, 106,
    129–30, 199
electronic health records (EHRs) 118,
    139, 259
Employee Benefits Research Institute
    21–22, 24

end of life 104–05, 109, 123, 137, 215–43
  do not resuscitate (DNR) orders 108,
    229–30, 241, 242
  hospice 219–23, 242, 261
  out-of-hospital DNRs 229–30, 242
  overtreatment 161, 224–25
  medical aid in dying 233–38, 243
  palliative care 219–23, 227
  portable medical order sets (POLST)
    229–32, 241, 242
  religious beliefs 232
  suicide 217, 233–35, 238–40
estate planning. *See* durable power of
  attorney; elder law attorneys; wills
exercise 10, 55, 65, 67, 81, 245, 247, 252,
  258, 260

faith-based organizations 59–60
Federal Highway Administration 143
Final Exit Network 238
financial abuse 98, 127
Financial Planning Association (FPA) 27
  information regarding pro bono
    services 27
financial planning for retirement 23–
  30, 43
  asset diversification 28–29. *See also*
    financial advisors
  defined contribution plan (401(k)) 24–
    25, 43
  delayed retirement credits 25
  disability insurance 24–25
  financial advisers 27–30, 36, 41, 43, 73,
    81, 128, 247
  individual retirement account (IRA) 25
  life insurance 24, 38–39, 43, 135
  long-term care insurance 30–38, 41,
    43, 212, 256
  low-income earners 27, 30
  retirement calculator 26–27
  reverse mortgages 39–40, 43
  Roth IRA 25. *See* individual retirement
    account (IRA)
  savings 17–20, 23–30, 36, 39, 43, 62,
    79, 247
Frances, Jane Wolf 31

friendships, importance of 47, 49, 52–53,
  68–69, 188, 247–48, 254, 261
funeral 134–35, 260

Gabinet, Leon xiv, 131
Gawande, Atul 165
geriatric care managers (GCMs) 86–
  88, 97–100
  benefits of employing 86–88, 97–100
  services provided by 87
  website 87
geriatricians 162–69, 171, 183
  geriatrician shortage 166–69
Gillick, Muriel 246, 254, 257
Golden Girls Network 57. *See also* shared
  housing services
GoGo Grandparent 154
guardian 89, 102–03, 126, 133. *See also*
  advance directives; durable power
  of attorney; elder law attorneys;
  incapacity; trusts

health care proxy 109–13, 118, 180, 228.
  See also advance directives; durable
  power of attorney
Hebrew Free Loan Association 30
Helpguide.org 163. *See also* Internet
  resources
Hemlock Society 238
HIPAA Privacy Rule 181
hobbies 52, 249, 254–55, 258, 261
home 91–97
  adapting 91–94
  professional organizers 94–95, 99
  selling 95–97
  staging 96–97
home care 21, 22, 23, 31, 60, 65, 69, 78, 87,
  93, 154, 182, 203–10, 211, 213, 251
  home care agencies 21, 65, 154, 182,
    203–07, 213
  home care aides 110, 203–10
  home health care 203, 206–07
Hopkins, Brooke 241
hospice 219–23, 242, 261. *See also* end of
  life; Medicare
hospital ethics committees 102, 124–25

incapacity 90, 102, 104, 117, 118, 121,
    126, 137, 138
  definition 104
  See also advance directives; durable
    power of attorney; guardian
independent living/55 Plus Communities
    52–54. *See also* continuing care
    retirement communities
in-home care. *See* home care
Insurance Institute for Highway
    Safety 145
  state license renewal requirements for
    older drivers 145–46
Intelius 154, 209. *See also* Internet
    resources
intellectual pursuits 12, 46, 53, 58, 61, 67,
    80, 249, 258
Internet resources
  accredited CCRCs 77
  adult day service centers 213
  certified elder law attorneys 90
  certified home health agencies 206
  daily money managers 84–85
  driving and transportation 150, 153–55
  financial planning 27
  home aides 59–60, 154, 207–08
  legal planning 106–07, 111,
    115, 129–30
  medical care 92, 179, 249
  nursing homes 193

Jewish Family Service Association 59

Kaiser Family Foundation 190, 241
Kosowsky, Joshua 177
Kushner, Rabbi Harold S., 50

legal documents 101–40. *See also* advance
    directive; anatomical gift form;
    durable power of attorney; living
    wills; transfer on death; trusts; wills
LegalZoom 129, 138. *See also* Internet
    resources
life expectancy 9
living wills 103–04, 107–09, 120, 137, 138
long-term care 185–213

costs 21, 185–86, 194–99, 204–05,
    207, 211
  facilities 187–203
  See also adult day services; assisted
    living; home care; nursing homes
long-term care insurance 30–39, 41–
    42, 43
  coverage 31
  hybrid products 38–39
  premiums 32–33
  recommendations regarding
    purchasing 37–38
  See also Community Living Assistance
    Services and Supports (CLASS) Act;
    Medicaid; Medicare
Lown Institute 161

meals on wheels 59
Medicaid
  coverage 34–35, 89, 105, 132, 194–95,
    199, 201, 204, 212, 249–50
  eligibility 34, 41–42, 61, 132, 197–
    99, 202
  See also long-term care insurance;
    Medicare; nursing homes
medical care. *See* concierge medicine;
    coordinated medical care, drug
    interactions; end of life; geriatricians,
    primary care physicians
medical aid in dying. *See* end of life
medical-legal partnerships 222, 242
Medicare
  beneficiaries 9, 61, 164, 197
  coverage for home care 204–05
  coverage for hospice 219–20
  coverage for medical expenses 20–21,
    168, 196–97, 213, 224, 250, 257
  coverage for nursing home 192–93,
    194–96, 199
  See also long-term care insurance;
    Medicaid; nursing homes
Medicare.gov 61, 193, 206
mental health treatment and professionals
    116–17, 138, 163, 183, 217–18. *See
    also* advance directive for mental
    health treatment; geriatricians

Menzel, Paul, 239
Moneychimp 26. *See also* Simple
    Retirement Calculator
middle-aged individuals 12, 46, 129, 143,
    169, 183, 255

National Academy of Elder Law
    Attorneys 90
National Adult Day Services
    Association 212
    checklist for visiting adult day service
      centers 212
National Alliance on Mental Illness 116
National Association of Insurance
    Commissioners 36
    premiums for long-term care insurance
      policies 37
National Association of Productivity &
    Organizing Professionals 94
National Center on Elder Abuse 210
National Council on Aging (NCOA) 9, 58
National Elder Law Foundation 90
National Hospice and Palliative Care
    Organization 219
National Institutes of Health 179
National Resource Center on Psychiatric
    Advance Directives 116
National Shared Housing Resource
    Center 57. *See also* shared housing
    services
naturally occurring retirement
    communities (NORCs) 54–55. *See*
    also retirement communities
nursing homes 21, 31, 34, 35, 61, 187–99,
    201–02, 203, 213, 230, 250
    costs 21, 194–99
    quality 188, 190–94
    See also Medicaid eligibility; Medicare
      coverage
Nurse practitioners 171
Nursing Home Compare 192–93

observational status 195–96
Ohio health care power of
    attorney 110–11
Ohio living will declaration 108–09

Older Americans Act of 1965 (OAA) 250
Oregon Death with Dignity Act
    (DWDA) 234–35
organ donation. *See* anatomical gift form

PACE programs 61
palliative care 219–23, 227, 237, 242. *See*
    also end of life
Parkinson's disease 6, 15, 17, 37, 92, 174–
    75, 178, 239, 246
Patient Protection and Affordable Care
    Act 42, 257
Patient Self-Determination Act (PSDA) of
    1990 105
personal emergency response and
    detection systems 92–94, 100
Pew Research Center surveys
    Adult children living with parents 18
    women who remain childless 11
physician assistants 163, 171
physician-assisted suicide. *See* medical aid
    in dying
portable medical order sets (POLST). *See*
    end of life
planned retirement communities.
    See independent living/55 plus
    communities
political action 255–56
power of attorney. *See* durable power of
    attorney
Presbyterian SeniorCare Network in
    Pennsylvania 60
primary care physicians 152, 164,
    169–74, 183, 257, 260. *See*
    also coordinated medical care;
    geriatricians
Prince Phillip 141
probate 131–33, 138, 260. *See also* transfer
    on death; trusts; wills
Programs of All-Inclusive Care for the
    Elderly. *See* PACE programs
professional organizers. *See* home
purposefulness 50–52, 254–55

Rauch, Jonathan 226
religious beliefs. *See* end of life.

relocation specialists 95–96
residential care homes 202–03
retirement communities 16, 46, 52–57, 61–81, 99, 153, 246–47, 254, 259
  benefits of 16, 46, 52–55, 61–62, 66–70, 99, 153, 254
  forms of. *See* continuing care retirement community (CCRC); independent living; naturally occurring retirement communities; shared housing services; village networks
retirement expenses 20–23, 249–50
retirement savings 23–30, 43. *See also* financial planning for retirement
reverse mortgages. *See* financial planning for retirement
rideshare services 153–55
Russo, Richard 160

senior centers 58–59, 80, 209, 260
shared housing services 57–58. *See also* retirement communities
shared decision making 177. *See also* coordinated medical care
Simple Retirement Calculator 26–27. *See also* Internet resources
six-bed board and care facilities 203
skilled nursing care 66, 72, 187, 195, 200, 203, 204, 206
smart homes 252–53. *See also* technology
social interaction 47–52, 142, 188, 189, 247–48
  importance of social life 47–52, 247–48 *See also* retirement communities, benefits
Social Security benefits 17, 25, 207, 249–50, 256
Social Security Administration 25
  delayed retirement credits 25
Span, Paula 78, 162, 166, 182, 187, 201
suicide. *See* end of life
surrogates. *See* default surrogates, durable power of attorney, health care proxy
Swan, Beth Ann 186
Sweden 251

Swift, Jonathan 216

taxes 24, 40, 73, 81, 83–84, 89, 185, 208, 213
technology
  for driving 155–57, 252, 260
  for health needs 93–94, 258
  for homes 251–53
  for social, intellectual, and physical fitness 254, 258
  use of 257–59
transfer on death (TOD) 133–34, 138, 260
transportation. *See* AAA, driving, Internet sources
trusts 131–33. *See also* elder law attorneys; probate
  revocable living trust 131
  special needs trust 132
trustee 131–33
two-midnight rule. *See* observational status

Uniform Power of Attorney Act (UPOAA) 127
US Bureau of Labor Statistics 186
US Department of Health and Human Services 114, 250
USLegal 129. *See also* Internet resources
Useem, Andrea 106

Veterans Administration 151, 204, 212, 221
veterans' benefits 89
Village Networks 56–57, 79. *See also* retirement communities
voluntary stopping eating and drinking (VSED) 239

Wen, Leana 177
Wife.org 27. *See also* Internet resources
Wills 101, 120–21, 129–31, 138. *See also* elder law attorneys; living wills
Wolff, Michael 225, 229

Zitter, Jessica Nutik 225